The No-Cry Sleep Solution for Toddlers and Preschoolers will eliminate some sleep problems instantly, with nothing more than a better definition of what is normal. It will help identify those few sleep problems that may require medical or professional attention. Of course, the majority of questions and struggles fall somewhere in between, and for these Pantley offers an extensive collection of gentle and loving tools from which to customize sleep plans that are considerate of the whole family's needs.

—*Norma Jane Bumgarner,*
author of Mothering Your Nursing Toddler

In *The No-Cry Sleep Solution for Toddlers and Preschoolers*, Elizabeth Pantley sweeps through the clamor of parenting philosophies with commonsense solutions. She provides parents with a virtual road map through the maze of sleep issues. Pantley manages the seemingly impossible: merging exhausted parents' desire for rest with their little ones' driving need for comfort and closeness. Her genuinely family-centered approach balances the demands of parents and children alike with respect, flexibility, and humor. Pantley's inclusive strategies offer alternatives for all sorts of families and all sorts of parenting styles. You can't find a more realistic, practical approach to solving sleep dilemmas.

—*Lisa Poisso, Editor-in-Chief,*
Natural Family Online *magazine (naturalfamilyonline.com)*

The No-Cry Sleep Solution for Toddlers and Preschoolers is a welcome alternative to "cry it out" advice. A crying child is a child in need, and leaving him or her alone to cry to sleep is not responding to the child's need or solving any sleep problems. Pantley's approach makes sense and is a child-friendly—and family-friendly—approach to sleep problems, something we have been in search of for a long time.

—*Jack Newman, M.D., FRCPC,*
author of The Ultimate Breastfeeding Book of Answers

Elizabeth Pantley offers parents a mindful, compassionate, and creative set of tools for a variety of sleep issues. Her welcoming tone is respectful of diverse parenting and lifestyle choices—inviting parents to find solutions that work best for their specific needs. I would be happy to recommend *The No-Cry Sleep Solution for Toddlers and Preschoolers* to sleep-deprived parents everywhere!

—*Nancy Massotto, Ph.D., Executive Director,*
Holistic Moms Network (holisticmoms.org)

As a physician and a parent there are no other resources that I recommend as highly or as often as Pantley's books. *The No-Cry Sleep Solution for Toddlers and Preschoolers* provides parents with the tools necessary to successfully guide their children (and themselves) sensibly and sanely to a good night's rest. Elizabeth Pantley has done it again.

—*Marianne Pinkston, M.D., family practitioner*
(and parent of previously sleepless children), San Antonio, Texas

The No-Cry Sleep Solution for Toddlers and Preschoolers is practical and well researched. Elizabeth Pantley has a unique ability to inspire the most exhausted parents and help them turn a time of trial into one of special bonding. Her techniques make the process of improving sleep one that is gentle, loving, creative, and even fun for both parents and children.

—*Daryl Grant, Ph.D., of sleep-baby.com, Brisbane, Australia*

One frustrating aspect of being a pediatrician is that it is often hard to give thorough advice for parenting problems in a short office visit. Elizabeth Pantley has once again provided me with a quick and helpful solution—writing a prescription to read *The No-Cry Sleep Solution for Toddlers and Preschoolers*.

—*Vincent Iannelli, M.D., pediatrician,*
president of keepkidshealthy.com, author of The Everything Father's
First Year Book, *and father of three, including twin toddlers*

the no-cry sleep solution
for toddlers and preschoolers

*Gentle Ways to Stop Bedtime Battles and
Improve Your Child's Sleep*

Elizabeth Pantley

New York   Chicago   San Francisco   Lisbon   London   Madrid   Mexico City
Milan   New Delhi   San Juan   Seoul   Singapore   Sydney   Toronto

Library of Congress Cataloging-in-Publication Data

Pantley, Elizabeth.
 The no-cry sleep solution for toddlers and preschoolers : gentle ways to stop
bedtime battles and improve your child's sleep / by Elizabeth Pantley.
   p. cm.
 Includes index.
 ISBN 0-07-144491-2
  1. Toddlers—Sleep. 2. Preschool children—Sleep. 3. Parent and child.
4. Child rearing. I. Title.

RJ506.S55P358 2005
649.'122—dc22   2004022730

19 20 21 22 23 24 25 DOC/DOC 1 5

ISBN 978-0-07-144491-0
MHID 0-07-144491-2

Interior design by Nick Panos

McGraw-Hill books are available at special quantity discounts to use as premiums and
sales promotions or for use in corporate training programs. To contact a representative,
please visit the Contact Us pages at www.mhprofessional.com.

This book provides a variety of ideas and suggestions. It is sold with the understanding
that the publisher and author are not rendering psychological, medical, or professional
services. The author is not a doctor or psychologist, and the information in this book is the
author's opinion unless otherwise stated. Questions and comments attributed to parents
represent a compilation and adaptation of reader letters unless indicated otherwise. This
material is presented without any warranty or guarantee of any kind, expressed or implied,
including but not limited to implied warranties of merchantability or fitness for a particular
purpose. It is not possible to cover every eventuality in any book, and the reader should
consult a professional for individual needs. Readers should bring their child to a medical
care provider for regular checkups and bring questions they have to a medical
professional. This book is not a substitute for competent professional health care or
professional counseling.

This book is printed on acid-free paper.

Contents

PART III   Customized Solutions for Your Family

Foreword

I adore toddlers and preschoolers. They're curious, fun, and charming. They have a contagious and boundless enthusiasm for life. These little folks have an abundance of energy and never seem to decelerate, even when it's time for sleep—whether it's naptime or bedtime.

In my work with families for almost thirty years, I have learned that sleep issues often dominate during the early years of a child's life, likely because when a child isn't sleeping well, neither are the parents. Furthermore, when a child's sleep is disturbed, his entire personality is affected. Lack of sleep brings an increase in health problems and negative behaviors, such as whining and tantrums.

Parents want nothing more than to see their children well and happy, and they want to enjoy raising their child. For many sleep-deprived parents, though, the endless fussing and crying that happens at bedtime, and in the middle of the night, creates tremendous stress. Parents don't know how to solve sleep-related problems, so the cycle of exhaustion and frustration continues night after night. While it may be common sense to know that good sleep is important for your child, and while it's normal to wish for your child to sleep well, it is not instinctual to know how to make this happen.

At last there's hope for all the confused and tired parents of sleepless children—*The No-Cry Sleep Solution for Toddlers and Preschoolers*. In this well-organized and easy-to-understand book, Elizabeth Pantley provides witty and wise insights into what causes children to have sleep problems. Even more, she offers a rich collection of practical and loving solutions that will help you help your child sleep better.

Typical of this mother of four's approach to teaching, she also includes plenty of reassurance and encouragement, so you'll never feel alone as you work through the process of setting up a plan and following it.

By adhering to the prescribed methods outlined in *The No-Cry Sleep Solution for Toddlers and Preschoolers*, your child will be sleeping better, and so will you. Your entire family can then reap the vital rewards of a good night's sleep—peace, health, and happiness.

—*Dr. Harvey Karp*

Dr. Harvey Karp is a nationally renowned pediatrician and child development specialist. He is an assistant professor of pediatrics at the UCLA School of Medicine, with a private practice in Santa Monica. He is the author of two bestselling books and DVDs for parents: *The Happiest Baby on the Block* and *The Happiest Toddler on the Block*.

Dr. Karp has appeared numerous times on "Good Morning America," "Dr. Phil," "ABC World News Tonight," CNN, Lifetime, and numerous national radio programs, and his work has been featured by the Associated Press and *Time*, *Newsweek*, and *People* magazines.

Acknowledgments

I am very grateful for the support of the many people who have made this book possible, and I would like to express my sincere appreciation to:

Judith McCarthy, at McGraw-Hill—thank you for your support and leadership, but most of all for your steadfast belief in my work.

Meredith Bernstein, of Meredith Bernstein Literary Agency, New York—thank you for your inexhaustible passion, dedication, and guidance.

Aisha Houghton, my research assistant—thank you for helping to gather and organize such a tremendous amount of family sleep information.

My family: Robert, Mom, Angela, Vanessa, David, Coleton, Michelle, Loren, Sarah, Nicholas, Reneé, Tom, Amber, and Matthew—thank you for your unwavering support, your love, and your devoted enthusiasm.

My fantastic group of test mommies—thank you for your many comments, questions, and ideas that you shared. I'm sending hugs to each of you and your children. Thank you to my friends: Alayne, Anne, Amy, Angela, Angelique, Candice, Christine, Denita, Diana, Donna, Emma, Erin, Esther, Frances, Gulie, Heidi, Honor, Jane, Janet, Jennifer, Jenny, Julie, Jolene, Kate, Kim, Kristin, Laura, Leona, Lisa P., Lisa R., Liz, Mary, Melanie, Michelle, Nichole, Samantha, Sara, Sharon, Shelia, Susan, Tiane, Tina, Tricia, and Vickie.

I would like to express my sincere gratitude to the following mothers, fathers, and children for participating in my research by completing sleep surveys and providing information about their family sleep situations: Aaron, Abbey, Abby, Abigail, Ace, Adam, Adrian, Adriana, Adriane, Adrianna, Aidan, AJ, Alan, Alayne,

AlecZander, Alexa, Alexander, Alexandera, Alexandra, Alice, Allison, Alnoor, Alyssa, Amada, Amanda, Amber, Ambika, Amelia, Amy, Andrea, Andy, Angela, Angelique, Angie, Anika, Ann, Anna, Annabelle, AnnaLena, Anne, Annette, Annika, Anthony, Antoinette, Aria, Arlin, Arthur, Ashley, Astrid, Audrey, Austin, Avery, Azaryah, Barbara, Barrielle, Beatrix, Bella, Ben, Benjamin, Benny, Bentley, Bert, Betty, Bill, Blake, Bobbey, Bonnie, Bradley, Bradon, Brandon, Braydon, Brian, Brianna, Bridget, Brigit, Brooke, Caitlin, Caleb, Cali, Callen, Calvin, Cameron, Camille, Candice, Carla, Carlene, Carli, Carmel, Carol, Caroline, Carolyn, Caspar, Catherine, Chad, Charlie, Charmaine, Chase, Cherie, Chester, Chris, Chrissy, Christabelle, Christi, Christian, Christina, Christine, Christy, Cielo, Cindy, Claire, Clare, Claudette, Cole, Collin, Cooper, Courtney, Curtis, Cynthia, Danette, Daniel, Danielle, Daphne, David, Dawn, Dean, Deborah, Deirdre, Del, Delaney, Delilah, Denise, Denita, Denny, Devan, Diane, Diana, Donna, Dylan, Edward, Eleanor, Elena, Elise, Elisha, Elizabeth, Ella, Ellen, Elliot, Elliott-Rose, Ellis, Elyse, Emiko, Emily, Emma, Eric, Erik, Erin, Ernesto, Esther, Ethan, Eve, Evelyn, Everett, Evyn, Ewan, Florian, Florina, Fran, Frances, Gabriel, Gabrielle, Garrett, Garrison, Gigi, Gina, Ginger, Ginnie, Gino, Gracia, Gracie, Gregory, Gulie, Hamid, Hannah, Harel, Hayden, Heather, Heidi, Helena, Holly, Honor, Ian, Isaac, Isabel, Isobel, Issac, Jack, Jackie, Jacob, Jade, Jake, James, Jamie, Jane, Janet, Jasmine, Jason, Jay, Jayda, JD, Jeff, Jenean, Jenn, Jennifer, Jenny, Jeremy, Jesse, Jessica, Jill, Jim, Joanna, Joanne, Joe, Joel, John, Jolene, Jori, Josh, Joshua, Julia, Julianne, Julie, Jun, Justin, Kaia, Kaitlin, Kaliska, Karen, Karin, Kate, Katherine, Kathy, Katie, Kaylee, Kazumi, Keaton, Kelsy, Ken, Kendyll, Kenny, Kim, Kimberly, Krissy, Kristin, Kyle, Kyler, Kylie, Kyra, Laura, Lauren, Leah, Leesa, Leeza, Lena, Leona, Licia, Lily, Ling, Linn, Lisa, Liu, Liz, Lo, Lorelei, Lorna, Louisa, Louise, Lucinda, Lukas, Mackenzie, Macy, Madeline, Madelyn, Madison, Madoka, Maezi, Malcolm, Manishi, Marcie, Margaret, Margie, Maria, Mark, Marty, Mary, Matthew, Max, Maxwell, Maya, MayaJun, Megan, Melanie, Mia, Michael, Michele, Michelle, Michon, Miguel, Miller, Miranda, Molly, Mona, Monica, Morgan, Nancy, Naomi, Natalie, Nathan, Nathaniel, Nicholas, Nichole, Nicky, Nicole, Nikki, Nikole, Nissa, Noah, Oliver, Olivia, Omeed, Owen, Pam, Patricia, Patrick, Paul, Penny, Peta, Peter, Phillippa, Pia, Rachel, Radiah, Raina, Raymond, Rebecca, Rene, Rhonda, Ricardo, Richard, Riley, Robby, Robert, Roberto, Robin, Robyn, Ronan, Rory, Rosa, Rose, Rowan, Ruby, Ryan, Ryder, Rylan, Sachi, Sally, Sam, Samantha, Samuel, Sara, Sarah, Satoshi, Savannah, Scott, Scout, Sean, Sebastian, Seneca, Shahin, Shannon, Sharon, Shaunna, Shayla, Shelia, Shelly, Sheridan, Sherri, Sinéad, Smita, Sonal, Sonja, Sophia, Spencer, Stacey, Stacy, Stephen, Steve, Sue, Summer, Susan, Suzanne, Sydney, Tallulah, Tamara, Tamsin, Tasha, Tasman, Taylor, Terri, Theresa, Thomas, Tiane, Tiffany, Tina, Trevor, Tricia, Tucker, Ty, Tyler, Valleri, Vicki, Vickie, Victoria, Vincent, Violet, Wade, Warren, Wendy, Wesley, William, Willow, Wilson, Wyatt, Xavier, XiuMei, Yasmin, Yonathan, Zachary, Zander, Zion, Ziva, and Zoey.

To my husband, Robert
Because
You are my life
My love
My knight in shining armor
My soul mate
My hero

My everything

And
Because
Life is wonderful
With you.

Introduction

The day I first became a mother, I set in motion a life-changing journey along the most extraordinary path of wonder, joy, challenge, and fulfillment: motherhood. Sharing my life with my four children brings me an almost indescribable happiness. As an author of books for parents, I have the pleasure of writing about my favorite topic, and the fun of chatting with people every day about our children and calling it work. I have three teenagers in my home now. My daughters are lovely young women: Angela is seventeen years old and Vanessa is fifteen. My son David is a fine young man of thirteen. My baby, Coleton, isn't such a baby anymore at five big years old. Still, some memories never leave us—and some experiences are common to nearly all parents with whom I speak. Possibly the most common topic that dominates the early childhood years is *sleep*—or, more accurately, *won't go to sleep*, *won't stay asleep*, and *won't let me sleep*.

I recently met my neighbor's six-day-old baby girl. My visit with this sweet, tiny, new person and her proud mommy and daddy made me think about how as parents we *expect* the sleeplessness when our babies are newborns. Even as we struggle with it, the challenge somehow seems normal, and in the blurry joy of getting to know our new baby, we expect and accept that the process involves less sleep for everyone. But when sleepless weeks turn into sleepless months and then into sleepless *years*, frustration builds. Before you know it, your baby isn't a baby anymore—an active toddler or curious preschooler has taken his place. Yet you're still a tired parent, and now you're wondering what you've done wrong along the way. At a loss with how to change things, you feel like you're the only one in the world who is *still* dealing with sleep issues.

I'm here to tell you: *You aren't alone.* One in three children under the age of five has disturbed nighttime sleep, an even greater percentage don't want to take a nap (even though they need one), and I'd wager that the vast majority of toddlers and preschoolers the world over present their parents with a nightly battle over bed-time. Even children who slept well as babies are not exempt, since a whole new crop of sleep issues can appear as children grow. So when you hear about those toddlers and preschoolers who will-ingly go to bed, stay there all night, and wake at a reasonable time in the morning—happy and refreshed, mind you—please know that they are the unusual, remarkable (and slightly odd) minor-ity! (Or else the storyteller is too embarrassed to admit that the four-year-old stays up until 10:00 P.M. watching TV and wakes up twice a night needing Mommy or Daddy to lie with him until he falls back to sleep.)

Dr. William C. Dement of Stanford University, who is often called the world's leading authority on sleep, says in his book *The Promise of Sleep* (Dell, 2000), "With young children, sleep prob-lems may be the rule rather than the exception. Sleep problems in these early years are so common, in fact, that people tend to think of them not as sleep disorders but as normal manifestations of childhood."

What makes the issue so much more complicated is that if our children aren't sleeping, we parents aren't sleeping. According to the National Sleep Foundation, adult sleep problems are most prevalent in households with children under the age of eighteen, and mothers are particularly prone to sleep disturbances. (Why aren't you surprised?) Dr. Dement explains, "The difference between sleep problems in young children and adults is that with children it is not the child who complains, but the parent. Sleep-deprived parents of sleepless children quickly reach a peak of frus-tration as they deal with their child's difficulties."

If you're a bleary-eyed, sleepless parent, you know how much damage the lack of proper sleep does to your day. Consider for a moment, then, what sleeplessness does to a youngster who by his normal and appropriate nature lacks your emotional control and resilience! If you're fatigued and miserable, your child may be, too. Daytime fussiness and discipline problems often have their roots in the nighttime hours. Healthy sleep carries with it magical properties for your child and fosters your child's health, attitude, intelligence, and growth.

I'm going to help you understand what your child gains from a good night's sleep and how much sleep actually constitutes a "good" night. I'll help you identify what you can and can't change about your child's sleep. The effective, realistic solutions that I provide will have your child—and you—sleeping better very soon. The goal is to help your child reap the most benefits from every night's sleep and allow you to join that giddy and well-rested minority of parents who have great little sleepers for children.

Why "No-Cry"?

It's an odd and disturbing myth that you have only two choices when it comes to changing your child's sleep problems: the slow, gentle method, or the quick-fix solution of putting a child to bed and letting him cry to sleep. The truth is that in some cases, either method can bring quick results. In most cases, however, both approaches—cry or no-cry—take weeks or even months of time before a child goes to sleep easily and sleeps all night.

If you've fallen into the trap of thinking that letting a child cry it out is a quick fix, talk to some parents who have attempted that approach, or visit any website message board for parents using a cry-it-out approach to "sleep training." You will see messages filled with the anguish of parents who must listen to their child cry for long periods of time, night after night after night, sometimes for many months. And just when it seems to be "working," along comes a vacation, a bad cold, an ear infection, or teething to disrupt the sleep pattern and set the family back to square one, starting the crying process all over again. Not only do these harsh extinction-based methods take as much time as gentler no-cry approaches, they may have long-term effects on a child's view of sleep, of being alone, or of his parent's ability and desire to meet his needs.

The bottom line is there are a wide variety of effective approaches to helping a child sleep better. If you could avoid making your child cry endlessly to achieve better sleep, then why wouldn't you?

Survey Families and Test Mommies

For this book, 245 families were kind enough, and motivated enough, to complete extensive surveys for me about their children's sleep issues.

Forty-four families volunteered to be test cases. They read through the manuscript and applied what they learned, and the mothers reported back to me on a regular basis. They asked questions, provided helpful tips, and let me peek into their naptime and bedtime routines, problems, and successes. The test mommies, as I affectionately call them, are a varied and interesting group, as you can see:

Test Family Information

Locations
- Seventeen from the United States (California, Colorado, Iowa, Michigan, New Mexico, Ohio, Pennsylvania, Texas, Virginia, Washington, Wisconsin)
- Eight from Canada (Alberta, British Columbia, Ontario)

- Eight from New Zealand (Auckland, Cambridge, Christchurch, Hibiscus Coast, Lower Hutt, Whangarei)
- Six from United Kingdom (Abingdon, Hampshire, Manchester, Oxon, Surrey)
- Two from Australia (New South Wales)
- One from South Africa
- One from Israel
- One from Japan

Children
- Twenty-eight boys
- Twenty-five girls
- Two sets of twins
- Thirty-two toddlers (twelve months to three years)
- Twenty-one preschoolers (three years to six years)

The test family configurations were quite varied. Married couples, single parents, and parent-partners were all represented. The parents' educational backgrounds ranged from high school graduates to college graduates to those who completed graduate studies. Some of the parents work full-time jobs, some work part-time jobs, and some work at home full-time with at-home business careers or in full-time domestic careers.

These 245 helpful families—those that completed surveys, including the test mommies—have provided thoughts and ideas that are interspersed throughout this book, along with photos of their wonderful children for you to enjoy.

Test Mommy Success Stories

To give you a boost of confidence in your own journey to improved sleep, I'll share a few excerpts from the letters I received from the test mommies during the process.

Kendyll, three years old

Lisa first wrote to me and said:

> My daughter Kendyll is almost three and still wakes up four times a night. She co-slept until five months ago but just does not like to sleep by herself. Now that her new brother is a co-sleeper, it is getting harder to keep her out of bed with us.

Lisa's update, just two months later:

> I wanted to let you know that Kendyll is now sleeping *all night* in her own bed *without* calling out to me! My husband has been taking care of bedtime for her (miraculous!), and she just gives me a kiss good night—that's it. He reads her a few books, tucks her in, puts up her bed rail, and leaves the room for her to fall asleep by herself and it *works!*

Jenn began her journey here:

My sixteen-month-old daughter, Abby, goes to sleep after her ritual with no problems, but she gets up in the middle of the night for up to four hours. Plus, she has been getting up rarin' to go before 5:00 A.M. She's still tired, but won't go back to bed.

Seven weeks later, Jenn reported:

Abby is now sleeping through the night—eleven hours!

In her first letter to me Frances wrote:

I have a twenty-month-old boy who has problems sleeping for more than two hours at a time. I am able to get him back to sleep, but it has to be me, not my husband, and he *has* to be breastfed before he will even try to go back to sleep. I do not believe in letting him "cry it out," as I see that it is a cruel way to treat him. So any help you could give would be valuable, as we are all very tired here.

One month later, Frances reported:

Samuel will now fall asleep by himself. Today when I said, "Bedtime," he went and got a book, went to bed, tucked himself in, and said, "Story." We read, and then I told him it was time to go to sleep. Five minutes later, he was fast asleep. He sleeps from 6:30 P.M. until 5:30 A.M. and only wakes once. Even when he wakes at 5:30 A.M., he has a quick feed and goes right back to sleep. Not bad for a boy who was waking every two hours!

Janet's first note to me read:

We desperately need help. Our son Wesley is nineteen months old and is addicted to nursing through the night in our bed. I did a sleep log last night, and he was up almost every hour! I only nurse in the middle of the night out of necessity and really want to stop doing this.

Two months later, Janet said:

Wesley can now sleep through the night without nursing. (Yay!)

The No-Cry Sleep Solution for Toddlers and Preschoolers

My previous sleep book, and the predecessor to this one, is *The No-Cry Sleep Solution: Gentle Ways to Help Your Baby Sleep Through the Night.* It provides answers for better sleep for parents of children from the day of birth through toddlerhood. My youngest son, Coleton, was a very frequent night-waking, all-night-breastfeeding baby. My experience with learning how to help him sleep all night was the incentive for me to write my first no-cry sleep book. Since then, I have corresponded with thousands of parents, and I have expanded my research up through the preschool years to bring you this new book, *The No-Cry Sleep Solution for Toddlers and Preschoolers.*

Because the magic of children is that they are all very different from one another and that they are unique in their transitions from one stage of growth to the next, this edition of *The No-Cry Sleep Solution* crosses paths with the first book for that in-between stage from baby to toddler. It then moves forward through the preschool years, and for many children, into the primary grades as well.

I hope now to guide you along a gentle, peaceful journey to good sleep for everyone in your family.

So let's begin.

Part I

Better Sleep Basics

Learn About Toddlers, Preschoolers, and Sleep

As the mother of four children, I know I don't have to convince you that your life would be easier if your child went to bed easily and slept the entire night—*every* night—waking up in the morning at a reasonable hour, refreshed and happy. I understand how frustrating it is to end the day with battles over bedtime, and I know the pain of being roused from a sound sleep every single night by a child standing near my bed. But I also know the pleasure of having my four children sleep all night while I, too, have my own good night's sleep.

Bedtime and sleep-related problems are far more challenging than many other aspects of parenting because we parents are *directly* affected by our children's lack of sleep, since when they aren't sleeping, we aren't either. We simply cannot function well as parents—or, as a matter of fact, even as people—when our own sleep is continually disturbed.

I think you will be surprised to learn that, beyond both the obvious parenting issues and the direct problems associated with bedtime and sleep, your child's sleep habits can affect every single waking moment of every single day. The quality of his sleep (or lack thereof) has a role in *everything* from dawdling, crankiness, and hyperactivity to growth, health, and learning to tie his shoes and recite the ABCs. *Everything*.

You are probably reading this book to learn how to end your bedtime battles with your child. Of course, that's the purpose of this book, and I'll share with you many tips for achieving that goal. But even more, you'll learn enough about sleep to be convinced that while the request for "one more drink of water" will fade in memory, the effects of good, healthy sleep in childhood can influence your child's health and welfare not only today, but for his entire life ahead.

Important Facts You Should Know About Sleep

When parents think of their children's sleep, they visualize a quiet child at rest. Actually, sleep is a dynamic activity: a complex series of phases, each of which contributes important aspects to health and well-being. Table 1.1 shows the various stages of sleep and describes what happens at each phase.

Each of the first four stages of sleep lasts from 5 to 15 minutes, and a complete cycle of the five stages of sleep takes between 90 and 110 minutes. Stages 2 and 3 repeat backward before dreaming sleep is entered, so the sleep cycle actually looks something like this: drowsy, stage 1, stage 2, stage 3, stage 4, stage 3, stage 2, REM (dreaming), continuing through the night by alternating between REM and non-REM sleep in a cyclical pattern. A full and healthy night's sleep that brings the best benefits of restfulness and rejuvenation allows an adequate number of these cycles, usually between four and six.

The Normal Flow Between Sleep Stages

Children (and parents, too) move through these sleep cycles each night, riding them up and down like waves. A child who falls asleep easily and sleeps well all night flows peacefully and contentedly through the stages of sleep all night long.

Now that you understand the concept of these sleep stages and how they work, you can begin to identify and understand some of the common sleep issues that occur with children:

Table 1.1 Stages of Sleep

Stage of sleep	Description	Depth of sleep	Body and mind processes
Presleep	Drowsy	Depending on conditions, can move into stage 1 or get a second wind and become alert and wide awake	Relaxed
Stage 1	Drifting off, very light sleep	Falling asleep, easily awakened	Floating sensation, relaxed muscles; slow heart rate and breathing; body may make a sudden jerk motion; eyes may roll slightly
Stage 2	Light to moderate sleep	Easily awakened	Regular, relaxed breathing; preparing to enter deep sleep
Stage 3	Deep sleep	Difficult to awaken	Regular, relaxed breathing; bed-wetting, night terrors, sleep-walking or sleep talking may occur
Stage 4	Deepest sleep	Very difficult to awaken; groggy or disoriented when awakened	Slow and regular breathing, no eye movement or muscle activity; bed-wetting, night terrors, sleepwalking or sleep talking may occur
REM stage	Dreaming	May be easy or difficult to awaken	Muscles immobile; irregular heart and breathing rates; eyes move around quickly (rapid eye movement or REM)
Sleep inertia	Awakening	The transition between sleep and complete wakefulness; may fall back to sleep or wake up fully	May act sleepy, groggy, disoriented, confused, or sluggish; reaction time and performance can be hindered

• There must be a preface to sleep—time for a child to wind down and relax. A child simply cannot go from wrestling with Daddy on the family room floor and an exciting, bouncy piggyback ride up the stairs directly to stage 1 of sleep. In that case, a second wind is a likely possibility.

• Children in the early stages of sleep wake easily. So when you have a child who fights sleep, he may begin to drift off but pull himself back just before he falls asleep, even if he's very tired. He may also be easily awakened by the sounds and activity of the household.

• Children enter sleep in a logical progression. If you are reading a bedtime story to a child who is relaxed and entering stage 1, maybe even beginning stage 2, but you get him up to use the toilet or move him to bed, he'll probably wake up fully. You've interrupted the normal flow of sleep stages and must begin the process again. (Oh, joy!)

• If your child requires certain conditions to fall asleep—such as your presence—she will wake easily when she senses she is going to lose the very thing she needs most to feel secure before she falls into a deeper sleep.

• Stages 3 and 4 are called delta sleep, which is regarded as the most restorative time of sleep. If a child lacks sufficient delta sleep, she will be sleepy the next day, regardless of how much stage 1 and 2 sleep she had. A child who fully awakens frequently throughout the night may not be getting enough delta sleep.

• Children spend substantially more time than adults in stage 4 sleep. This is when growth hormones are released, making deep sleep very important for your child's physical development.

• While scientists still debate the exact reasons and purposes for dreaming sleep, it appears to be a mechanism by which your brain sorts through the day's events, processes new information, explores issues that you are worried about, stores memories, and "cleans house." Research has demonstrated that REM sleep is crucial at all ages for proper functioning of the brain and psyche. The duration of REM sleep periods increases over the course of a night, so the longer a child sleeps, the more time he will spend in REM sleep time. An adequate amount of REM sleep enables a child to wake up feeling refreshed, happy, and energetic.

• Normal sleep follows a cyclical pattern throughout the entire night, but periods of deep sleep (stages 3 and 4) are longer at the beginning of the night. This explains why many children have a long sleep period followed by more frequent awakenings during the second half of the night.

• Sleep inertia, which is the gradual awakening process that occurs when a child first comes out of sleep, can be affected by the amount and quality of the child's sleep. The confusion and sleepiness of this state may last longer and be more intense if a child has not had enough sleep. Researchers are still trying to confirm a direct correlation, but if your child remains sleepy and dull for more than a few minutes after waking, it may be a sign that she's not getting the sleep she needs.

Brief Awakenings Between Sleep Stages

All human beings wake up five or more times each night, particularly when shifting from one stage of sleep to another. For a good sleeper, these brief awakenings aren't noticeable or remembered. You might fluff a pillow, straighten a blanket, or check on your child sleeping beside you, and then fade right back to sleep.

These brief awakenings have different consequences in babies and children. While a content sleeper will find a comfortable position and go back to sleep, a more finicky sleeper will become fully awake in search of whatever she needs to go back to sleep. Thus the series of sleep stages must begin anew.

A child can make a very strong sleep association wherein he associates certain things with falling asleep and believes he *needs* these things to fall asleep. When he begins to fall asleep or comes to the surface in a brief awakening between sleep stages, he may prevent himself from falling back to deeper sleep until he locates what he needs to comfortably ride his wave of sleep stages once again.

Remember that although all human beings wake periodically throughout the night, this association process is one of the main reasons that babies and young children call out to a parent in the middle of the night. They need a parent to right their sleeping situation so they feel secure and comfortable and are able to fall back to sleep.

The Biological Clock

Human beings have an internal clock, called a circadian rhythm, that regulates wakefulness and sleep. When it's working properly, people feel awake and alert during the day and sleepy at bedtime. The actual internal clock runs on a twenty-five-hour cycle, but it easily resets itself each day based on the person's sleep habits, timing of meals, and exposure to light and dark.

Some children have internal clocks that set easily; others have a finicky system that can be upset by any kind of external cue: lights that come on after he falls asleep, noise from dish-washing in the kitchen, or the beeping of a parent's alarm clock early in the morning. Haphazard nap- and bedtimes, irregular mealtimes, too much light or activity at bedtime, or not enough light in the morning can skew a child's biological clock as well, disturbing his state of biochemical equilibrium and causing an inability to fall asleep, poor-quality sleep, or too early waking.

The human biological clock needs resetting every day, and the components of a healthy bedtime routine, as will be discussed in the next chapter, will help keep your child's biological clock working properly.

How Lack of Adequate, Restful Sleep Can Affect Your Child

When I began to research sleep and children, an idea began building in my mind. With each piece of research I read, the idea became clearer until I finally reached that "Aha!" moment: for many children, the main reason for temper tantrums, fussiness, irritability, dawdling, and stubbornness is the *lack of adequate, restful sleep.*

Perhaps an even bigger catastrophe is that poor-quality sleep sets Mom or Dad adrift in that same fog when a child isn't sleeping in a way that allows parents to replenish their reserves. This creates chronic fatigue in the parent—from tending to a child's night waking and other sleep issues month after month, year after year—which can seriously reduce the parent's ability to navigate the day effectively. So the family ends up with a grumpy and noncooperative child handled by a parent with a very short fuse. In short, everyone in the family suffers.

Fascinating yet frightening new studies demonstrate that children who do not get enough quality sleep may suffer from a long list of problems, including the following:

Mood and Behavior
- Irritability
- Depression
- Exaggerated emotions
- Increased aggressive behavior
- Behavioral problems
- Hyperactivity

Health
- Reduced physical performance of small and large motor skills
- Delayed recovery from illness
- Disruption in natural growth and development

Learning
- Impaired hand-eye coordination
- Memory lapses
- Lack of concentration
- Impaired memory
- Compromised decision-making processes

Sleep
- Unrestful sleep
- Inability to nap
- Increase in nightmares and night terrors
- Increase in sleepwalking and sleep talking

Dr. James Mass, an expert on sleep from Cornell University, writes in his book *Power Sleep* (HarperCollins, 1998), "Sleep plays a major role in preparing the body and brain for an alert, productive, psychologically and physiologically healthy tomorrow." He sums it up by saying, "If we don't get adequate sleep, our quality of life, if not life itself, is jeopardized."

How Sleep Affects . . . Sleep

It's a vicious circle: a consistent lack of adequate, restful sleep creates chronic sleep deprivation. Sleep deprivation brings fatigue, but this tiredness is coupled with an ironic inability to fall asleep and stay asleep. The quality of sleep is compromised. Sleep is often fitful, with an increase in nightmares, night terrors, sleepwalking, and sleep talking. Furthermore, in many households the stress over

Gabriel, three years old, and Daphne, one year old

children's sleep issues creates sleep deprivation in the adults, and this stress is felt by the child. So worry and tension add to why everyone in the entire family is short on quality sleep.

How much sleep does your child need? The actual number of hours that your child sleeps is an incredibly important factor for his health and well-being. A sleep study completed by Dr. Avi Sadeh at Tel Aviv University demonstrates that even a *one-hour* shortage in appropriate sleep time will compromise a child's alertness and brain functioning and increase fatigue in the early evening. That's an amazing finding, and it calls for parents to look very closely at the total number of hours their children are sleeping.

The following table is an important guide to your child's sleep hours. All children are different, and a few truly do need less (or more) sleep than shown here, but the vast majority of children have sleep needs that fall within the range shown in Table 1.2.

If your child is not regularly getting *close to* the amount of sleep on this table, he may be "chronically overtired." This will affect the quality and length of both his nap- and nighttime sleep, which will directly affect his daytime behavior, learning, and growth.

Your child may not *seem* tired, because overtired children don't always act tired—at least not in the ways parents expect. Regardless of how your child's actual sleep hours match up to the table (because each child's needs are individual), the following signs may indicate he's not getting an adequate amount of sleep. Do any of these apply to your child?

- Tends to be whiny, fussy, or clingy
- Sucks his thumb, finger, or pacifier at times other than bedtime

Table 1.2 Average Hours of Daytime and Nighttime Sleep

Age	Number of naps	Total length of naptime hours	Nighttime sleep hours*	Total of nighttime and nap-time sleep**
12 months	1–2	2–3	11½–12	13½–14
18 months	1–2	2–3	11¼–12	13–14
2 years	1	1–2½	11–12	13–13½
2½ years	1	1½–2	11–11½	13–13½
3 years	1	1–1½	11–11½	12–13
4 years	0–1	0–1	11–11½	11–12½
5 years	0–1	0–1	11	11–12

*These are averages, and they do not necessarily represent unbroken stretches of sleep, since brief awaking between sleep cycles is a normal process of sleep.
**The hours shown don't always add up, because when children take longer naps, they may sleep fewer hours at night and vice versa.

- Carries a blanket, stuffed animal, or other lovey around during the day
- Is hyperactive, especially at times when you think he should be tired
- Is overly stubborn
- Has regular temper tantrums or easily becomes upset or angry
- Has difficulty falling asleep when put to bed
- Falls asleep frequently when in the car, bus, or train
- Falls asleep in front of the television
- Sometimes falls asleep on the sofa or floor before bedtime
- Sleeps later in the morning on days when the house is quiet
- Takes a long time to become awake and alert in the morning
- Does not appear to be well rested and full of energy
- Doesn't seem as happy as she should be

Children who are chronically overtired will often resist sleep, not understanding that sleep is what they really need. It's up to you to help your little one get the sleep he needs.

Experts tell us that sleep habits formed in childhood can affect health, mood, learning, and performance—both now and in the future. That's why it's so important to help your children establish good sleeping habits now, so they can reap the benefits for the rest of their lives.

Does Your Child Have Sleep Problems That Need to Be Fixed?

This may seem like an odd question in the first chapter of a book on children's sleep. But before going a step further, take a look at your situation to make sure you are looking at things clearly. I've found that during the early years of a child's life, everyone has opinions about how you should be raising your child, and other people's opinions may sometimes cloud your perceptions of reality. So take a deep breath, clear out all the cobwebs that other people have placed in your path, and first go over what's *not* a problem.

The Sleep Situation That Doesn't Need to Be Fixed

Your child is getting enough sleep, you're getting enough sleep, and everyone in your household is happy with how things are going. The problem is that your in-laws, your friend, or your neighbor is telling you that something in the way you are doing things is wrong and must be changed. Perhaps your child is up with you until midnight and then sleeps until noon. Maybe your king-size bed is where the entire family sleeps and your toddler's crib holds only his collection of stuffed animals. Possibly Mommy sleeps in the toddler bed, Daddy sleeps on the sofa, or your preschooler sleeps on the floor in your bedroom. Maybe the whole family plays musical beds every night, and you never know where anyone will end up. Or perhaps your bedtime routine is two hours long and includes everything from reading to singing to back rubs. Maybe your two-year-old is still nursing to sleep for bedtime and naps, or your three-year-old sleeps with five pacifiers and the family dog.

Here's the bottom line: *if* your child is getting enough sleep, you are all sleeping well, and the people who live in your home are happy with the way things are working out, then *nothing needs to be fixed*, regardless of what anyone else has to say about your family's sleeping situation.

If this is the case for you, then the only thing you need to change is your response to unwanted advice about how you are running your own household. You may want to change the subject when the topic of bedtime comes up in conversation, or do a

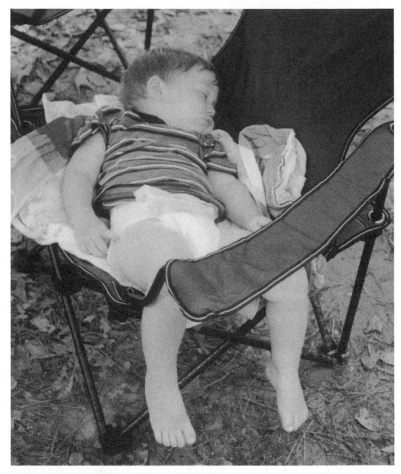

Matthew, twenty-two months old

little research so you can back up your parenting choices more confidently.

There's no harm in reading this book and learning more about healthy sleep. Perhaps your entire family can benefit from some tips for healthier sleep. But please don't feel compelled to change anything that is already comfortable for you and working for your family.

Sleep Situations That Do Need to Be Fixed

Now look at the other side of the coin. Perhaps the sleeping situation in your house isn't good. What used to work doesn't work any longer. Or it has never felt right, but you have never known how to change things. Possibly your child isn't getting quality sleep and is demonstrating a variety of the signs of overtiredness covered earlier. Maybe your child's sleep is perfectly fine, but *your* sleep has been disrupted for far too long by midnight child-tending, and you truly yearn for your own uninterrupted night's sleep. In any of these situations, your entire family will benefit if you take a month or so to create and follow a more conscious sleep plan for your child.

In these cases, the rewards for improving your child's sleep are overwhelming: A child who is happier, healthier, stronger, and better able to learn and enjoy life. And, possibly just as important, a parent—*you*—who can truly enjoy the daily process of raising a happy, well-rested child.

So take a deep breath and pause a moment to absorb the information you've just learned about the importance of sleep and about meeting your own family's needs. Next, you'll learn the basics of good sleep and find specific solutions to the issues that stand in the way of a good night's sleep for *everyone* in your family.

Create Sleep Logs

When you first begin to work on improving your child's sleep, it can be helpful to pick one typical day and night and create logs to record your child's current sleeping patterns. These logs can help you analyze how your child is sleeping now and will help you determine which ideas best apply to your situation. The other advantage of doing these logs is that you'll have a baseline for judging the effectiveness of your sleep plan. By doing one new set of logs every two to four weeks, you'll be able to see just how your little one's sleep routines are changing, and thus be better able to make adjustments in your plan, if you need to.

The logs are intended to help you through the process and should give you a feeling of control over what now may be an out-of-control situation. They are a tool to guide you through the process of change.

If, however, you have log-phobia, or if one look at them gives you hives, then by all means skip the logs and go directly to creating your plan. The last thing I want to do is create any stress for you. Many parents find, however, that making one day's logs every two to four weeks helps them better understand how their child is sleeping, which leads to clearer decisions about what needs to change and how implemented changes are working. Don't be tempted to log any more frequently than every two weeks, though, as you might create unnecessary tension for your child and yourself over sleep issues.

What follows are three logs: naptime, prebedtime routine, and night waking. Each one shows a sample entry. (These can also be found on my website at nocrysleepsolution.com.) Following the logs are lists of questions to help you evaluate your child's sleep patterns and a worksheet to help you set a plan.

Satoshi, one year old, and Elise, two years old

The nap log is important not just as it relates to naps but also because daytime sleep has a very powerful effect on nighttime sleep. The log will show how long it takes your child to fall asleep, where and how he falls asleep, and when and how long he naps—which will all be valuable to analyze as you put your plan together.

The prebedtime routine log will help you see how evening activities either help relax your child for bed or hinder your little one's ability to settle down for a good night's sleep. For this log, simply record the activities your child is engaged in and the environment surrounding the activity from roughly two hours before bedtime until the time he is actually asleep in his bed.

The night-waking log will display how many times your child wakes up, what you do when he does, how long your child is awake, and how long his sleep stretches are between awakenings. (It's easiest to place a pencil and pad near your bed and scratch down the information during the night, then transfer it to the form in the morning.)

All of these logs will direct you toward your best solutions and help you monitor your progress.

Nap Log

Name: _____

Age: _____

Date: _____

Time child fell asleep	How child fell asleep	Where child fell asleep	Where child slept	How long child slept
1:15	In front of TV	On sofa	In his bed	1 hour 20 minutes

Prebedtime Routine Log

Name: _____

Age: _____

Date: _____

Activity: active, moderate, or calm
Noise: loud, moderate, or quiet
Light: bright, dim, or dark

If your child gets up after being put to bed, include those details in this log.

Time	What we did	Activity level	Noise level	Light level
6:00	Ate dinner	Moderate	Moderate	Bright
	Asleep in bed			

Night-Waking Log

Name: _____

Age: _____

Date: _____

Time	How child woke me up	How long awake; what we did	How child fell back to sleep	How long child has slept since last falling asleep
10:40	Cried and called me	15 minutes; rocked	Being rocked	2 hours 10 minutes

Night-Waking Log Summary

Asleep time: _____

Awake time: _____

Total number of awakenings: _____

Longest sleep span: _____

Total hours of sleep: _____

Sleep Plan Questions

Take some time to review the logs you've created as well as the sleep facts in Part I and read the eight tips in Part II. Then answer the following questions:

1. Review Table 1.2 on page 12:
   How many hours of nighttime sleep should your child be getting? _____
   How many hours of nighttime sleep is your child getting now? _____
   How many hours of daytime sleep (naps) should your child be getting? _____
   How many hours of daytime sleep (naps) is your child getting now? _____
   How many total hours of sleep should your child be getting? _____
   How many total hours of sleep is your child getting now? _____

   How do the suggested hours of sleep in the table compare to your child's actual hours of sleep?
   Gets _____ hours too little daytime sleep
   Gets _____ hours too much daytime sleep
   Gets _____ hours too little nighttime sleep
   Gets _____ hours too much nighttime sleep
2. Does your child have any of the signs of sleep deprivation listed on pages 12 and 13? _____ How many? _____
3. Does your child have a wind-down or quiet time before bed? _____
4. Is the hour prior to bedtime mostly peaceful, quiet, and dimly lit? _____
5. Is your child's bedtime consistent (within a half hour) every night? _____

6. Do you have a formal, reliable bedtime routine (one that has a specific ending task and an ending "lights out" time)? ⎯⎯⎯⎯⎯⎯

7. Are the foods that your child eats for a prebedtime snack the right quantity and type to induce a feeling of calm and drowsiness? ⎯⎯⎯⎯⎯⎯ (See Tip 6, on pages 82 and 83.)

8. Does your bedtime routine help your child relax and get sleepy? ⎯⎯⎯⎯⎯⎯

9. Is your child's sleep environment conducive to a good night's sleep? ⎯⎯⎯⎯⎯⎯ (See Tip 5, on page 65.)

10. Do you "help" your child go back to sleep every time or nearly every time he or she awakens? ⎯⎯⎯⎯⎯⎯

11. What things do you do for your child (breastfeed, rock, provide a bottle, etc.)? ⎯⎯⎯⎯⎯⎯

12. Does your child wake up at roughly the same time (within a half hour) every morning? ⎯⎯⎯⎯⎯⎯

13. Does your child get adequate daily physical activity to feel tired at the day's end? ⎯⎯⎯⎯⎯⎯

14. What have you learned about your child's sleep patterns by doing these logs and answering these questions? What problems do you see? What do you think needs to be changed?

⎯⎯⎯⎯⎯⎯⎯⎯⎯⎯⎯⎯⎯⎯⎯⎯⎯⎯⎯⎯⎯⎯⎯⎯⎯⎯⎯⎯⎯⎯⎯⎯⎯⎯⎯

⎯⎯⎯⎯⎯⎯⎯⎯⎯⎯⎯⎯⎯⎯⎯⎯⎯⎯⎯⎯⎯⎯⎯⎯⎯⎯⎯⎯⎯⎯⎯⎯⎯⎯⎯

⎯⎯⎯⎯⎯⎯⎯⎯⎯⎯⎯⎯⎯⎯⎯⎯⎯⎯⎯⎯⎯⎯⎯⎯⎯⎯⎯⎯⎯⎯⎯⎯⎯⎯⎯

⎯⎯⎯⎯⎯⎯⎯⎯⎯⎯⎯⎯⎯⎯⎯⎯⎯⎯⎯⎯⎯⎯⎯⎯⎯⎯⎯⎯⎯⎯⎯⎯⎯⎯⎯

⎯⎯⎯⎯⎯⎯⎯⎯⎯⎯⎯⎯⎯⎯⎯⎯⎯⎯⎯⎯⎯⎯⎯⎯⎯⎯⎯⎯⎯⎯⎯⎯⎯⎯⎯

⎯⎯⎯⎯⎯⎯⎯⎯⎯⎯⎯⎯⎯⎯⎯⎯⎯⎯⎯⎯⎯⎯⎯⎯⎯⎯⎯⎯⎯⎯⎯⎯⎯⎯⎯

⎯⎯⎯⎯⎯⎯⎯⎯⎯⎯⎯⎯⎯⎯⎯⎯⎯⎯⎯⎯⎯⎯⎯⎯⎯⎯⎯⎯⎯⎯⎯⎯⎯⎯⎯

⎯⎯⎯⎯⎯⎯⎯⎯⎯⎯⎯⎯⎯⎯⎯⎯⎯⎯⎯⎯⎯⎯⎯⎯⎯⎯⎯⎯⎯⎯⎯⎯⎯⎯⎯

⎯⎯⎯⎯⎯⎯⎯⎯⎯⎯⎯⎯⎯⎯⎯⎯⎯⎯⎯⎯⎯⎯⎯⎯⎯⎯⎯⎯⎯⎯⎯⎯⎯⎯⎯

⎯⎯⎯⎯⎯⎯⎯⎯⎯⎯⎯⎯⎯⎯⎯⎯⎯⎯⎯⎯⎯⎯⎯⎯⎯⎯⎯⎯⎯⎯⎯⎯⎯⎯⎯

Develop Your Sleep Plan

Throughout this book you'll find a multitude of sleep solutions. A collection of important ideas are presented in Part II, Eight Sleep Tips for Every Child; I strongly recommend that you incorporate as many of these into your plan as possible. The remaining ideas in the book are subject specific, and you can choose any that suit your situation, your personality, and your family.

How quickly you experience positive changes in your child's sleep will depend on how well you evaluate your child's current sleep patterns, how much thought you put into creating your plan, how persistently you follow your plan, and your child's personality. Writing down your plan will consolidate all your ideas in one place for easy reference and will help you remember the things you are going to do, especially at the end of the day when you're simply too tired to recall the details. Even if you begin by making a few subtle changes, you may see sleep *improvement*. So go ahead and begin using ideas that make sense to you along the way, even before you settle on an exact plan. The sooner you get started, the better.

As you work through your plan, try to stay relaxed about it, but be consistent. Do give each idea enough time to have an impact— at least two or three weeks. A night or two isn't enough time to judge an idea's value. This is not a quick-fix plan; rather, it will enable you to help your child sleep better over the next few months. After all, it has taken longer than a day or two to get where you are now, and habits and conditions take some time to change, not to mention that biology and maturity are part of the picture, as well. Keep in mind that parenting isn't a sprint—it's a marathon. You've only just begun, so there's no reason to rush yourself or your child.

You can copy and fill in the following pages (or check my website at nocrysleepsolution.com for PDF files to print). The general ideas are outlined for you. When you use solutions that relate to specific situations, you can jot down the page number for future reference.

Plan Worksheet

Before making a plan, it may help to think about and write down the things that are most important to you, what every family member hopes to gain from a sleep plan, and what your specific sleep goals are. You can fill in answers to these questions.

The things that are most frustrating or disruptive to us now are:
Sample: He wakes us up three to five times every night.

_____

_____

This is what we hope to achieve from a sleep plan:
Sample: To understand and define the problems, create solutions, and reduce stress

_____

_____

Our sleep goals are:
Sample: No wake-ups from 10 P.M. to 6 A.M.

_____

_____

_____

Our Sleep Plan

We will begin our sleep plan for _____ on
                                     (name)

_____ .
   (date)

We will start our nightly bedtime routine at: _____ .
                                               (time)

This is our bedtime routine:

Approximate time	Activity

Bedtime (lights out) is: _____ .
                            (time)

Consistent wake-up time and regular naps:

- Morning wake-up time will be: _____ .
                                            (thirty-minute range)

- My child's naptimes will be: _____ .

Specific solutions for our situations:

From page _____ *Section heading:* _____

Description of the idea and what we will do:

_____

_____

_____

_____

From page _____ _Section heading:_ _____

Description of the idea and what we will do:

_____

_____

_____

_____

From page _____ _Section heading:_ _____

Description of the idea and what we will do:

_____

_____

_____

_____

From page _____ _Section heading:_ _____

Description of the idea and what we will do:

_____

_____

_____

_____

From page _____ _Section heading:_ _____

Description of the idea and what we will do:

_____

_____

_____

_____

Planning with Patience, Perspective, and Persistence (and a Sense of Humor, Too)

When your child's nighttime patterns prevent *you* from getting a full and uninterrupted night's sleep, your own sleep deprivation and desperate need for sleep stand solidly in the way of reason and thwart any possibility of rational thinking.

To make matters worse, other people might lead you to believe that your child's sleep habits are wrong and unusual, and that it's entirely your fault that your child doesn't go to bed easily and sleep soundly all night long. You're too weak, they say. You've created your own problems, they declare, because you breastfeed at night, or give him a bottle when he wakes up, or bring him to your bed, or don't make him nap, or let him nap too much, and on and on. Of course, these same folks tell you that you could solve your problem in a day or two if you would just put your child to bed, lock the door, put earplugs in your ears, and let her cry it out until she falls asleep. This advice just makes you feel worse. So, let's first clear up your confusion.

Is It Your Fault?

Let's start with the idea that it's a parent's fault if a child isn't sleeping well and that something is wrong if a child isn't sleeping perfectly. The National Sleep Foundation conducted a poll of 1,473 primary caregivers about their children's sleep. One of the ques-

Christi, Evyn, two years old, and Robert

tions was related to changing a child's sleep patterns. Seventy-seven percent of those with toddlers and 82 percent of those with preschoolers said that *they would change something about their child's sleep if they could*. Tell me something: are all of these parents doing things wrong? Or could it be that young children simply *don't* sleep the same way that adults do? Perhaps the only thing wrong is people's perception that children *should* sleep the way that adults do.

Yes, the things that we parents do have an effect on how our children sleep. But children are complicated beings, and if you did everything differently, you'd still have sleep issues—they'd just be different ones! Trust that I know this—I get hundreds of letters from sleep-deprived parents every single month, and although they all have sleep issues, they all have entirely different lives. It is the same among my test mommies and the parents who completed my surveys. These families are from all over the world. Some are two-parent families, some single-parent households, and some are extended-family households. In some families both parents work, in others only one does, and in some both are home all day. Some children attend day care full-time, some attend part-time, and others don't attend at all. Some children co-sleep; others sleep in a crib, in a toddler bed, on a mattress, on a futon, or on the family room sofa. Some breastfeed, some bottle-feed; some take pacifiers, some don't. The mix of family types, sleeping arrangements, and the array of problems and issues are almost endless. No single right way to address sleep will guarantee a child who puts himself to bed at 7 p.m. and wakes cheerfully at 7 a.m. There just isn't one.

Would Letting Him Cry Solve the Problems?

If a day or two of letting a child cry to sleep would solve all problems, there is no way that the previously quoted percentages would be so high. In addition, if those who tried it found immediate, simple success, it would be impossible for word not to spread quickly around the world. The truth is that even though cry-it-out advocates try to tell you that it's a quick fix, it often takes weeks or even months of very intense crying (and very little sleeping) for a child to finally succumb and start sleeping better, only to relapse after teething, illness, vacations, schedule changes, and growth spurts. So to imply that "a few nights of crying" would solve everything is naïve and unrealistic. As a matter of fact, I'd like to share with you a few actual quotes from messages posted to a sleep-training message board on a popular website to help dispel any confusion you still have over "crying it out" meaning quick, painless success:

Six Weeks Unsuccessful Training . . . Desperate!
HELP! I am feeling very worn down and can barely take the crying anymore. I'm very frustrated and angry! This is a horrible cycle . . .

he is crying all the time and is tired all the time and is no longer the happy child he normally was . . .

At the End of My Rope! AAAHHHH!

At twenty-two months, we put a gate up and made her just stay in there no matter what. She eventually started going to her bed, but remains awake until at least 9:30. Then without fail, she wakes up AT LEAST four times a night. We let her cry it out each time she wakes up. It never gets better. She screams and cries after waking, then falls asleep at the gate for a while, and then wakes up and starts over again. She's now three years old and is still not sleeping. It has been over a year, and it is still going on.

Getting Worse: Now up to Four Hours CIO Daily

Things are getting worse and worse. DS naps are getting shorter, and he is crying longer and longer and waking more frequently. He is getting only a little more than ten hours of broken sleep after four hours of crying. At what point do I say that I am just torturing this kid? I'm feeling tired, sad, angry, and guilty.

Persistent Crier—Retraining Nineteen-Month-Old . . .

This has become a nightmare. The problem is that when he gets back on track after any setback (bad cold, cough, teething, vacation, etc.), we have another setback and have to start all over again with hours of crying. I guess my question is, How much crying is too much?

So How Much Crying Is Too Much?

I'm a firm believer that babies should never be left to cry until they fall asleep. I also believe that toddlers and preschoolers should not be left for endless amounts of tears and anguish, contrary to some sleep books, which suggest doing this even to the point of vomiting. There are hundreds of ideas for helping a child sleep better without resorting to shutting the door on him and wringing your hands while he wails for hours. I have learned, however, that allowing an older toddler or preschooler a few minutes of fussing or moderate crying is not necessarily evil. Many loving, attached parents have put together complete and considerate sleep plans for their children and allowed a small amount of tears along the way. Many breastfeeding-ten-times-a-night toddlers have spent some time crying while being rocked in Daddy's loving arms, while a desperately tired mother catches a few hours of uninterrupted sleep. There is a huge difference between putting a child in a crib, shutting the door, and abandoning her to hours of crying versus creating a complete and thoughtful sleep plan that includes a loving before-bed routine and then allowing a few minutes of protest at the time the lights are turned out. There's also a considerable difference between letting a tiny baby cry in the night and letting a four-year-old cry when he's put to bed but would rather stay up and watch a movie. After all, when your toddler or preschooler cries for candy before dinner, or because you won't let him paint the kitchen cabinets, or because you told him not to give the dog a haircut, you don't second-guess yourself, do you? So if your no-cry plan turns into a little-bit-of-cry plan, don't feel like you've been a failure. Just provide your child with lots of love and attention during daytime hours, and of course, make sure you're following a complete sleep plan so you can keep the tears to a minimum.

Every parent has his or her own tolerance level for tears, and it's right to listen to your own heart. Every child is affected differently by his own crying. Some children can protest for twenty minutes before falling asleep and suffer no ill effects. Others experience a heart-wrenching sadness if left alone to cry for even a few minutes. Much of this depends on a child's personality, the sleep issues involved, and how the parents have responded to him for the first few years of his life. Among my own four children, even

Mother-Speak

"I've been studying the sleep hours chart and realized that Jayda has been substantially short of hours, especially since she stopped napping six months ago. After lunch on Monday, she was being her usual fussy, grouchy self so I decided to try putting her down for a nap. I gave her some milk, read her a book, turned on her white noise, closed the blinds, put her in her crib, and closed the door. Jayda cried for ten minutes, and although normally I would have taken her out after five minutes, I left her this time. I told myself it was a 'test project' that I had to complete so I could report the results back to you. Well, she FELL ASLEEP! And she slept for over an hour! Again on Tuesday and Wednesday she took naps that were over an hour long. Both times she cried for about ten minutes, but she woke up happy and was cheerful the rest of the day. What I didn't understand about sleep—I thought she was a stubborn child, not a tired child—cheated me out of six months of 'afternoon breaks.' It's almost embarrassing to admit that I had been denying her of sleep and then calling her fussy and stubborn."

—Jolene, mother of two-year-old Jayda

as they grow, I find that they each have very different ways of expressing and dealing with their emotions. Part of the job of a parent is to learn how to read each child and provide what each most needs in return.

The goal, of course, is no crying. And you can achieve this, or close to this, by making thoughtful changes in your child's sleep situation and then being patient as you put your plan into action. The key is to listen to your child, listen to your heart, and know that if it feels wrong, it probably is wrong for you. This doesn't mean you should give up on the idea of making changes if your child resists them. It just means you need to put additional thought into adjusting your plan.

A Persistent, Consistent Sleep Plan

Changing your child's bedtime, naptime, and sleep patterns is a very complicated undertaking. So many different aspects are involved that the solutions aren't always simple to identify or to apply, and it takes dedication to make the necessary changes. In addition, children grow and change along the way, and their sleep needs change, too. If you randomly choose one or two ideas and make a halfhearted attempt to apply them, you'll likely see little or no improvement in your situation. When the agony of night waking is greater than the torture of following a sleep plan, however, you will be motivated to do it. (Why do you think people do their taxes on April 14th?) In order to see the most pleasant and long-lasting changes, you'll need to follow these steps:

1. **Make a commitment to identify your child's sleep issues.** Every child is different, and every family situation is different, so it is impossible to create a one-size-fits-all sleep solution. It takes some detective work to clearly identify your child's sleep issues. These also differ for each parent based on the parent's needs, which must be taken into consideration as well.

2. **Find the right solutions.** Each family has their own personality and philosophy about life. You cannot blindly accept someone else's prescribed solution and expect it to work for you. It's important to choose solutions that suit your family, your beliefs, your child, and your sleep needs.

3. **Organize these solutions into a complete plan that encompasses naptime, bedtime routine, sleep, and awakening.** Reading about good ideas is, of course, only the beginning. You must

choose your solutions and organize them into a plan so you can actually remember all the parts of it as you go through your day and night. Writing them down will be most helpful for those times when you are simply too tired to think.

4. **Follow your plan in total every day and every night.** Making a grocery list but then going out for a walk in the park won't fill your refrigerator any more than will making a sleep plan but leaving it in the book solve your sleep problems. It takes effort, yes. But the results are very worth it. Commit to following your plan, and positive changes are inevitable.

5. **Be flexible enough to make adjustments as necessary.** It's not always possible to make a perfect plan from the get-go. Sometimes it takes a few adjustments as you learn more about your child's sleep and as you work through the ideas. While you should give each idea enough time to settle before you judge its effectiveness, you should also be looking to make adjustments along the way to customize your original plan until you feel that you've settled on the right solutions.

6. **Be realistic enough to have reasonable expectations about the amount of change you are expecting and the length of time it will take to achieve these changes.** Just as in most life situations, it takes time to experience change. Let's face it, no matter how good your plan is, there are times it will be impossible to follow: you'll be out at a birthday party past bedtime, your child will come down with a cold, or you'll have a hectic day and simply be too tired to walk down the hall again and again, so you'll plop your child into your bed and accept the easiest route to sleep. Don't beat yourself up over these very natural digressions. Just dust yourself off, and start anew. Parenting isn't a race to be won in a day— it's a lifelong journey. No prizes are given for the ones who get their child to sleep through the night the quickest. So relax, and take the time you need. If you stay the path, you will all be sleeping well soon.

Beatrix, two years old

And a Sense of Humor, Too

Do you remember what you had for lunch a week ago last Tuesday? What clothes you dressed your child in for his outing last month? Likely not. The sleep issues that you are facing today will fade in memory that same way. These issues loom large today, more than most parenting problems, because they occur at night when you are tired. When you need rest and a respite from the vigor of raising an energetic toddler or preschooler, sleep becomes an obsession. But over time, these feelings fade, and new concerns will take their place. In comparison to some of the situations you'll face over the next eighteen or so years (trust me here, I have three teenagers—two with driver's licenses!), these huge sleep problems of today will shrink into very minor blips in your history.

It's not always easy, but it is immensely helpful to maintain a feeling of joy and a sense of humor. Children are little for a very short time, and almost all parents of older children will tell you that these early years are the most magical of childhood. The things you'll remember most are the adorable little antics and joy-filled pleasures of raising a little one, and you'll probably wish you had basked in them a little more often when you had the chance. So why not do it now?

So when you get poked in the ribs at 3 A.M., or your little jack-in-the-box pops out of bed for the fifteenth time asking how long 'til his next birthday, or you painstakingly choose and purchase the perfect toddler bed but your child refuses to even sit on it, try to see the joke. When your child is finally sound asleep, stand over the bed and drink in the sweetness of your precious little person. Finally, let love guide you as you solve all your sleep problems, all in good time.

Part II

Eight Sleep Tips for Every Child

Beginning the Journey to Better Sleep

Once you've decided to make changes in the way your child sleeps, it helps to understand that the process of helping a child to sleep better is like putting together a hundred-piece puzzle. As much as you may want to see it finished, you must put it together patiently one piece at a time, and frequently the whole picture doesn't look right until most of the pieces are in place.

Each child's particular combination of sleep issues is unique: some children have nightmares, some are scared of the dark, some make frequent visits to Mommy and Daddy's bed in the middle of the night, some wake up too early, or some stay up too late. These situations are all filler pieces to the puzzle that needs to be completed section by section.

Just as with a puzzle, you can put your child's sleep plan together in any way you'd like, but it's often easier and more orderly if you put the frame together first and then fill in the middle. Sleep researchers have learned that human beings, as different as they are from one another, have certain similarities when it comes to sleep. Some ideas are of value to almost any sleeper, regardless of age or the particular issues preventing a good night's sleep. The following eight general tips are like a border that can be put around the edge of nearly any child's individual sleep puzzle.

If you will commit to spending the next thirty days working with these eight ideas alone, you'll likely see noticeable improvements in your child's sleep. In addition, if you also use the ideas in Part III that address specific sleep issues, you should see major improvement not only in your child's sleep but also in her mood.

Last, but certainly not anywhere near least, you'll see improvements in your own sleep and outlook as well.

So let's begin with the sleep tips that work well for almost every
toddler and preschooler. (A bonus is that these ideas work for
older children and adults, too. Go ahead and apply them to anyone in the house who would benefit from better sleep.)

Tip 1:
Maintain a Consistent Bedtime and Waking Time Seven Days a Week

As explained in Part I, your child's biological clock has a strong influence on her wakefulness and sleepiness. Just like a clock that is running properly, when your child's biological clock is ticking in time with her daily activities, she will be tired at naptime and bedtime, fall asleep easily, and wake up refreshed. If, however, her waking time, naptimes, and sleep time aren't in sync with her natural rhythm, she'll likely have resulting sleep problems along with daytime moodiness or other physical or emotional problems.

Remember that the human clock runs on a twenty-five-hour cycle and must be reset daily to work effectively. The first key to this process is to establish a set time for two important components: bedtime and wake-up time. A handful of children are very flexible in regard to their sleep schedule and can easily adapt to an inconsistent pattern of sleep times. I suspect, however, that since you are reading this book about sleep, your child isn't one of these wonder kids and would benefit from a regular sleep and wake schedule.

The good news is that when you get to the point where your child is sleeping well consistently, you will be able to be more flexible. Once your child's sleep is regular and undisturbed, you'll find that veering from your schedule from time to time doesn't disrupt anything. But in the meantime, finding the right sleep schedule is an important key to better overall sleep, so it's worth making it a priority for now.

A very important point here, and one that is often missed, is that your child's clock has its own rhythm. A schedule *can* be forced upon a child to adapt to a parent's chosen time agenda, but this often backfires if the times selected don't correspond to the child's natural rhythms. Plus, working too hard to adhere to a rigid schedule can create stress for your family. What works best is to discover and work with your child's natural patterns so that you can eliminate many of the battles that arise over forced schedules, while taking advantage of the benefits a regular bedtime brings.

Timing of Bedtime

Numerous studies have shown that the vast majority of young children have a natural bedtime that is early in the evening. There are exceptions, but most toddlers and preschoolers respond best with a bedtime between 6:30 and 7:30 P.M. Studies have shown that a child's blood pressure, heart rate, and release of cortisol (a stress-regulated hormone) are all affected in a positive way by an early bedtime. Although it may seem backward, most children who go to bed late have more night wakings and wake up earlier in the morning. Most children will actually sleep *better* and *longer* when they go to bed earlier. So this is definitely an idea worth exploring, even if it means forgoing evening after-work playtime with your child in favor of a morning play session.

While an energetic child may appear to be running on full steam until late in the evening, a toddler or preschooler who stays awake until 9:00 or 10:00 P.M. often was ready for bed many hours earlier and is up late functioning on overdrive—usually indicated by fussiness or hyperactivity. Or he may in fact be ready for a night's sleep when he takes a late afternoon nap, which can, with a little coaxing, be adapted to become a much earlier bedtime instead.

It's beneficial to find a bedtime that corresponds to your child's biological ready-for-bed time. In *The Promise of Sleep*, sleep

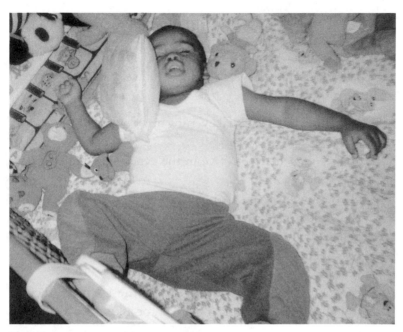

Ricardo, two years old

researcher Dr. William C. Dement states, "The effects of delaying bedtime by even half an hour can be subtle and pernicious [very destructive]" when it comes to babies and young children. A child who is awake past the time when his body calls for sleep is often grumpy and whiny, finds it difficult to fall asleep, sleeps poorly, and may even wake up too early, further compounding his own sleep problems.

How Can You Tell If Your Child's Bedtime Is Too Late?

Watch your child. In the few hours before he goes to bed, is he happy and relaxed? Is he in a pleasant frame of mind during your prebedtime routine, and does he go off to bed easily? Then his bedtime may be right for him, even if it happens to be 10 P.M.

If, on the other hand, you are dealing with any of the following issues, your child may be sending you a sign that his current bedtime is too late:

- Your child has a habitual evening meltdown when he is fussy and out of sorts.
- Your child gets hyperactive in the evening and finds it hard to settle down for bed.
- Even though you know she's tired, your child fights going to bed at bedtime.
- When you're in the car in the evening he often falls asleep.
- She seems almost hypnotized by the television in the evening.
- He increases his tired behaviors in the evening, such as thumb sucking, hugging a blanket, or asking for a bottle or to nurse.
- Your child has frequent temper tantrums or crying spells during her bedtime routine (while you're putting on pajamas, brushing teeth, etc.).
- You must wake him up in the morning, and when you do, he doesn't wake easily.

If any (or all) of these apply to your child, it's very likely that his current bedtime is too late, and you would all benefit from an earlier bedtime.

How to Find the Right Bedtime

If you suspect that your child has been going to bed too late, it's time to make a change. This may be easier to accomplish than you expect. According to my surveys of children's bedtime behavior, a truly amazing 97 percent of kids gave the same exact answer to the question, "How do you know it's bedtime?" The answer they gave? "Mommy (or Daddy) tells me." Think about it! This gives you more power than you have realized to determine a bedtime for your child, since you are the keeper of the bedtime clock. You may have never known that setting a bedtime is as simple as . . . setting a bedtime!

You can use one of three approaches to finding your child's best bedtime:

1. Set your child's bedtime earlier than his current time by fifteen to thirty minutes every two or three nights. After a few days, you can judge the effect by taking note of how pleasant he is during the bedtime routine, how easily he falls asleep, how well he sleeps at night, and his mood upon waking up in the morning.

2. If your child must be awake at a certain time in the morning—for example, if he must be up to leave the house for day care—then the best approach is to review Table 1.2 on page 12 to determine how many hours of sleep your child should be having and base his bedtime on his awaking time. Remember that the hours are based on *sleeping* time, so you'll need to begin your prebedtime routine an hour or so before the actual sleep time begins. Keep in mind that your child's sleep hours may differ slightly from the table, but it's always a good idea to plan for more sleep to start with. After a week or so of using a new bedtime, you can gauge your child's mood upon awakening and his daily disposition to tweak the exact times.

3. A third approach is to watch your child closely beginning at around 6:30 P.M. and as soon as he exhibits signs of tiredness, take him off to bed. For about a week, you can note the time that this happens. You can determine the best bedtime for your child by tracking his behavior, and then set your prebedtime routine to begin an hour or so before. Children show their parents in many different ways that they are tired, but what follows are the more typical telltale signs of fatigue:

- Losing focus or having poor concentration
- Becoming easily agitated or frustrated
- Decreasing the pace of his activities
- Fussing, whining, and getting cranky
- Lacking energy or losing interest in usual playtime activities
- Having tantrums
- Becoming hyperactive, wired, or wound up
- Quieting down, talking less
- Rubbing eyes or pulling at ears
- Looking glazed or acting distracted
- Becoming clingy, wanting to be held or carried
- Complaining of a headache or stomachache
- Yawning
- Lying down on the floor or a chair, or closing the eyes for long blinks
- Caressing a lovey (such as a blanket or stuffed animal)
- Asking to nurse or asking for a pacifier or bottle

As you watch your child more closely for these signs, you'll be better able to determine the best bedtime for her. You can use this list of signs to help you decide when your child should have a nap, as well.

Timing of Awakening

Establishing a regular wake-up time that is the same seven days a week can be an important key to maintaining a perfectly functioning biological clock. Again, some people—adults and children—are more flexible, but if sleep problems exist, then this is a great step to take toward consistent sleep.

You may have never thought about awakening time as a key to better sleep, but it's quite possible that you have actually felt the effects of this phenomenon in your own life. Often, adults have a

Madison, eighteen months old, and Betty

consistent wake-up time during the week because of a work or school schedule, but then they sleep in on the weekends. This results in extreme tiredness on Monday morning and the urge to hit the snooze button repeatedly for just a few more minutes of sleep. Then by midweek the morning routine is easier to accept, and by the week's end you may even be waking just before your alarm goes off—a signal that the human biological clock is working perfectly. But then the pattern begins anew—sleeping in over the weekend, followed by that Monday-morning-can't-get-up routine. Sleeping late on weekends is similar to giving yourself jet lag every week—living in one time zone Monday through Friday and a second time zone on the weekends.

This same thing happens with children who have different awakening times over the course of a week's time; they end up with a poorly functioning biological clock. You can easily gauge the effects of this technique with your own child by setting a consistent wake-up time for a few weeks and watching what effect this has on his sleep and behavior. Some children respond to this idea much better than others, but give it a few weeks to be sure you

can see how it works with your child. It's an easy enough approach
to try out.

How Consistent Do You Need to Be?

What's important about a consistent wake-up time is that it's based
on a reliable bedtime and regular naptimes, which all come
together to result in the correct amount of sleep for your child
every day.

The awakening time is somewhat flexible, within an hour or so.
This means that if you have no morning commitments, you certainly don't have to wake your child simply because it's wake-up
time. A child with irregular bedtimes and staggered awakening
times, however, will generally continue to have sleep problems.
After a morning of sleeping in late, that day's nap becomes late
and that night's bedtime is pushed later, which means another
morning of sleeping late, and the dreaded cycle continues. Sometimes the best way out is to decide on an awakening time and stay
close to that time seven days a week.

Settling into a Good Schedule

What matters most is to find a daily routine that works for you and
your family and try to stick with it every day. Once your child is
sleeping well, you can experiment with the flexibility of your routine, since you'll know what behaviors signal more sleep is needed,
and you can make adjustments when you need to.

Tip 2:
Encourage Regular Daily Naps

A daily nap is important because an energetic young child can find it very difficult to go through a full, long day without a rest break. A nap-less toddler or preschooler often wakes up cheerful in the morning but becomes progressively moodier, fussier, or hyperalert as the day goes on and as he runs out of steam. Furthermore, the length and quality of naps affect nighttime sleep. (And conversely, nighttime sleep affects naps.)

A midday nap refreshes a child in a number of ways:

- Children have a natural dip in energy and alertness at midday, even after a full night's sleep, and a nap that corresponds with this dip follows a child's natural biological need for rest.
- A midday nap enables the body to release hormones that combat daily stress and tension.
- Napping can help a child recover from any problems in the prior night's sleep, as any night sleep time that was missed is made up during the nap.
- A child is typically more alert and happier following a midday snooze, which is as good for the parent as it is for the child.
- Adequate sleep is crucial to proper brain development, and some studies indicate that daytime napping may play a role in learning by helping convert new information into a more permanent place in the memory.
- A child who needs a nap but doesn't get one will become overly tired and then may find it difficult to fall asleep at bedtime.

- Research shows that children who nap have longer attention spans and are less fussy than their non-napping peers.
- The benefits of napping extend to caregivers, since adults sometimes need children to nap just as much as children need the nap. During naptime, moms, dads, or caregivers can have a little bit of quiet time. They can rest and reenergize or do a few things for themselves so they can enjoy their little napper more when she wakes up.

Timing of Naps

Choosing the right time for naps is important for a number of reasons. First, a nap taken too late in the day will negatively affect nighttime sleep, since your child will get that second wind and not be tired at bedtime. Also, a very late nap may be long after the best biological naptime for the child. When you miss that window, then your child either finds it hard to fall asleep or she crashes from being overtired, sleeps too long and too late, and then isn't tired at bedtime.

Another problem with a late nap is that it may actually be a child's natural *bedtime* that is being treated as a nap. If so, a natural awakening that occurs between sleep cycles is seen as the end of the nap—and wake-up time! If your child is a too-late napper, try treating it as bedtime. Let him sleep in a dark room with white noise and see if it actually works as an early bedtime.

Yet another reason to pay close attention to naptimes is that there is a natural phase of sleepiness that occurs midday (the traditional siesta time). A child has a period in the afternoon that is conducive to a daily nap—his body is physiologically ready for sleep—and if you take advantage of this natural dip in energy, a child will more willingly accept a nap.

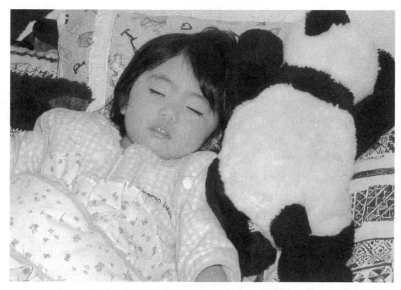

Elise, two years old

Certain times are better for napping because they fall during the natural phase of sleepiness that occurs in your child's biological rhythm, and they don't interfere with nighttime sleep.

Generally, for most children, the best times for naps are as follows:

- If your child takes two naps: midmorning and early afternoon
- If your child takes only one nap: early afternoon

As is typical with so many features of these little people, they don't always give clear signals about what they need. So a tired child doesn't always slow down and yawn; in fact, quite the opposite can happen. A child needing a nap may suddenly become inattentive, hyperactive, or fussy or display any of those signs in the previous list (page 48).

How to Set Naptimes

The first step is to review Table 1.2 on page 12, which outlines the typical sleep needs of children. Once you've determined where your child fits in the table, you have a starting point for figuring out the best nap schedule.

Begin by noting your child's current bedtime, naptime, and awaking time. Then according to the table, set new times when you think these events *should* be occurring. (If your child currently has a sporadic sleep schedule, it may take a week or two for you to figure out what the best plan will be.)

In order for your child to welcome naptime, you need to get him to bed when he's tired. Use the list of signs of fatigue on page 48 as indicators, along with your predetermined times as a guideline. Keep your eye on your child as your chosen naptime approaches. As soon as your child shows signs of being tired, it's time for a nap. If setting a regular naptime is new to you, then focus on watching your child's behavior as a key to naptime. Don't begin a lengthy prenaptime routine if your child is clearly ready to sleep, because she may work through her tired spell and get a second wind. When that happens, she'll likely wind down long before bedtime, and you will spend your evening with a tired, fussy child.

Once you've established a nap routine and followed it for a week or two, take a good look at your child's behavior before and after naps, and in the evening. Does he seem happy and well-rested? Is he tired at bedtime but not overtired? These are signs that your new nap schedule is working well.

If your child isn't a very good napper, if you are in the process of changing from two naps to one, or if your child seems to be giving up naps altogether, look for specific napping solutions in Naptime Problems on page 241.

Tip 3:
Set Your Child's
Biological Clock

N ow that you know how important consistency is in your little one's sleep routine, you can go one step further and take advantage of his natural biology so that he's actually *tired* when his predetermined bedtime arrives. Nothing is quite as frustrating as knowing your child should be in bed and trying to adhere to an early bedtime, but finding him wide-eyed and energetic when this bedtime arrives.

Everyone has heard the comment, "You can't make a child sleep, but you can make him go to bed." This statement is true enough, but this theory creates all kinds of chaos in the house when said child is jumping on the bed, playing in the bed, popping out of the bed, and generally doing everything in the bed but sleeping. The missing link here is actually having him be tired enough to lie on the bed and go to sleep.

How Sleepiness Is Regulated

Several brain processes regulate a person's wakefulness and sleepiness. The first is simply a factor of how long a person has been awake. If a child is awake long enough, he eventually will become tired. This is why a long late-afternoon nap can destroy the idea of an early bedtime: a late napper simply hasn't been awake long enough to become tired. The second regulating factor is light and darkness. Bright light stimulates and energizes, while darkness brings on feelings of relaxation and tiredness.

Morning Light

Bright light orchestrates an array of functions in your child's body, from temperature to blood pressure to the release of hormones. Morning light provokes the release of your child's wakefulness hormones. Exposing your child to morning light is like pushing a Go button in her brain that says, "Time to wake up and be active."

Use this to your advantage: expose your child to bright light first thing in the morning. Daylight is most powerful. So set up your child's breakfast, morning cuddle, or the wake-up breast-feeding in a room with windows. If you don't have such a room or if the morning is dark outside, start your child's day in a well-lit area of the house.

The Dark of Night

As much as bright light is your child's biological Go button, darkness is the Stop button. Darkness causes an increase in the release of melatonin, the body's natural sleep hormone. You can help align your child's sleepiness with his bedtime by dimming the lights in your home during the hour or two before bedtime.

Use night-lights judiciously. Choose small and dim ones. If possible, select a night-light that emits a more blue tone of light (like moonlight) rather than yellow (like sunlight). When you understand the power of light and dark as biological signals, you can see that a bright night-light glowing in your child's bedroom can be counterproductive to helping her sleep soundly all night. When she wakes between her sleep cycles, that night-light actually can push her Go button—even a very dim light and even if it's

2:00 A.M. You can also see that if your child wakes in the night for a diaper change, a bottle, or a trip to the potty, things like turning lights on or opening the refrigerator and flooding the room with light can accidentally signal morning's arrival.

Dr. Charles Czeisler, who studies sleep at Brigham and Women's Hospital, completed years of research on the biological resetting effect of lights. He discovered that even the light of a hundred-watt bulb held ten feet away is powerful enough to reset your biological clock! Keeping this in mind, use the least amount of light you can for your middle-of-the-night duties—the tiniest night-light or a penlight flashlight—and turn it off as soon as possible.

Incidental lights can affect your child's sleep, too. A streetlight outside his window, car lights flickering past, early morning sunlight, or the neighbor's kitchen lights coming through his window can call out to the sleeping child, waking him in the night or earlier in the morning than you'd like. Do what you can to prevent light from entering your child's bedroom. Use light-blocking curtains or shades, or cut cardboard boxes or aluminum foil to fit inside windows.

Pay attention to lights inside the house that enter your child's room through his doorway or around his doorjamb. His room may be dark, but if you're up and about, the light seeping into his room (not to mention the noise of your activities) will keep your little one from falling asleep. This also can cause his repeated waking after you've put him to bed but before you've gone to bed yourself.

A child who fears the dark often finds comfort in the dimmest of night-lights or in a child-sized flashlight at his bedside that he can use if he finds waking in the dark scary. (For ideas on easing these fears, see page 229.)

Keeping a child's bedroom as dark as possible from bedtime to awakening time can be a very powerful tool to define his sleeping hours.

Lights, Camera, Action!

Even if the lights are dim, you'll find that noise and action can override the light- and dark-regulated biological need for sleep. In other words, if the lights are dim, but the television is loud and your child is racing around the room with Daddy or her siblings, then her brain will override that Stop button and convince her to push through the tiredness. She'll become alert, often *hyper*alert, since she'll be forcing herself to stay awake despite an inner voice that's calling her to sleep.

The key is to keep the prebedtime hour as peaceful as possible:

- Turn the television off, or keep the volume low and the picture dimmed, and avoid loud, stimulating programs.
- Turn the radio to soothing, relaxing tunes.
- Keep video, computer, and electronic games turned off.
- Direct playtime toward quiet and restful activities.
- Prevent your child from engaging in physically active play; avoid having him run, dance, jump, or wrestle during the hour before bedtime.
- Avoid scheduling social events, running errands, or entertaining visitors during the hour before your child's bedtime whenever possible.

Tip 4:
Develop a Consistent
Bedtime Routine

Creating a specific bedtime routine usually isn't suggested or even necessary for newborns. When they are hungry, we feed them; when they are tired, we put them to bed. Not much preparation or structure to that process is necessary. The problem is that some parents are led to believe that routines are *always* a bad thing and that if parents would just let their children fall asleep when they are tired and wake up when they are ready, then there wouldn't be any bedtime or sleep problems at all. While free-form sleep and going-with-the-flow sound like good ideas, a number of problems can arise when there is a total lack of bedtime routine.

The first problem is that if your toddler or preschooler is sleeping and waking on his own erratic schedule, it can be difficult for you to organize your days. Busy parents often have other children to tend, car pools to drive, errands to run, and work to complete. Never knowing when you'll be getting your child ready for bed, how long the process will take, what time your child will sleep, or how long she will sleep, can make it difficult for you to feel in control of your day. Furthermore, if your little one is suddenly ready to sleep when you have other plans on your agenda, you'll be forever juggling your schedule as you go through your days. In addition, once your child starts school, the whole family will go through a major adjustment from free-form to a necessary routine. This will just add to the already major adjustments involved in beginning school, contributing stress to what should be a very exciting time in your child's life.

Why Bedtime Routines Are Important to Your Child—Even If You Don't Believe in Routines

It may seem that if you follow your child's lead, he will naturally fall into a predictable schedule and pattern of activities. Although anything is possible, this result is unlikely simply because of an interesting twist to the internal human biological clock: remember, it doesn't run on a twenty-four-hour day. Numerous studies have been done where people volunteer to live in cavelike homes where they are isolated from the external world and given no cues to the time of day or night. These subjects are allowed to sleep and wake whenever they feel the need. The studies show that most people function on an almost twenty-five-hour day, and some settle on cycles that range anywhere from sixteen-hour days to thirty-hour days. These schedules also tend to gradually drift, so the test subjects become totally out of sync with the real world.

What these studies show is that allowing a child to sleep and wake on his own whim would most likely result in a chaotic nonschedule. Instead of becoming a relaxing flow, your days would rather resemble those times when you had a newborn in the house.

I've already discussed the biological advantage of using the same sleep time and wake-up time seven days a week. By adding a specific bedtime routine—a series of rituals performed at the same time each night before bed—you'll not only help your child's biological rhythm but also enjoy a predictable pattern to your days

Mother-Speak

"We recently had another baby, and it totally disrupted Samantha's sleep. I realized that we had abandoned her regular routine. Once we returned to her usual before-bed pattern of activities, her sleep problems disappeared."

—**Wendy, mother of two-year-old Samantha**

and nights. You'll be able to schedule activities easier, knowing in advance when your prebedtime activities will begin. Your child will begin to expect and flow with the bedtime routine, instead of fight against it.

Why Your Child Will Love a Routine

Consistency and routine create feelings of security and reliability in your little one's life. It's a very big world, and children learn so much every day that the enormity of it all can easily overwhelm them. When certain important key points always remain the same, they create anchors of security. Young children look for these anchors and thrive on their consistency. Children enjoy routines; they easily adapt to them and even look for them. I remember one Sunday morning when my husband woke early to discover our boys, David and Coleton, already awake. Since they were the only ones awake in the house, Daddy decided to take the boys out to breakfast. The following Sunday morning, our girls were away at sleepovers and I was busy writing, so Daddy decided again to take the boys out for breakfast. The third week, Robert and I were awakened by the boys standing at the side of our bed. "Daddy! Wake up!" they were whispering. "It's Sunday and we *always* go out to breakfast on Sunday!"

Sinéad, six years old, and David

In my sons' analysis of their world (time being a slow-motion version of how we adults view life), two weeks in a row equaled "always." If you think about this, it may bring to mind similar situations that have occurred with your child—a certain book that *must* be read, a specific path your stroll *must* follow, a certain order a game *must* take, and a particular phrase that *must* be said before you leave out the door.

Parents can take advantage of this natural desire that children have for routine by actually creating a very specific before-bedtime routine that naturally and easily ends with sleep. Since most children share the same reasoning as my two sons about *always*, it takes thirty days or less for them to adopt a bedtime routine as the normal and usual way to end the day.

Yet More Reasons to Create a Consistent Bedtime Routine

Beyond the biology, convenience, and stability of a regular bed-time routine, there are lots of other reasons why you'll find this to be a helpful key to overcoming your bedtime woes.

- A consistent, peaceful bedtime routine allows your energetic child to transition from the constant motion of the day to the tranquil state required for falling asleep.
- An organized bedtime routine helps you coordinate the specifics that must occur before bed: taking a bath, putting on pajamas, brushing teeth, and so on.
- A specific bedtime routine helps you to function on autopilot at the time of day when you are most tired and least creative.
- Following a standard routine every night often replaces a disjointed and unhappy bedtime battle scene with a satisfying and peaceful process.
- An established routine helps you get your child into bed at the same time every night so he can get plenty of sleep and feel well-rested and happy.

Keys for a Good Routine

Now that you know the reasons why a bedtime routine is good for both you and your child, you can take the steps to create and follow a plan that works best for you. Here are some tips:

- First, use Table 1.2 on page 12 to figure out how much night sleep your child should be getting. Based on this, and the details of your daily schedule, set a bedtime.

- Start your child's bedtime routine early: allow at least an hour from start to finish. Rushing through the process will create tension, and your child may not be sleepy by the end of the process. In most homes this isn't an extra hour you need to find; it simply replaces an hour (or more) of dealing with a child who is arguing, dawdling, crying, and fussing about going to bed.
- The entire hour of your child's bedtime routine should be relatively quiet, dimly lit, and peaceful. This creates the transition from daytime activity to sleep time.
- Reading books, listening to audiobooks, or storytelling are all wonderful ways to end the bedtime routine. In addition to being very natural sleep-inducers, they are critically important keys to your child's emerging intelligence, making this a peaceful, enjoyable, *and* productive use of your time.
- View your routine as a special time to be treasured with your child. The bedtime routine should be as much about enjoying the loving connection between you and your child as it is about donning pajamas and brushing teeth.

For more ideas on how to create and maintain your child's bedtime routine, go to Bedtime Battles on page 105.

Tip 5:
Create a Cozy Sleep Environment

My daughter Vanessa has always been a super sleeper. When she was young, we'd often find her sleeping wherever she happened to be when tiredness hit. We have adorable photos of her asleep on the stairs, in her high chair, and on the grass at a picnic. She's sound asleep in one family portrait because try as we might she just would not wake up. Some children, like my Vanessa, are able to sleep anywhere at all; they can fall asleep on a cement floor just as easily as they do in their beds. Others are like the princess and the pea: any little discomfort prevents them from sleeping at all. Most children, though, fall somewhere in between, and with a bit of effort you can make certain that your child's bedtime environment is conducive to a good night's sleep. Even if your little one seems to be one of those easy sleepers, it can be helpful to go over the following things to consider as you create a cozy place for your child to sleep.

Your Child's Bed

You may have never given much thought to the surface your child sleeps upon, but it can be one of the keys to better sleep. It's common knowledge among adults that people all have different preferences when it comes to beds and mattresses. Some people spend a great amount of time and money choosing the right mattress with the perfect level of firmness and comfort. Children's mattresses, however, often aren't even selected. Parents simply take whatever comes with the crib or toddler bed without question. But these standard mattresses are notoriously uncomfortable; often they're hard and plastic-covered. Parents often use mattresses handed down from a sibling, cousin, or friend, which may be worn out from prior use. A good mattress may help your child sleep better, so when deciding on a mattress for your child, keep in mind the points that follow.

- **Support.** Mattresses can be made of coil springs, foam, or air, and there are a variety of gauges and types. (A water bed is not a safe choice for a toddler or preschooler.) A child's mattress should be of good quality and relatively firm without being uncomfortable.
- **Construction.** Mattresses and mattress covers are made in a variety of materials such as polyester, rubber, vinyl, cotton, and wool. While it's nice to have a water-resistant surface to protect against diaper leaks or bed-wetting accidents, your child's comfort should be the primary concern.
- **Space.** Make sure your child has enough space in bed to move around comfortably. If siblings share a bed, they need a large mattress. If your family practices co-sleeping, a large mattress is a necessity for everyone's comfort. If your child has outgrown her crib or toddler bed, she may find her old mattress increasingly uncomfortable despite her attachment to and the security of a familiar bed. (See page 287 for moving a child from a crib to a bed.)
- **Safety and health.** A child's bed and mattress should be perfectly safe for him. (See the safety checklists on page 371.) If your child has allergies or asthma, look into mattress and pillow covers (or specially made pillows) made especially for reducing typical allergens.

Vanessa, two years old

- **Level.** If your child sleeps in your bed, then check often to be sure that the place where your child sleeps is level. Frequently flipping the mattress can prevent dips and valleys in the place where your little one ends up sleeping. Also, run through the safety list for co-sleeping on page 375.

Pillows

A good pillow can be just as important as a good mattress in ensuring a restful night's sleep, and it's even common for children to adopt their pillows as their nighttime lovies. There's no rush, however, to introduce your child to a pillow if she sleeps well without one. To keep your little one safe, it's wise to hold off on pillow use until your child is at least eighteen months old. Even then, choose a pillow wisely.

A child's pillow should be soft enough for comfort yet firm enough to be safe and to provide proper support. Shop for a crib pillow or toddler pillow, which is much smaller than a regular pillow, and use the special small pillow cases made for these types of pillows. Stick to a thin, flat, stiff pillow, and avoid fluffy goose down or feather pillows. To test a pillow's resilience, place it on a flat surface and push it down firmly in the middle. The quicker the pillow regains its shape, the firmer it is. If it hardly moves at all, it's too soft for your child.

If your child has allergies, or if you do (therefore, your child might), choose a pillow made of a hypoallergenic material and cover it with a tightly woven or specialty pillowcase. (Also see Allergies, Asthma, and Gastroesophageal Reflux Disease [GERD] on page 335.)

Blankets

As a matter of safety, you may have avoided using a blanket when your child was an infant, resorting to thick sleeper pajamas as an alternative source of warmth. Many toddlers and preschoolers are perfectly happy to continue in this familiar way. As long as they are comfortable and warm enough, wearing thick sleeper pajamas is a fine way for a child to sleep. Other children enjoy using a tiny, lightweight, child-sized blanket.

In the grand tradition of Linus from the Peanuts comic strips, a large percentage of children adopt a blanket as their nighttime comfort object, or lovey. For these children, their blanket serves two purposes, warmth and security, and its importance shouldn't

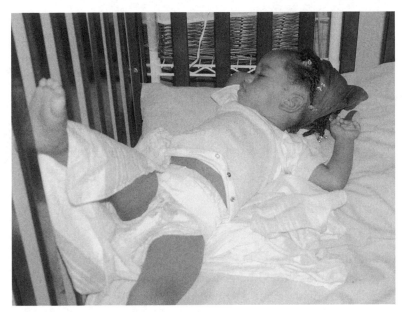

Camille, twenty-three months old

be underestimated. A child who has a lovey can sometimes overcome nighttime fears and separation anxiety more easily than a
child who doesn't have a security object to turn to.

If your child has a special blanket that he now sleeps with, it
would be an act of brilliance to find an exact duplicate and trade
off between the two. Usually the second must be precisely identi-
cal—even a frayed hem can make them different to your child. It's
important that you keep your spare blanket hidden or cycle the
blankets, giving your child only one at a time. If your child dis-
covers there are two, he may adopt *two* blankets as his typical
nighttime companions, leaving you to find two more spares just
in case.

Even among those children who don't have a blanket-lovey,
most have definite preferences when it comes to their nighttime

covering. A simple way to determine the best blanket for your child is to provide two or three choices and ask your little one which he would like to sleep with. As a safety precaution, avoid heavy bedspreads or puffy down quilts—you don't want him entangled in a spread that he can't easily control. Beyond that, you can experiment with different textures and weights to see which type most appeals to your child. The right blanket can increase your child's level of comfort in bed and help him sleep better.

Pajamas

Your child's pajamas should be clean and comfortable. The thickness of pajamas should be geared to the weather: when it's hot, dress her in lightweight pajamas, and when its cold, use warmer styles. Just like adults, children have preferences, and learning what your little one likes to wear to bed is one more key to relaxed sleep.

Consider safety factors when you choose pajamas for your child. Flame-retardant materials or tight-fitting cotton sleepwear (as a nonchemically treated choice) have both been shown to protect children should they be exposed to fire. Because oversized cotton T-shirts pose a burn threat, they aren't a good choice for children. Pajamas should fit snugly around the legs, arms, and chest to keep a child safe from fire.

Pajamas are a sleep-time cue for many children. The ritual of putting on pajamas is often a key part of the bedtime routine. Many kids love the comfortable fit of pajamas and like to stay in them throughout the morning. You can reinforce the sleep-cue properties of jammies, though, by putting your child in his pajamas at bedtime and getting him dressed in daytime clothes first thing in the morning.

Darkness

Earlier I talked about the powerful influence that light and darkness have over a child's biological clock. Basically, light equals awake time, dark equals sleep time. It's been discovered that even the glowing face of a digital clock can trigger wakefulness. This is an important reason to keep your child's room dark from the time he goes to bed until the time you want him to wake up in the morning.

Another reason you may want to keep your child's room dark for sleep is for the sake of her eyes. Some studies have shown that children who sleep with a light on all night have a greater chance of growing up to be nearsighted than children who sleep in the dark. "Our findings suggest that the absence of a nightly period of full darkness in early childhood may be a risk factor in the future development of nearsightedness," says Richard A. Stone, M.D., a professor of ophthalmology at University of Pennsylvania Medical Center Scheie Eye Institute and senior author on one such study. These reports are not yet conclusive and the direct connection has not been proved, but since it is a possibility and since darkness helps set your child's biological clock anyway, it makes sense to work toward having your child sleep in a dark room.

If your child has any fears of the dark, go to page 229 for specific ideas on handling and overcoming those fears.

Temperature

When a child goes to bed in a room that is too hot or too cold, he will tend to have disturbed sleep. While all people, adults and children, have their own preferences for the right temperature, sleep research shows that the majority of people sleep best in a cooler room. *Cooler* has a different definition for different people, but generally the range from 60°F to 70°F (15.5°C to 21°C) is cited as best for sleeping.

In addition to the temperature in a room, the quality of the air can make a difference for sleeping, too, particularly if a child has allergies or asthma. It may help to pay attention to the level of moisture in the air and use a humidifier, dehumidifier, or air purifier to create the best air quality.

Quiet and White Noise

The level of noise that disrupts sleep is different for each child. Some children can sleep through a home smoke-detector siren (I have one who actually did!), but some kids are awakened by the slightest noise. Many children will actually wake themselves up if they hear voices and think they might be missing out on some fun.

Many children whose sleep is affected by noises will sleep better with the gentle hum of white noise. Even children who aren't awakened by noises can benefit from falling asleep to white noise. White noise is sound that contains a combination of sound frequencies in equal amounts. It can be described as nonspecific noise that exists in the background without definition. The best example is the sound that is made by a fan or air conditioner, a hum that people hear but don't really register with active thought.

White noise can be a critical component to getting some children to sleep all night without waking. It is helpful in three aspects. First, the gentle, consistent sound can be very effective at soothing a child to sleep. Second, it can filter out other noises that may jar her awake—sounds from siblings, kitchen dishes clinking, the television in another room, traffic, or a dog barking outside. Third, it creates a cue for sleep.

Many people have discovered the benefits of white noise for better sleep (not just for children, but for adults as well), so there are a wide variety of white-noise CDs and digital white-noise machines that offer realistic, tranquil sound environments such as rhythmic ocean waves, sounds of a summer night, or the sounds of rain or waterfalls. An alternative to these is to take advantage of a household object. Use the hum of a fan or an aquarium tank, create a white-noise effect by tuning a radio between stations for a static hum, or even make a recording of your clothes dryer!

If white noise is helpful to your child, there's no harm in leaving it on all night long (think of the times you've slept well listening to the sound of a fan or air conditioner). If you wish, however, you can let your child fall asleep to white noise and turn it off when you go to bed.

Many white-noise machines function as alarm clocks, so you can set one to begin working in the morning just before you wake for work or before older children rise for school. That way, the noises from the outside world won't so easily wake your little one before he should be up. (See the chapter The Early Bird: Waking Up Too Early.)

Encourage Your Child's Attachment to a Lovey

A lovey is a transitional object that comforts your child in your absence, and it can be especially valuable to a child when falling asleep or when she awakens in the middle of the night. A soft toy or small blanket that can be held closely can give your child a sense of security. Since young children have strong imaginations, these lovies can seem very real to them and can ward off any feelings of being alone.

A good way to promote this practice is to provide your child with two or three possible lovey choices and have them nearby

Melanie, four years old

throughout the day and before bed. Watch your child to see which she spends more time holding, and then put the toy in bed with her for naps and nighttime sleep.

Ideal lovies are small enough for a child to handle, don't contain any potentially removable pieces such as button eyes, and are soft enough for cuddling. A peaceful expression on the toy's face is important, as well. A wide-eyed, plastic-faced doll may not be as comforting as a doe-eyed teddy bear. A wonderful option is a widely available bear designed for babies called the Original Slumber Bear. (Coleton is holding one on the cover photo of this book.) This bear has the added features of a tiny, soft blanket for cuddling and a soothing white-noise recording of womb sounds, which are similar to ocean waves. While created for newborn babies, this combination of soft, gentle bear and soothing sounds can be just as comforting to toddlers and preschoolers. Specially created bedtime friends for children come in a wide variety, so shop around for one that suits your child's personality.

If your child does indeed become attached to a lovey, try to purchase at least two of them to prevent any future lost-lovey disasters—or at least choose one that is easily replaceable or widely available.

Television in the Bedroom

No matter your child's bedtime habits, evidence strongly suggests that the worst thing to have in a child's bedroom is a television set (second place goes to computers). Watching TV can be a stimulant to many children, preventing them from falling asleep. There are many other reasons to banish the set from your child's bedroom:

- Unsettling programs can create fears and nightmares.
- A child with private access to a television may be watching unacceptable programs without your knowledge.
- A child can develop a habit of TV viewing at bedtime and find it very difficult to fall asleep without it.
- A child who watches TV before sleeping may be staying up long past a healthy bedtime.
- Having a TV in the bedroom increases the overall number of hours watched, which can lead to obesity, anxiety, and depression.
- TV watching at bedtime takes the place of a very important prebedtime activity: reading.

A Place Specifically for Sleeping

Children's bedrooms very often double as playrooms. Frequently, an abundance of exciting toys and activities are just an arm's reach away from the bed. Although a child may spend many happy play-time hours in her room, these same toys can create too much of a distraction when bedtime comes. A partially completed Lego structure, a half-finished puzzle, or the latest collectibles can all call rather loudly to a child who should be focused on relaxing for sleep. Some children aren't sidetracked by their playthings, but others can't settle for sleep when thinking about all the exciting things of the day left undone. If your child won't fall asleep easily, wakes up in the night, or gets out of bed too early in the morning, you might consider making the bedroom a sleep-only zone and see how this affects the sleep situation.

Creating an Inviting Sleeping Cubby

While it's a good idea to separate a play space from a sleeping place, it's not always practical or possible to make one whole room for sleeping and one for playing. There are ways to make this idea work without remodeling your home! One way is to separate the sleeping place from the toy area by rearranging the room. Create a sleeping nook by separating the bed from the rest of the room with a wall of dressers, chairs, or bookcases between the spaces. You can also hang curtains, sheets, or fabric from the ceiling to separate the bed area, or use folding screens for the same effect. The sleeping area doesn't need to be large; simply the size of the bed will do. You may even want to get your child involved in designing the area, choosing fabrics, or designing the partition.

The only things included in your child's sleeping area should be a few stuffed animals for sleeping company, a selection of books, a white-noise machine or CD player, a reading light or night-light, and a glass of water. Once you've created this wonderful bed nook, you can explain to your child that it's her special place for sleeping, reading, and resting only. (Let Daddy or big brother or sister know that this means tickling and wrestling should be done in the playroom!) This new arrangement can help create a strong mental association between your child's bed and sleep. This tip might even make going to bed—and staying in bed—more interesting!

A Safe, Secure, Happy Sleeping Place

In order for restful sleep to occur, a child must feel safe and secure in her bedroom. Toddlers and preschoolers often fear being alone, even during sleep. They are of an age when they start to understand more about the world and begin to have more concerns and fears. The safer their bedroom feels to them, the more likely they will go to sleep willingly and stay sleeping soundly all night.

A child's room should bring about feelings of peacefulness. This means eliminating the bedroom as a place used for time-outs or punishment. It also suggests taking the time to clean, organize, and decorate the room so that it is an inviting and happy place for your child to retreat to for peace, relaxation, and sleep.

Tip 6:
Provide the Right Nutrition to Improve Sleep

What children eat, what they *don't* eat, when they eat, and how much they eat can all affect their sleep. If your little one isn't sleeping as well as you'd like, or if your child takes a long time to fall asleep, then take a look at her overall nutrition and daily meal schedule. Making a few simple changes might help improve both naptime and nighttime sleep.

What Children Eat

Many foods can affect energy level and sleepiness. Some induce a feeling of calm and even drowsiness, some can create feelings of alertness, and others are neutral. This phenomenon is due to certain chemicals contained in food and certain biological responses to food that affect brain function. Some, for example, contain serotonin or tryptophan, which are amino acids that make you feel sleepy. Other foods stimulate the production of chemicals in the brain that cause alertness. Foods can affect the regulation of insulin in people's bodies, resulting in either alertness or tiredness.

You may see sleep aids such as melatonin or tryptophan sold in health food stores, but these can be very dangerous when given to children (and in some cases can be dangerous for adults, as well). It's important that your child receives these nutrients in their natural forms in foods.

Once you've reviewed the following information, you can experiment with the type, quantity, and timing of foods in your child's daily diet. Watch to see if any of these appear to have an effect on your child's ability to fall asleep at naptime and bedtime. Make a few changes, and note how they affect your child at naptime, bedtime, or early in the morning.

Foods That Create Calm and Drowsiness

Some carbohydrate-rich foods are known to have a calming, relaxing effect on the body. Pure carbohydrate snacks can be helpful for creating a ready-to-sleep mood. Highly processed carbohydrates don't have the same sleep-inducing effects, which means that a before-bed bowl of sugary breakfast cereal isn't such a good idea.

It can take thirty minutes to an hour for the sleepy effect to occur, so aim for a healthy carbohydrate snack a half hour before naptime or just before beginning your prebedtime routine (which you have now, right?).

Other foods that are known to help create a calming effect similar to that of carbohydrates are green, leafy vegetables and sunflower and sesame seeds.

Foods That Stir Up Energy or Prevent Sleep

Many foods that are high in protein generate alertness and energy, particularly when eaten alone, without the addition of fat or carbohydrates. Avoid giving your child a high-protein meal or snack for two hours before bedtime, since that's how long the effect can last.

Here are a few examples of high-protein foods to avoid before bedtime:

- Red meat
- Bacon and pork
- Sausage
- Ham

Some foods can create sleep problems through the digestive process because they can cause indigestion and gas, as well as aggravate reflux. Other foods have a stimulating effect on the nervous system. So avoid giving your child any of these foods before bedtime or naptime:

- Caffeinated beverages such as cola or tea
- Chocolate
- Peppermint
- Fatty or greasy foods
- Spicy foods
- Orange juice and other citrus juices
- Cream sauce
- Butter and margarine
- Additives and preservatives
- Monosodium glutamate (MSG), often found in Asian food
- Carbonated beverages
- Sugar
- Simple carbohydrates: white rice, white potatoes, white bread

Foods That Break the Rules

The following foods don't fit the previous descriptions given. Because of unique characteristics, they are good choices for before-bed nutrition:

- Breastmilk: contains sleep-inducing properties for both mother and child

- Cow's milk: can be a relaxing choice, particularly when warm, as it contains tryptophan, calcium, and magnesium, which can bring sleepiness (Avoid cow's milk if your child has allergies, and don't add chocolate!)

Other foods that contain tryptophan, the sleep-inducing chemical, include the following:

- Turkey
- Tuna
- Almonds, cashews, or walnuts (not whole nuts, which are a choking hazard for young children)
- Natural peanut butter without sugar (Spread a small amount on bread, crackers, or fruit. Peanut butter alone can pose a choking hazard.)
- Cottage cheese
- Hard cheese
- Yogurt
- Soymilk, tofu, and soybeans
- Eggs
- Bananas
- Avocados

Here are a few ideas for prebedtime snacks for your child:

- Whole-wheat toast and cheese
- English muffin with low-sugar jam
- Oatmeal with bananas
- Whole-grain cereal and milk
- Bagels (especially whole wheat) with cheese or turkey
- Whole-grain crackers with tuna
- Peanut butter sandwich
- Low-sugar oatmeal cookies with warm milk
- Whole-wheat pretzels with cheddar cheese

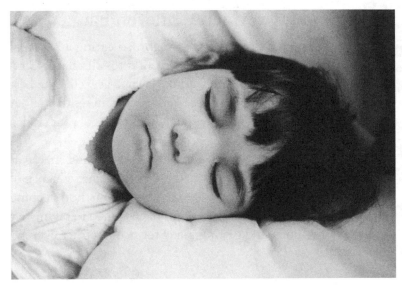

Sachi, three years old

- Apple slices with natural peanut butter
- Brown rice pudding
- Yogurt and low-sugar granola

What Children *Don't* Eat but Should

In today's fast-food world, many children aren't getting nearly enough whole grains, fruits, and vegetables in their diets. Vitamin and mineral deficiencies that are due to consistently unhealthy food choices can affect a child's overall health, including her sleep. Make your best effort to provide your child with a daily assortment of healthy foods, and ask your health care provider if your child would benefit from a daily multivitamin supplement.

When and How Much Children Eat

The digestive system slows down at night, so eating a big meal right before bed can make it hard for a child to fall asleep. Conversely, feeling hungry can keep a child awake as well. The best choice is to provide a small snack about thirty minutes to an hour before bedtime, using the previous guidelines to make your choice for a before-bed snack.

It may be helpful to schedule your child's meals and snacks at about the same time every day or at least in the same sequence of daily events. This can often work as a cue to anchor sleeping times. For example, a child can become accustomed to taking her daily nap after lunch and getting ready for bed after her evening snack.

Food Allergies, Food Sensitivities, Diabetes, and Reflux

Many health conditions are aggravated if a child is eating the wrong foods, and one of the troublesome side effects of this is poor sleep. If your child has any health issues or possible issues based on family history, it would be wise to talk with your health care professional about supplements, daily diet, and bedtime snacks. (For more information on this topic, see page 335.)

If your child takes any medications, check the label or talk to your pharmacist or medical provider about the possibility of the medication causing sleep problems.

Tip 7:
Help Your Child Be Healthy and Fit

It's a simple yet important fact that being healthy and fit helps a child sleep better. In today's world, though, many children are not getting the daily physical activity they need. Too much television watching and computer time coupled with a lack of activity amount to a sedentary lifestyle, which is common among children—even toddlers and preschoolers. Some studies show that although children are physically active during parts of the day, less than 2 percent of their time is spent in activities of a high enough intensity to promote cardiovascular health and better sleep.

Little Couch Tater Tots

The average American or Canadian preschooler watches as much as five hours of television per day—up to twenty to thirty hours a week—that's nearly a full-time job! It's been found that children who have television sets in their bedrooms watch the most TV of all and have the most health and fitness-related problems.

The main sleep-related problem with this much TV watching is that it robs a child of the physical activity needed during the day in order to get a good night's sleep. In the case of a TV in the bedroom, it often causes a child's bedtime to be much too late and can even create the unhealthy habit of watching in bed while falling asleep.

The Canadian Paediatric Society suggests that parents limit their preschoolers to no more than one hour of television per day. The American Academy of Pediatrics recommends that children under age two watch no television at all. Some parents may view this as extreme, but it is definitely in your little one's best interest: for his overall health, development, and for better sleep, too.

To keep it simple, here are the best TV tips for parents of toddlers and preschoolers:

- Choose programs wisely.
- Limit daily viewing times to an hour a day or less.
- Don't put a TV in your child's bedroom.

How More Activity Helps Your Child

There is a direct relationship between physical activity and healthy sleep. According to sleep research completed at Stanford University, exercise can produce statistically significant improvements in the quality of sleep and can increase time spent in stage 3 and stage 4 of sleep, which are the deepest, most restful stages of sleep. In addition, adequate daily physical activity accomplishes the following:

- Tires and relaxes the body, preparing it for the upcoming night's sleep
- Controls blood pressure, improves blood circulation, and keeps the heart healthy
- Reduces the anxiety, tension, and stress that can prevent a child from falling asleep easily
- Improves the flow and transition between sleep cycles
- Reduces the likelihood of sleep disorders and insomnia

- Diminishes the probability of daytime tiredness
- Improves overall well-being, which allows for peaceful sleep

In addition, the studies that I suspect you would find most appealing demonstrate that children who get enough daily physical exercise fall asleep more quickly, sleep better, stay asleep longer, and wake up feeling more refreshed.

Mother-Speak

"I always dismissed this advice because I thought Sebastian was getting plenty of exercise, but I've found that he needs a great deal more than he was getting. We've added daily outside activity such as hiking on rugged terrain, ball games, climbing in the playground, and working in the garden. He's having a grand time and sleeping so much better."

—Candice, mother of three-year-old Sebastian

Playtime Is Exercise Time

Toddlers and preschoolers don't require a formal exercise program, and they don't need to be put on a workout plan! They just need to have plenty of time every day for movement: running, jumping, and other physical pursuits. The American Heart Association recommends the following:

- All children age two and older should participate in at least thirty minutes of enjoyable, *moderate-intensity* activities every day.
- They should also perform at least thirty to sixty minutes of *vigorous* physical activities at least three to four days each

week to achieve and maintain a good level of cardiorespiratory (heart and lung) fitness.

These recommendations are simply guidelines for you to keep in the back of your mind. What's most important is that you opt for active playtime instead of letting your little one veg out in front of the TV or movies for long periods of the day. Sprinkle this with bursts of all-out action, such as running at the playground, riding a tricycle in the driveway, skating, swimming, dancing, or jumping on the bed (when the "bed" is a mattress on the floor, of course!).

When to Play

There is one important caveat to keep in mind. You'll want to keep physical parts of your children's day separated from the prebedtime hours. Avoid letting your children have their bursts of physical activity in the hour or two before bedtime, since exercise is stimulating and has a physical alerting effect. Too much activity too close to bedtime will increase adrenaline and make it difficult for children to settle down and fall asleep—they'll be bouncing on the bed instead of snoozing in it.

Tip 8:
Teach Your Child How to Relax and Fall Asleep

Have you ever forced yourself to go to bed when you weren't tired? Perhaps you had an early meeting or an airplane to catch the next day, so you went to bed early. You weren't tired, so you lay there staring at the ceiling, shifting positions on the bed, arranging and rearranging your covers. You knew you should sleep, but sleep eluded you. Your frustration in knowing that you *should* sleep may have made you more wide awake, so it took you even longer to settle to sleep.

What I've just described is how many children feel when they are put to bed. Mommy or Daddy says, "Go to sleep now," and the child lies awake, waiting for sleep to happen. Wide awake, she might decide she needs a visit to the bathroom, a drink of water, or some company. She hops out of bed and roams the house. A parent shows up to usher her back to bed with the same words, "Go to sleep." Not knowing how to respond, but feeling stressed and confused, she thinks, *"I don't know how!"*

> **Kid-Speak**
> ("Is it easy to fall asleep?")
> "Never ever ever ever."
>
> —Naomi, age six

To catch a glimpse of how some children feel about falling asleep, here are a few of the answers I received from children as part of their sleep surveys:

Name	Age	"Do you ever lie awake in bed at bedtime?"	"Have you tried any ideas to fall asleep? Did it work?"
Sean	6	Yes, all the time.	I close my eyes and try to fall asleep. It doesn't work—it takes a long time.
Alexandra	4	I lie awake every night.	No. I don't know what to do.
Atticus	5	Yes, that's what I do.	Counting. Singing. Talking. Asking. Thinking. Wondering. Jiggling. It all makes me awake.
Jackie	3	Yes, I open my eyes.	Go to the bathroom sometimes.
Daniel	6	Sometimes.	Thinking about something nice like kittens playing. It doesn't work.
Chase	4	Yes, I have to always.	Just wait.
Emily Rose	6	Always! (laughed)	Sometimes lying still and keeping my eyes shut works—mostly it doesn't.
Cielo	4	Yeah.	Sometimes and I keep my eyes open, but I don't get up. [Does it work?] Nope.
Austin	7	Yes, but I try to fall asleep.	I was going to try to sleep with my stuffed animal whale. No, it didn't work.

(continued)

Name	Age	"Do you ever lie awake in bed at bedtime?"	"Have you tried any ideas to fall asleep? Did it work?"
Jessica	6	Yes.	Just close my eyes. No, it doesn't.
Sinéad	5	Sometimes.	Dad says that when you count sheep you can fall asleep. One time I tried it, but it didn't work.
Janet	6	Sometimes.	Staring at the posters on the wall. [Does it work?] No. But I always fall asleep before morning.

I think that these answers demonstrate that many children get in bed but aren't sure what to do when they get there. It can be helpful to follow a soothing prebedtime routine (page 59) that helps create feelings of sleepiness. That is the first step, but sometimes a routine by itself isn't enough. It may help to teach your child *exactly how* to relax and fall asleep once in bed.

There are many different approaches to relaxation, and what follows is information on some of the techniques. Look them over and decide if any seem right for your little one; then spend a few weeks experimenting with the process. You can even customize your own approach based on what you learn.

Reading at Bedtime

A very common component in many families' bedtime ritual is storytime, and for good reason. A child who is listening to a book will tend to lie still and focus his attention on the story. This quiet stillness will allow him to become sleepy. In addition to the relaxation value of a good book or story, there are a number of other reasons that it's a great idea to end your child's bedtime routine with stories:

- A parent who can relax and enjoy the reading portion of the evening will find it a peaceful way to end the day with the child.
- Reading together with your child is something pleasant that you can share. It becomes an enjoyable bonding process.
- If you are putting more than one child to bed, you'll find that a reading session can keep everyone happy and in one place. (Many a mother—myself included—has nursed the baby while having a child cuddled on either side of her during storytime!)
- Reading to your child is the most important key to her future academic success.

Often the days get too busy to fit in much reading time, so reading books as part of your *bedtime* routine ensures that your child gains the benefit of a daily reading session. In our family, we've always had a very long and wonderful reading time before bed with all of our children. Part of the ritual involved going to the library every two weeks and filling a large plastic tub with a new assortment of books. (They are free, you know!) Not only has the bedtime reading become a tradition in our home, but all of our children have become superb readers.

Storytelling and Audiobooks

While reading books is a great way to help a child relax for sleep, some kids who aren't tired enough will easily have you read book after book after book, and the only person falling asleep is the one reading them! If your child is like this, then you should definitely continue to read books, since it is such an important component to intellectual development, and one that he obviously enjoys. You don't, however, have to read for endless hours. Put a limit on the number of books or the length of reading time, and then shut off the light and play a children's story recording or tell a story yourself. Playing a recording or telling a tale in the dark will not only keep your little scholar happy but will also help him relax and fall asleep.

If you choose to be the storyteller, you may find your child becoming attached to a particular story or theme. If the story features your child as the main character, it's even more likely to happen. While you may find this boring, your child will love the predictability of hearing his regular nighttime story.

A wonderful assortment of children's audiobooks is available at bookstores, online, or at your library. Just choose soothing stories. Avoid those that are too exciting or rousing, and avoid any that could be scary or disturbing right before sleep.

Massage

Very often children are so full of energy that they find it hard to relax enough to allow sleep to happen. A lovely way to end the day and help a child settle to sleep is with massage. Massage can help promote relaxation and relieve stress or tension. Some studies have even demonstrated that massage can help young children develop a more regular, consistent sleep cycle and, in some cases, can help them sleep longer and more soundly.

A prebedtime massage can be as simple as a back rub or foot massage, or a more practiced full-body rub after the evening bath. There are many massage classes available to parents, often through hospital education programs or massage clinics. Also, a number of books have been written on the topic of massage for children. The key is to be gentle and to respond to your child's reactions. After a few sessions, you'll learn what works best with your little one.

Massage is often effective as a specific last step in the bedtime routine. You'll want your child to brush his teeth, use the toilet (or put on the nighttime diaper), and get that last drink of water before you begin your nighttime rubs. Then he can drift off to sleep after you've helped his body to relax. Having your child pop out of bed for a last-minute potty break can defeat the purpose of the tranquil massage!

Regular bedtime massage can help your child associate relaxation and sleep with his bed, and that association is an important factor in helping him fall asleep. Children love to be held and caressed, and incorporating massage into your nightly routine can be very special and bonding for both you and your child.

Progressive Muscle Relaxation

This effective technique has been practiced since the early 1940s. It involves focusing on each part of the body in turn and causing relaxation one part at a time. You can talk your child through the process for a number of weeks, and eventually he'll be able to do this on his own.

Here's one example of how this might work: At the end of your bedtime routine have your child lie in bed. Sit or lie beside him and talk to him in a gentle, soothing voice, giving relaxation instructions starting from the toes and working up toward his head. You can even use a gentle massage as you talk him through the relaxation exercise, either gently massaging the part you're talking about, or just giving a head or back massage throughout the process. You can say something like this:

Ewan, fourteen months old, and Ken

Relax. Breathe in. Breathe out. It's time for your body to go to sleep. Wiggle your toes. They are really tired. Your toes are relaxed and sleepy. Your feet are tired now. They are warm and sleepy and comfortable. Your legs are tired. And so are your feet and your toes. They are tired and calm and warm and sleepy.

Continue this pattern up through his hips, back, chest, shoulders, arms, neck, face, and head, taking time with each body part.

There are many different ways to use progressive muscle relaxation. Some people envision a warm blanket covering each body part or the sun warming each section, or they imagine they are a sleepy cat or a rag doll. You can make up your own version or check out a book on the topic.

This can be a very helpful technique with young children, since they can be susceptible to your gentle suggestions of relaxation and sleepiness.

Clearing the Mind to Welcome Sleep

Just like adults, some children find that when they lie quietly in bed, their mind begins to race with a review of the day's activities or worries and thoughts about tomorrow or the future. Several techniques can be used to help a young child calm his mind so he can fall asleep more easily. You can try one of these with your little thinker:

- **White paper.** Have your child imagine a blank, white sheet of paper. She can then imagine a paintbrush with light-blue paint, and she can imagine painting dots or lines of light blue on the paper. Talk your child through the imagery for the first week or two when she is in bed. Then see if your child can imagine it all by herself.
- **Quiet ears.** Complete your child's bedtime routine, and have him relax and lie comfortably in bed. Have him put his hands over his ears and listen to the sound. When you try this, you'll see it makes a lovely, quiet white-noise sound. Depending on your child, you can just have him listen, or have him pretend he is hearing the sounds of the ocean or the wind. You can go one step further, if you like, and have him imagine that he is on the beach or standing in the grass and hearing the wind. He can do this for five to ten minutes until he feels sleepy.
- **Peaceful imagery.** Have your child lie on her bed with her eyes closed. Explain that you are going to tell her a story. In a gentle, soothing voice describe a peaceful place that your child would find familiar, such as a beach, swinging in a hammock, or lying on a blanket in the grass. You may want to enlist your imagination and be a butterfly floating in the wind. Describe the details of the surroundings quietly and slowly. Use this same place and this same story every night. Eventually, your child can use the story even when you aren't there to tell it.

Yoga

If you use yoga in your own life to unwind and relax, then you may want to use some of the simple stretches to help your child, as well. Yoga movements, breathing meditations, and relaxation exercises can all be used to take children through a wind-down bedtime routine that helps them to stretch and relax every part of their body. You can even incorporate soft music, dim lighting, or aromatherapy into the routine to enhance the relaxing properties of the exercise. A number of books and programs teach yoga movements especially for children.

Music or White Noise

When in bed, either at night or early in the morning, many children are easily distracted by sounds from other family members, the television, dogs barking, or cars driving by outside. They hear something—anything—and they feel like they are missing out on the fun, or they're simply distracted from the process of relaxing, so they can't fall asleep. You can mask these sounds and create a sleep-inducing environment by using soft music or white noise (a subtle monotonous hum of sound).

Many children enjoy listening to soothing music as they fall asleep. Choose bedtime music carefully, though. Some music (including jazz and much classical music) can be too complex and stimulating. Also watch for how songs progress, since abrupt changes in rhythm or volume from one song to the next can disrupt the relaxing effect. For music to be sleep inducing, stick to simple, repetitive, predictable music, like traditional lullabies. Recordings created especially for putting babies to sleep are great choices. (Disney has a lovely collection of lullaby CDs worth investigating.) Pick something that *you* will enjoy listening to night after night, too. (Using a player with an automatic repeat function is helpful for keeping the music going as long as you need it to play.)

Widely available and very lovely "nature sounds" recordings work nicely, too, as well as those small sound-generating or white-noise devices and clocks you may have seen in stores. The sounds of these—raindrops, a bubbling brook, birdsong, or running water—are soothing to adults as well as children. A ticking clock or a bubbling fish tank can also make wonderful white-noise options.

You can find some suitable tapes and CDs made especially for babies or children or those made for adults to listen to when they want to relax. Whatever you choose, listen to it first and ask your-self: Does this relax me? Would it make me feel sleepy if I listened to it in bed?

As always, though, children are unique, and sometimes you'll discover your child's own version of any idea works best.

Mother-Speak

"We tried white noise, lullabies, classical music, and whale song, but Samuel didn't take to any of them. My husband thought he needed something more substantial, so he put on the Bee Gees—their greatest hits, to be precise. Samuel loves it and goes to sleep to it every time."

—Frances, mother of three-year-old Samuel

If you must put your child to bed in a noisy, active house full of people, keeping the music playing (automatic replay) will help mask noises. This can also help transition your sleepy child from a noisy daytime house, to which he subconsciously has become accustomed, to one of absolute nighttime quiet. If you are dealing with a child who wakes up during naptime or the nighttime, you can leave the music or sounds turned on for an entire nap and even all night (think of how peaceful it is when a fan, air conditioner, or heater is running all night).

Once your child is familiar with her calming sounds or music, you can use these to help her fall back to sleep when she wakes up in the middle of the night. Simply show her how to press the play button to turn on her music if she wakes in the night.

If your little one gets used to his sleep-time sounds, you can take advantage of this and take the tape with you when you are away from home at naptime or bedtime. The familiarity of these sounds will help your child sleep in an unfamiliar environment.

Eventually your child will rely on this technique less and less to fall and stay asleep. Don't feel you must rush the process; there is no harm in your child falling asleep to these gentle sounds. When you are ready to wean him off these, you can help this process along by reducing the volume by a small amount every night until you finally don't turn the music or sounds on at all.

Prayer

Many families follow a tradition of saying nighttime prayers before bed. These can be very comforting to a child, and if done as a part of the bedtime routine, they can become a cue for sleep and set your child up for a secure and peaceful night's sleep.

A child's bedtime prayer can be a conversation with God; it can involve giving thanks for the day, asking for guidance, or reciting a prayer. A prayer time that you share with your child can be a very special way to end each day and can help your little one develop his faith.

If you choose to teach your child a nighttime prayer, try to avoid one that refers to death or fear, as many traditional children's prayers do. Look for one that creates feelings of security.

Garrison, nineteen months old, and Gabrielle, four years old

Don't be in any rush for your child to memorize a prayer; doing so may create tension and a negative association, and prevent sleep, as well. If you say a prayer to your child every night and over time begin to say it together, eventually your child will learn the prayer on his own. Take your time choosing a prayer that is uplifting and comforting, as it may become a lifelong prebedtime ritual. Here's a wonderful example:

A Child's Bedtime Prayer
Thank you, Lord,
for the day I had.
Thank you for
my mom and dad.

Help them take
good care of me.
God bless my friends
and family.
Help me sleep well,
all night long.
Guard me with
Your angels strong.
When I wake up
on a brand new day,
Help me love,
and learn, and play.
Amen
(*Author unknown*)

Aromatherapy for Relaxation

Aromatherapy is the art of using natural essences and oils of plants
to promote peace and well-being. Young children are very receptive to smell, and children can come to associate specific smells
with security and sleep. Certain scents—lavender and chamomile
—are known to produce a relaxing response and are perfect for
use at bedtime. These are available as fragrances, oils, and mists
or as fillings in sleep pillows or teddy bears. It's best to use products specially created for children and avoid using aromatherapy
for infants.

Using the Bed for Sleep Only

If your child finds it hard to relax at bedtime, take a look at how
he uses his bed. If he plays in it, jumps on it, builds forts around

it, and entertains friends there, it won't carry an association with sleep. Consider making a change to using the bed for sleep and only sleep. Save getting into bed for the last step in the bedtime routine. It's fine to include relaxing presleep rituals once in bed, such as reading, listening to soft music, massage, breastfeeding, or drinking a bottle.

If Relaxation Techniques Become a Crutch

Dr. Meir Kryger, chief editor of *The Principles and Practices of Sleep Medicine*, warns that toddlers and preschoolers who rely on relaxation techniques to fall asleep might have hidden sleep disorders. Therefore, if you have a good sleep plan, and a consistent nap and bedtime schedule, but your child still finds it difficult to fall asleep, you should review the chapter When a Sleep Plan Doesn't Work: Analyzing Problems and Identifying Sleep Disorders.

Part III

Customized Solutions for Your Family

Bedtime Battles: "I Don't Want to Go to Bed!"

Every night in our house brings a struggle to get my children into bed. The minute that I even suggest putting on pajamas, they both go into overdrive. They're not the least bit interested in cooperating, and our nights usually end up with me yelling and one or both of them crying. How do I solve our bedtime battles?

If it is any consolation, this scene is played out in millions and millions of homes around the world every single night. Parents and children view bedtime in totally opposite ways. By understanding how children feel about bedtime and then applying solutions that take their needs—and yours—into account, you can banish the bedtime battles from your home.

Why Don't Children Want to Go to Bed?

As an adult who treasures that moment at the end of a long day when you can finally fall into your bed and close your eyes to welcome sleep, you may have a hard time understanding why your little one resists bedtime with such vehemence. So let's begin by looking at the typical reasons that children don't want to go to bed.

- **Not tired.** Nothing is worse for a child than being put to bed when he's wide awake. He'll do just about anything to prevent you

105

from shutting off the light—one more book, one more glass of water, one more trip to the potty. To determine if this is the issue for your little one, refer back to the table of typical night sleep and nap hours on page 12. Take a good look at your child's nap schedule as well, since a nap that occurs too late in the day will keep your child refreshed and alert far past bedtime. An adjustment to the time or length of daytime naps, plus more activity in the early afternoon, including outdoor play when possible, may help your little one to actually be *tired* when it's time for bed.

- **Overtired.** Very often young children are tired quite early in the evening, around 6 to 7 P.M., but parents think that it's just too early to put them to bed. Or the family gets busy, and two hours fly by without you realizing it. What happens in this case is that your child becomes so overtired that he gets a second wind—propelling him into a wired-tired-can't-sleep state. He's running on adrenaline and will need some help to wind down enough for his condition to transform into sleepiness. The solution to this dilemma is an earlier bedtime, preceded by a peaceful, hour-long prebedtime routine.

- **Too busy.** Chasing a toddler or preschooler for a day can wear out a triathlete, but these amazing little people never seem to want to stop their continual activity. They view the world as an endless supply of entertainment created just for them. The idea of giving up the next exciting endeavor—whatever that may be—to go to bed doesn't appeal to them in the least. Creating a consistent and pleasant bedtime routine, plus avoiding any new or exciting toys or events right before bedtime, can work wonders to help a too busy child cooperate at bedtime.

- **Too curious.** Children sometimes have a vision that when they are confined to their bed, magical and marvelous things are happening in the rest of the house. As they lie in bed, they listen to people's voices, the television, and sounds of activity in the house. Something convinces them that they really need to find out what's happening, since they certainly are missing out on something wonderful. If you can keep the household quiet after your child is in bed and use white noise or soft music to mask any enticing noises, you may be able to keep your curious little one from coming out of bed to see what he is missing.

- **Is afraid of something.** The dark, monsters lurking under the bed, the troll in the closet, the sounds of dogs barking outside, or the roar of a truck passing by. Because of their emerging intelligence and their active imagination, this is a common age for fears to surface. If you suspect that fears are one of the reasons why your little one doesn't want to go to bed, read Nighttime Fears on page 229.

- **Lacks an *enticing* bedtime routine.** I've already mentioned (OK, I'll admit it—repeatedly) the importance of a bedtime routine for any child. If your little one resists getting ready for bed, the key word I've added for you here is *enticing*. A good bedtime routine is one that's reliable and predictable. A great bedtime routine is one that your child looks forward to each night and willingly participates in. (Tips on how to create a great routine will follow.)

- **Wanting to be with you.** The dark, quiet, lonely night is a time that separation anxiety often surfaces in toddlers and preschoolers. They want to be with the people they love the most and with whom they feel safe and secure. Given a choice between being with their parents or being alone, almost all toddlers and preschoolers will choose company.

I have a preschooler, plus I have three teenagers, too. Having both older children and a young one allows me tremendous clarity on many issues, and this is one of them. I sometimes seem to be an innocent bystander in the lives of my three teens as they race through their days. Our bedtime routine . . . isn't. Well, in a way it is, and it's very simple: they put down their phone to give me a quick kiss and hug good night. Yes, they love me and I know it—but their desire to be with me has been replaced by so many other things in their young adult lives. (Excuse me, while I get a tissue . . .)

In the meantime, my little Coleton still needs me and wants to be with me as much as possible. I relish his hint of separation anxiety when he doesn't want to be parted from me. I'm really in no rush to have him grow up!

Change the Way You Look at the Bedtime Routine

We parents today have demanding schedules and juggle multiple tasks all day long. There's too much to do and never enough time to do it. The bedtime routine often gets slotted as one more "thing to do," after which we can get on to yet another task on our never-ending to-do list.

I'd like to present you with a new way of looking at your child's bedtime routine: as a wonderful opportunity for a nightly ritual of quiet connection and bonding. It is like a forced savings account—a daily slice of time out of a busy day, given to you so you can bask in the joys of parenthood and build the foundation for a close lifetime relationship. Pretty heady stuff when you look at it this way, isn't it?

Simply said, you must get your child ready for bed each and every night. *The time will be spent, one way or another.* Would you like it to be peaceful, nurturing, and bonding—or rushed and stressful? You have the power to set the tone of your evenings, so why not choose a pleasant routine? You will enjoy it more, and your child will no longer resist bedtime. Won't that be marvelous!

Solutions for Ending Your Bedtime Battles

What follows are a variety of ideas from which you can choose. Don't feel you have to implement all of them; just pick the ones that suit your family and see if they create positive changes.

Begin Your Routine Earlier

If you are starting your child's bedtime routine fifteen to twenty minutes before you'd like him to be asleep, it will inevitably create problems. This provides barely enough time for the essentials, little time for pleasure, and no time at all for the inevitable dawdles and delays. As a parent, you're watching the clock move forward, stressing over the time, and trying to rush things along. Your child, who senses your tension and feels pressured, reacts by dawdling or fashioning new requests that simply must be met, but there's no time, so a meltdown occurs. Following this pattern night after night makes both parent and child dread bedtime, further increasing the stress and making things even worse. So goes the cycle from bad to worse, night after night.

The answer to all this turmoil is to allow plenty of time for the prebedtime routine. For most families, this means allocating at least an hour between the beginning of the process and lights out. While an hour or more may seem like a lot to spend on a bedtime routine, most families with bedtime struggles end up spending more time than this dealing with a fussy child who won't cooperate. And said fussy child gets so worked up that once in bed, he's wide awake and takes a long time before nodding off.

Decide in advance on the best bedtime for your child, and then identify a specific time that you will begin the getting-ready-for-bed routine. You may have to work backward from this time to schedule dinner and post-dinner activities so they are completed by the time you wish to start your prebedtime plan.

Once you understand the power a long-enough routine has to ward off bedtime problems, and if you look at this bedtime routine as an opportunity to spend some peaceful time connecting with your sweet child, then this hour can be something wonderful to look forward to each night.

Coordinate Multiple Children's Routines

When you have only one child, particularly when your child is a baby, it can be an easy thing just to allow your little one to set the schedule. If you have more than one child, it may be better if you avoid simply going with the flow each night and, instead, set a specific plan. Try to coordinate as many activities as possible. For example, no matter the age, they all have to put pajamas on, so have them all do it at the same time. You might even gather them into one room and make it a putting-on-pajama-party. (Just don't let the party get too wild!)

When my older three children were little, I kept them all on the same bedtime routine schedule. We—all four of us—would have a snack, don pajamas, and brush teeth together. Then we would snuggle on their big bed to read books. I'd have a daughter on either side of me and David nursing in the middle. When he was weaned, he continued part of the routine: he would lie across my lap during storytime and almost always fell asleep. When he was three, I remember commenting to him that he was getting to be a big, heavy boy to lie on me. He looked at me with a puzzled expression and with all seriousness asked, "But what will you do when I'm thirteen?" (David is thirteen now and finds this story funny and embarrassing!)

Avoid Television Time Before Bed

A recent study demonstrated that children who watch television before bed have more trouble falling asleep, have less restful sleep, and sleep fewer hours overall, typically falling far short of recommended sleep hours. Those children with sets in their bedrooms had the worst overall sleep problems, and children who fell asleep watching TV had the most sleep disorders of the group studied. Children who watched evening television also had more nighttime fears, since even fleeting images of disturbing content can linger in a child's mind.

Another report demonstrated that young children who get in the habit of falling asleep to the television tend to retain the habit and the sleep-related problems as they get older. In addition to all this, TV-related sleepiness had a negative effect on the children's waking lives as well.

So letting a child fall asleep to the TV as a temporary way out of bedtime battles creates far too many problems to even consider it as a solution. In light of all these reasons, it would be wise to avoid evening television time for your little one in favor of other more enriching and better sleep-producing activities, such as playing with toys, going for a walk, or reading.

Write Down Your Routine

To help you organize and remember your new routine, take the time to write it down. Doing so will help you get a timely start each night and will keep you organized as you go through your nightly ritual. When you write down your routine, take a guess at the length of time it takes to complete each task on your list so you know how much time to plan. You'll likely see that you need to schedule an hour or more to fit it all in, and you'll be shocked that previously you attempted to squash everything into twenty minutes!

How to Put Together Your Routine

When you create your bedtime routine, think carefully about your child's personality and likes and dislikes. Set things up to work with his natural behavior, not against it. For example, some children find a bath relaxing, but others enjoy the splashing so much that it's almost as if they've been in a swimming pool, and afterward they're refreshed and ready to play. Some children enjoy a snack early in the routine; others do better with a light snack just before bed. Try to balance maintenance tasks, like getting into pajamas and brushing teeth, with some pleasant activities.

Keep in mind that it doesn't take any more time to make routine tasks a bit more fun. Here are some ideas to get you thinking:

- Give your routine a fun theme and a name, such as Countdown to Sleep Space, Jungle Campout, Bedtime Circus, or Sleep Parade.
- Play "I Spy" or walk in the dark with flashlights.
- Play hide-and-seek along the way: you hide in the bathroom, your child hides in the bedroom.
- Make the pajamas talk as they walk over to your child; give the toothbrush a singing voice as it does its work.
- Give your child funny choices along the way: "Do you want to brush your teeth while sitting on the floor or sitting in the bathtub?"

- Let your child pick out the books to read and line them up in the order she'd like them read.
- Sing a special song to your child during routine tasks: pick any tune you'd like and sing about his day or things that he can look forward to tomorrow.

These seemingly little things can make your child look forward with eager anticipation to this special time with you each night. And in his joy, you'll find your own reward.

Reading Before Bed

If at all possible, fit in a bedtime reading session of at least fifteen minutes or longer—in fact, as long as you'd like it to be. There are countless reasons for including reading time as part of your bed-time routine, as discussed earlier (page 91). Schedule this reading time to occur at the very *end* of the bedtime routine process, when your child is in bed. Many children become very drowsy—some even fall asleep—as they listen to wondrous stories told with their

Mother-Speak

"Both of my boys would try to finagle extra books every night. To avoid the issue I say, 'This is the last book. What happens after this?' They are accustomed to the question and always respond, 'Lights out and time to sleep.' This seems to prepare them for what's coming."

—Judith, mother of three-year-old Harry and eight-year-old Robbie

loving caregiver's reassuring voice. The last thing you want to do is reach this point only to rouse her out of bed to brush her teeth, change location, or use the toilet.

If your child seems to be wide awake and alert after reading time, then try ending with a short storytelling session after the lights are out. You can make up a very simple tale to please your child. Often, using her as the main character is well-received. She can do just about anything in your story: go to the park, play on the beach, take a boat ride, go on an airplane, or visit magical places. Some children enjoy this part so much that they ask for it nightly. Interestingly, at this age the very same story told with little change is not only acceptable but desired, so you don't have to be too creative!

Make a Bedtime Chart

While a young toddler can be easily directed through your chosen routine, it is often helpful to involve an older toddler or preschooler in the process. An easy and fun way to do this is to create a poster that displays your routine in a step-by-step series of images. Here's how:

1. Get a large piece of poster board.
2. Gather colorful markers, crayons, and stickers.
3. Cut out pictures of children from magazines, advertisements, and the newspaper. Look for pictures that demonstrate the steps in your routine, such as a child brushing his teeth. An alternative is to take photos of your child doing the steps in his bedtime routine.
4. Use the pictures, markers, and stickers to create a fun, colorful poster that clearly demonstrates the steps to bedtime.
5. Hang the poster on your child's bedroom door at his eye level.

6. Have him help you follow the chart each night by asking, "What's next?"
7. Praise him for following the steps ("Good job!").

Here's a sample bedtime chart:

Sonya Gets Ready for Bed
1. Put on pajamas.
2. Brush teeth.
3. Go potty.
4. Read three books.
5. Sing Sonya's "nighttime song."
6. Turn on Winnie-the-Pooh night-light and lullaby music.
7. Have Mama's milk.
8. Give kisses, hugs, and back rub.
9. Sonya goes to sleep: Night night!
10. Mommy and Daddy go to sleep: Night night!

For many young children, the chart alone will provide the consistency and routine that will ease them happily into bed each night. If you have a little yo-yo who likes to pop out of bed after your routine, asking for a drink of water, for a hug, or "How many days 'til my birthday party?" you can solve this in one of two different ways.

The first option is to finish off your routine by lying with your child until she is asleep. If you choose this method—and many parents do—keep in mind that you can't skip this part on nights when you don't feel like lying with your child or if you're too busy to do it. You become an integral part of the bedtime routine. Actually, you become the most important part, and without this step your child will not be able to fall asleep quickly. Parents who lie with their children nightly after a pleasant, peaceful routine report that it usually takes only five to fifteen minutes for their child to fall asleep. And the majority of parents discover that this step is naturally weaned from the bedtime routine when their child is ready. Every child is different, and with encouragement the process can be moved along, but when left to the child, weaning from the need to have a parent lie with her as she falls asleep usually happens between five and ten years old.

If you'd prefer not to lie with your child until she's asleep (or if you've been doing it and wish to stop), the second option is a fun method that is often successful with older toddlers and preschoolers. The second option for a little yo-yo child is to add this step to your chart, which will help to eliminate the exasperating process of a child popping out of bed repeatedly after lights are out:

- Sonya will get two Get-Out-of-Bed-Free cards. She may come out for potty, water, kisses, or hugs TWO times. When Sonya's tickets are gone, it is time to stay in bed and go to sleep.

These "cards" are simply pieces of paper that you create with your poster supplies. At the end of your routine, give your child the tickets. She has to give you a ticket each time she gets out of bed. You can choose the number of tickets based on the current number of bed escapes you are dealing with, minus a few. That is, if she normally climbs out of bed five or six times, start with four tickets. After a week or two, change to three tickets, then two, and eventually, one.

If your child doesn't quite respond to the get-out-of-bed-free tickets, there is something you can do to persuade her: offer a prize. I provide this idea because almost all of the children of my survey families said they would change their sleep habits if given a prize. You may be able to entice your child to cooperate by letting her turn in any unused tickets in the morning for a small reward or prize. Interestingly, it doesn't have to be anything elaborate, a small plastic animal or a sticker can do the trick.

Different Homes, Different Schedules

If your child divides his time between two homes, make a duplicate bedtime chart for his second home. Having the same routine followed in the same way will keep bedtime consistent at both places.

Sometimes family schedules aren't consistent from day to day. If in your family one person puts your child to bed several days a week and someone else has the pleasure on other days, or if work or day-care arrangements require a different bedtime on certain days, don't fret. Simply make several charts for specific days, such as a "Daddy & David Bedtime Chart" and a "Mommy & David Bedtime Chart"; "Day-Care Bedtime Chart" and "Home Bedtime Chart"; or charts labeled for certain days of the week. In this way your child will become used to the idea of a nightly chart and will adapt to the changes in his schedule more easily.

Write a Family Bestseller

Most toddlers and preschoolers enjoy reading books, especially books with pictures of real children or of fantasy characters doing realistic, recognizable things, like getting ready for bed. Reading books about sleep to your child at bedtime can be helpful. I've found that most of these books depict a predictable, typical bedtime routine. Seeing that other children (or creatures!) go to bed in the same way he does can help your child do the same.

This is a great time to write your child his own book about sleep. This idea has helped many parents overcome disastrous prebedtime chaos and create a more peaceful, organized process. It has also helped many parents successfully and gently wean their children from breastfeeding, drinking a nighttime bottle, or having a pacifier. I first used this idea with my older son, David, when he was weaning from breastfeeding and the family bed. Here's how it works:

Use poster board or very heavy paper. Cut it so that your book ends up to be about 8½ inches by 11 inches or bigger. Tape the pages together with heavy tape, but don't do so until you've created the entire book. That way, you can easily replace any pages you may mess up during the creative process.

Here I'll describe making two different types of books. Make either one, or even both!

Book One: My Sleep Book

Cut out pictures of children from magazines, books, or the newspaper. Use pictures that show steps from your own bedtime routine, such as a child in a bathtub or a father and child reading a book. Also cut out pictures of related objects: a toothbrush, pajamas, blanket, night-light, and so on.

Use the pictures to create a homemade book that demonstrates your exact bedtime routine, step by step. Write a simple story on the pages to go along with the pictures.

Read this book every night at the start of your bedtime routine.

Book Two: The Personalized Growing-Up Book

Title your book *All About [insert child's name]*. This book will depict the story of your child's life, with the focus on sleeping, as well as feeding if you are using this idea to help your child wean from the breast or bottle. You can also use this idea to wean your child from the pacifier or, for that matter, to help her adjust to any major change in her life, such as introducing a new pregnancy, dealing with divorce, adjusting to a parent's marriage, or preparing to enter day care or preschool.

Eric and Zion, fifteen months old

Gather photos of your child right from the time of birth. Start with a shot of her as a newborn, and progress through her life, finishing up with those pictures that feature actions and items in your bedtime routine. Pictures of her breastfeeding, drinking a bottle, using a pacifier, wearing pajamas, reading a book, lying in bed, and sleeping are the most helpful. If possible, take photos of your child during every step of your current bedtime routine—including several of her sleeping soundly. In one of the sleeping photos, you might have Mommy or Daddy in the background smiling and watching over her as she sleeps.

Each page in your book will show a picture of your child and explain briefly what is happening. The book's ending will show your *goals* for your child. (For example if she now sleeps in your bed, but you want her to sleep in her own bed, then the book will end with her sleeping happily in her own bed.)

This book will be customized to your family. The following are excerpts from the book I created for my son David many years ago. (As a lovely bonus, you'll have this book to cherish as your child grows up. Excuse the tearstains as I write the following portion.)

(Newborn photo: David nursing) David is a brand-new baby. His mommy and daddy love him very much. They are so happy he was born. David loves nursing and having Mommy's milk.

(Six-month photo: Angela giving him a bottle) David is getting bigger. He can crawl now. He loves to play with Angela and Vanessa. He still loves nursing and having Mommy's milk, and now he likes his bottle, too, especially when Angela or Vanessa help him have his bottle.

(Eleven-month photo: David walking) David is growing so much! He is starting to walk and throw a ball. He can have some real food, too, and his favorite drink is chocolate milk. He still loves nursing and having Mommy's milk, and he likes his bottle, too.

Continue on in the book through your child's life. Don't make the book so long that your little one will lose interest, because the ending is, after all, the real goal of the book. You know your own child and how long of a book she enjoys.

The last section of the book will be your bedtime and sleep (or weaning) goals, outlined very clearly and specifically. Here is our ending:

(Second birthday photo) Happy birthday, David! You are a really big boy now. You can run and play and eat ice cream. You can go down a slide. You can take the dog for a walk. Big boys like David have a snack and then get in bed to go to sleep. They don't need Mommy's milk anymore—they just need lots of Mommy cuddles! Mommy and David can cuddle at bedtime, and then they both sleep all night long.

(Two-year-old photo: David sleeping) Mommy and David cuddle in the morning when the sun comes up. Everybody can hug and cuddle David in the morning. Congratulations, David! You are a big boy now.

(Pictures of everyone in the family with David)

The End

Once you've created your wonderful book, read it to your child every night. (She may like it so much that she wants to read it during the day, too—and that's perfectly fine.) Talk about what you read. Help your little one do the things you talk about in the book: "Remember? You can go in your own bed, just like in your book!"

After I made this book for David, we read and talked about it. He loved it. After a few months of reading and talking, David was weaned. The process was simple and loving, and we both felt good about it.

I've heard from many families who have used this idea successfully to ease their child into a better bedtime routine, to get their child ready to move from the family bed to his own bed, to move

a child from the crib to a toddler bed, or to prepare him for a new
sibling or a family move. It may be worth a try for you!

Evolution and Flexibility

Keep in mind that your child's bedtime routine won't remain the
same forever. As he gets older or as your daily schedule changes
to include a new sibling, school, or other changes, your routine
will change as well. Be open and flexible enough to change things
when necessary.

Once your child is sleeping well and bedtime and sleep-time
issues aren't so all-encompassing, you can experiment with relaxing your routine a bit. Don't stray too far from your established
routine at first, as it may be a key to ongoing sleep success. Over
time, however, you'll find things won't require as much orches-
tration as they do now.

"Mommy, Stay!": Needing a Parent's Help to Fall Asleep

Every single night, for the past three years, I've had to stay with my daughter until she falls asleep. If I try to leave when she's awake, she cries and carries on. I actually left her once—she cried and screamed, "Mommy, stay!" It took two hours for her to settle down on her own before she fell asleep on the floor in front of the door! I felt so cruel! I don't want to repeat that horrible night, but I'd really like her to fall asleep on her own. Help!

Before getting into the ideas and solutions part of my answer, I'd like to set the record straight on that television scene we know so well: parent tucks blanket around child, kisses child's forehead and says good night, shuts off the light, and leaves the room. Child smiles, closes eyes, and goes to sleep. You know, that scene? Pure fantasy. Unrealistic, inconceivable, la-la land. It just ain't gonna happen in real life.

According to the National Sleep Foundation's 2004 *Sleep in America* poll, more than two-thirds (69 percent) of all children experience one or more sleep problems. Two of the most common issues cited include having difficulty falling asleep and resisting going to bed. Among parents of toddlers and preschoolers, almost half report having to be present in the room while their child falls asleep. (Incidentally, for those of you with a baby in the house, 68 percent of you are staying with your baby until he is asleep.) Interestingly, by school age, more than a quarter of parents are still staying in the room at least once a week until their child is asleep.

In the same poll, parents and caregivers were asked if the children put themselves to bed. In the toddler age group *less than* 1 percent did, and among preschoolers 1 percent managed this amazing feat. Only 12 percent of school-aged children put themselves to bed.

> **Mother-Speak**
>
> "Even now, at nine years old, she needs one of us to walk with her to bed, tuck her in, and spend a few minutes closing the day, rubbing her back, and saying good night. She simply cannot fall asleep without this ritual. It used to bother us, but as she is growing up, we find that this special time keeps us connected to her every day, no matter how busy the day was."
>
> **—Pia, mother of nine-year-old Gracie**

So what does this all mean? First, if you stay in the room until your child is asleep, you are not alone. As a matter of fact, you are clearly in the majority. Second, and more important, this indicates that the "problem" isn't really a problem at all, but normal childhood behavior.

Why Your Child Wants You There

There are a number of reasons why your child wants you beside him until he falls asleep:

• **He loves you.** You represent security, safety, and love. Falling asleep brings the vast unknown. If a big, strong parent is in the room, then all is well and a child can relax enough to sleep.

- **She's scared.** The dark brings frightening shadows. The quiet invites mysterious noises. The stillness brings scary thoughts. A parent in the bed, or beside the bed, is the ultimate protection from all things scary.
- **He's worried.** When the activity of the day grinds to a halt, your child's unoccupied mind begins to sort through the day's events. Worries enter your child's thoughts—things that have happened, "Oh, no! Where did I put my red truck?" and worries about upcoming events, "Did Daddy say we have to go to the doctor's tomorrow?" Preschoolers worry about bigger things—"Will my dog run away?" "Will our house burn down?" "Will Mommy or Daddy die?" These worries loom large when a child is alone in the quiet and dark. Having a parent nearby is the ultimate protection against scary thoughts.
- **He's not sleepy.** If you put your child to bed when he's not tired—or overtired—he won't willingly stay put. He's wide awake and would rather be doing anything else than lying in bed, so your company is the only thing that keeps him there.
- **She nurses to sleep.** The 2004 *Sleep in America* poll uncovered some very enlightening information about toddlers and sleep. When breastfeeding mothers were asked if their toddler fell asleep nursing, the answer was as follows:

67 percent	Every night/Almost every night
11 percent	A few nights a week
11 percent	About once a week

This means that almost 90 percent of breastfeeding toddlers fall asleep nursing at least once a week and almost 70 percent do this every night or almost every night! Let me repeat that tidbit of amazing information for you: *almost 90 percent of breastfeeding toddlers fall asleep nursing.*

The sucking-to-sleep association is the most difficult and complex sleep association to change, and so this (obviously!) becomes a key component to your child needing you with her as she falls asleep. (For specific solutions turn to The Nighttime Nursling on page 165.)

- **She wants Mommy—and nobody but Mommy will do!** No matter how wonderful and loving Daddy, your partner, the babysitter, or Grandma is, nature and biology take a role in causing your little one to prefer Mommy above everyone and everything else in the world—especially when it comes to bedtime! Although parents may instinctually understand this preference, it can be a challenge when Mommy is also dealing with the child's siblings or when she's just all mommied out from a long day of child-tending. When it comes to bedtime, many mothers have conflicting emotions: they want to be a loving, comforting mother, but they also just want a moment (just one!) to themselves. This conflict can be conveyed to your child through both your conscious and unconscious acts and words. So if your loving partner offers to take over the bedtime routine, but your child inevitably rebels with tears or tantrums, it may hurt everyone's feelings, further complicate the stressful evening, and drag out an already too-long bedtime process.

- **It's a routine.** I've talked a lot about bedtime routines and how critical they are to a peaceful process, and believe it or not, you are demonstrating just how powerful these rituals are. You have a bedtime routine now that involves staying with your child until she is asleep. Remember that it takes about a month for a new routine to be formed. Whether you've been staying with your child until sleep from the day she was born, after her sibling was born three months ago, or after your move six weeks ago, you've likely been reinforcing this routine—night after night—for a long, long time. It will take patience and a plan to create a new routine.

What Is It That Bothers You?

When I interviewed parents to find out what exactly bothers them about having to stay with their children until they fell asleep, the following were the five most common answers (and many included a combination of all five):

1. "It takes a long time for her to fall asleep, and I have things I need to do, so I get very antsy about lying there."
2. "Sometimes I even fall asleep before he does, so I'm in bed much earlier than I plan to be."
3. "She gets used to my staying beside her, so if she wakes up during the night she wants me back."
4. "I have a baby and a husband that need me too, so I feel pulled in all directions."
5. "At the end of the day, I just don't have the energy to deal with bedtime. I want to just tuck him in and get on with it."

Before proceeding with the solutions, take some time to figure out what it is that bothers *you* about having to stay with your child until the sandman arrives. Understanding your own feelings will help you choose the correct plan of action to take as you begin to make changes to your current bedtime practices.

Choose a Path

You may have never looked at it this way, but there are two paths you can follow. Either choice can work beautifully. But you need to make a decision and follow it up with a plan:

1. Continue to stay with your child until he or she falls asleep, but do so in a way that encourages your child to fall asleep quickly.

2. Take steps to help your child learn how to fall asleep on his own.

Stay or Don't Stay—but Don't Whiffle-Waffle

Very often parents feel "stuck." They don't want to stay, but they do it to prevent tears or a tantrum. So some nights it works fine— their child falls asleep peacefully and quickly. Other nights parents have pressing issues to get to so they try to rush the process, or their child is too wired to sleep, but either way, their child reacts by staying wide awake for far too long. The lying-with or staying-with ritual drags on for an hour or more, often with the parent becoming angry and the child resorting to tears. In the end, parents get stuck with both: they get to stay and they get the tantrum too.

This aspect can be further complicated when parents disagree about how to handle bedtime, each pulling in opposite directions, with a tired child in the middle. Parents tend to avoid talking about the situation during the day, but the stress and anger about the routine rears its ugly head every night at bedtime. This situation can also become confusing when a child lives in two households and each home has a completely different bedtime ritual, with no communication about bedtime rituals. If you waver between the two choices, or if different caregivers use different approaches, your child will never know what to expect, so bedtime will remain tense and perhaps even a struggle of wills. Two different plans *can* work, but only if both are intentional plans, not haphazard whatever-happens confusion.

There is no "correct" answer here—either approach works for many families. So decide which path you are going to follow, stay or don't stay, and have everyone involved be consistent with whatever choice you make. When you maintain a pattern, and apply other sleep-inducing ideas from this book, you will end up with a more peaceful bedtime hour.

Deciding to Stay

Like the majority of parents, you may decide that when your child falls asleep quickly, it's not an inconvenience to stay in the room with him. Also, if you knew he'd always fall asleep promptly, you wouldn't mind the stay. If this is what you decide to do, let your child know and he'll relax into the new bedtime routine! Tell him in a very pleasant tone of voice, as if offering a gift, *"From now on I will stay with you until you fall asleep. Then I will go to my own bed. We both sleep all night, and then we can cuddle in the morning."*

What About Night Waking?

Many, many toddlers and preschoolers are able to go to sleep with a parent's company and then sleep all night without further help. Some, though, continue to depend on a parent's company anytime they wake up throughout the night. Remember that all human beings have night wakings—it's how your child falls *back* to sleep that can create problems for you. As you work through the various solutions in all the appropriate chapters of this book, you'll learn what category your child falls into, and this will help you as you organize your own approach to your child's sleep situation. Also, the sleep routines you choose can change and modify over time. Just because you choose one path doesn't mean you can't change approaches later. Do give each plan enough time to work through the kinks *before* you make modifications. Unless you have a deadline for change, allow a month or so to judge an idea's true effectiveness.

How to Stay and Promote Sleep

The key to staying, and making it a pleasant routine for everyone involved, is to set up a plan that works. The plan should involve a specific bedtime routine that ends in quiet, peaceful darkness. The finale to your bedtime routine should be your *quiet* presence as your child nods off. If you continue to talk and interact with your child, you may be actually keeping him awake! So do all your usual things—reading, storytelling, nursing, back-rubbing—and then *turn off the lights and be quiet*. The only noise you should make is a quiet "Shhh, Shhh" in response to any movement or noise from your little one.

The exception to this is a child who falls asleep easily to a parent's quiet singing, humming, or storytelling *under one condition*, and this is an important condition: do this only if you enjoy it too. Don't get into a habit of doing something to please your child if you hate it! You'll just begin to resent the process, and your emotions will prevent bedtime from being the peaceful, loving time it should be.

Invite Tiredness

When bedtime arrives, you want your child to be perfectly tired. If he isn't tired or if he is overtired, he'll struggle against your desire for him to go to sleep. Revisit the sleep hours table on page 12, and determine if your little one is getting the right amount of nighttime and naptime sleep. Take a look at your child's daily nap schedule, and make sure that naps aren't too long or too late in the day.

Look at your child's daily flow of activity and bursts of energy. You should be encouraging lots of energetic play between morning and dinnertime, and planning quiet time from dinnertime until bedtime. You'll want him to get plenty of fresh air and exer-

Sheila and Megan, two years old

cise during the day, and provide him enough time to wind down before sleep time.

Have an early enough bedtime so that your child doesn't become overtired. Make sure the time is consistent (try to stick with the set bedtime seven days a week) so that your child's biological clock is ticking in tune to his scheduled bedtime.

Have a Long-Enough Bedtime Routine

In the *Sleep in America* poll, it is reported that more than half the preschoolers and almost half the toddlers take fifteen minutes or longer to fall asleep *once the lights are turned out*. Add this to the time it takes to prepare for bed (taking a bath, putting on pajamas, brush-ing teeth, reading books, etc.), and you'll need at least an hour ded-icated to putting your child to bed. If you rush through this process, your child won't fall asleep easily or more quickly; the steps to going to bed are very important to a peaceful falling-asleep process. Of course, there are exceptions. On any given night, if your little one is truly tired, then a very short routine is in order! Don't keep a tired child awake just to make it through your traditional getting ready for bed routine. You may find it helpful to stick with your usual sequence of events, but shorten each step as much as possible—for example, pick one brief book rather than the usual three.

It helps to remember that it will likely take your child ten to twenty minutes to fall asleep once the lights are turned out. These twenty minutes seem like sixty when you're anxious to get up and get on to other things you need or want to do. Ironically, if you are quiet and peaceful yourself, your child will fall asleep much more quickly. So when you begin your new routine, glance at the clock when you turn the light off and then again when your child is asleep, noting how long it takes. Check again in a week, and compare the two. You may discover that it takes your little one far less time to nod off than you thought, particularly when he real-izes that you will stay every night until he's asleep.

Think of Your Needs, Too

As you wait for your child to fall asleep, what do you do with the time? Do you tap your toe impatiently while waiting, telling your-self that you're wasting valuable time or that you wish you didn't have to stay? This is a common response and is part of the reason why parents so dread this little nighttime ritual. Once your sleep plan is ticking perfectly, it's likely that your child will take much less than fifteen minutes to fall asleep every night. So choose wisely how you spend those minutes. While you are waiting for your child to fall asleep, perhaps you'll want to do one of these things:

- Think about some of the highlights of your day; enjoy your memories.
- Plan tomorrow's calendar.
- Watch your child and enjoy the beauty. They grow up so fast, you know.
- Daydream about an upcoming event or something fun.
- Put on headphones and listen to music or an audiobook.
- Meditate or pray.

No-Cry Solutions for Changing to the Don't-Stay Option

You may decide that you really do want your child to fall asleep independently and you don't want to stay in the room as he falls asleep. You can achieve this goal, but as with most sleep situations, no single right method works for every family, nor is there a quick-fix, easy solution. Merely leaving the room and letting your child cry to sleep isn't easy, and for the vast majority of families, it is not quick, either. In addition, new research is showing that such crying-it-out approaches may be only a temporary solution, because in many cases, sleep problems resurface and new ones appear.

What follows is a list of gentle, practical solutions and ideas for you to consider as you put together your own plan to encourage your child to begin falling asleep without your continued presence. Choose a few and add them to your current plan for better sleep based on Part I of this book.

Annette and Julia, twenty-two months old

Weaning from the Routine: "I'll Be Right Back!"

If you have decided that you really would like to have your child fall asleep on his own, you can do so gradually. Begin by following your usual pattern. Once the light is off and your child is sleepy, however, use an excuse to get up for just a minute or two: "I have to go potty, I'll be right back." "I need to get some socks, be right back." "I have to check the time—be right back."

Return to your child in a few minutes—before he has a chance to get out of bed or to get upset. After five minutes or so, repeat the exercise. Because you continue to come back to him, he should relax and not keep himself awake waiting for you to return—since you always do.

If your child won't stay in bed should you leave the room, then don't. Get up to close a window, put socks in the hamper, adjust the blinds, do some yoga stretches or a few crunches, or do something that gets you up and away from your child, but still in the room, for a few minutes. After he gets used to this step, move on to leaving the room for short errands.

Gauge your child's reaction after you have done this for a few nights or a week, and if things are looking good, leave his side for longer periods. Eventually, change your phrase to, "I'll be back." (leaving off the "soon"). Before long this will mean, "I'll be back . . . in the morning."

Weaning from Your Current Routine— Step by Step by Step

If you are currently lying with or near your child in her bed until she is sound asleep, you can use a step-by-step approach to literally move yourself out the door. This idea involves expanding the space between you and your child as she falls asleep, and doing it over a period of time. You'll need to customize this, depending on your current routine, your goal, and your sleep arrangement.

What's important during this phasing process is that you also use many of the other sleep ideas you've picked up through this book, particularly the eight tips in Part II, which begin on page 41. Tips such as using music or white noise and making the room dark and cozy will increase your success. By creating a comfortable routine and a relaxing sleep environment, you will help your child adapt more easily to change. This phasing process can be used when your child first goes to sleep at night, as well as for any subsequent night wakings as well. (You can read more about using this technique for night wakings on page 160.)

As you move from phase to phase, don't make a big production out of the modification. Simply ease into it without much fanfare.

Here is a sample plan—again, this is a *sample* and is not intended to be followed religiously. You'll need to create your own plan based on your family situation.

Sample Plan for a Toddler Who Sleeps in Her Own Bed

• **Currently.** You lie beside your child until she is totally asleep. She's usually curled up tightly beside you, perhaps with an arm or leg draped over your body.

• **Phase One.** Move yourself an arm's length away from your little one so that you're in bed but not touching, except to place a hand on her to reassure her if she needs it. If you don't already use it, it's a good time to introduce a lovey (a special stuffed animal or blanket), white noise, soft music, or an audiobook as a sleep-time cue. This will help create a consistent thread for falling asleep as you move from phase to phase.

• **Phase Two.** Sit in a chair moved tight beside the bed. Place your hand on your child if necessary, or put your feet up on the bed near her. Allowing your child to listen to music, white noise, or an audiobook can help her stay peaceful and welcome sleep. You may want to use your own headset to listen to music or a book on tape, meditate, pray, or catch up on your knitting to keep yourself relaxed. If she resists this change, begin by doing it for brief periods, "I'll just sit here for a minute, then I'll lie with you." This will help her get used to your being farther away.

If your child has a lovey, put it in her bed with her. Some older toddlers or preschoolers respond well if the bed is *filled* with stuffed animals. This is also a good excuse for you to sit in the chair, "Gee, there's no room for me, I'll just sit right here." Invite her to say good night to each one and tuck them in, since this makes them more like friends to sleep with. They will become even more helpful as you move on to the next phases.

• **Phase Three.** Move your chair a few inches from the bed. Remember to keep the rest of your bedtime routine the same, and keep all the other sleep cues consistent, such as white noise and stuffed animals.

• **Phase Four.** Move your chair to the other side of the room. (You may want to provide a simple reason for moving your chair, such as, "I'm going to sit here by the night-light and read tonight. Can you and your stuffed animals be quiet for Mommy so I can read?")

• **Phase Five.** Move the chair so that it's just outside her door, but she can still see you. ("I need more light to read, so I'll just put my chair here tonight.") When you do this, make little noises, like gentle coughs, humming, or rustling page turns. This helps your child know that you are still nearby.

• **Phase Six.** Move the chair so that it's outside her door and she can't see you, but close enough so you can talk to her if she needs to know that you're there. For the first few nights you can make your quiet noises so she knows you aren't too far away. If all goes well, sit quietly for a few nights. If your child falls asleep without calling out to you, then you're free to go about your business after putting your child to bed from then on. (Hurray!) Keep an ear open or a baby monitor tuned in, though. If she has a nightmare or wakes calling for you and you don't appear, this could set you back, and you won't want that to happen!

How Long at Each Phase?

You can spend a few days, a week, or even a month on each phase; there's no set rule. This will vary depending on your child's age and personality, and on your own patience and goals. It also may take longer to complete some phases than others. But keep in mind that parenting isn't a race, and sometimes the harder you push, the longer the process will take. Be patient.

Make It Clear and Predictable

Once you decide on how you are going to handle bedtime, communicate the news to your child. Of course, every parent knows that telling a toddler or preschooler something one time can be about as effective as not telling him at all! The key is to find a way

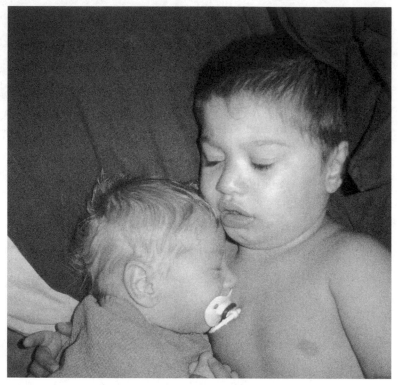

Ty, two months old, and Chad, two years old

to explain to your child what exactly you'll be doing and to remind him nightly of the plan.

You can explain the parts of your bedtime routine each night to your child, one or two steps at a time. Begin before the first step, and let your little one know what's happening at each point, giving forewarning before each major item. The preparation in advance is important because it allows your child to anticipate what's next and to prepare for it mentally. I call this the *power of 5-3-1*. Here's what your announcements might sound like:

"We're going to have a bath in five minutes."
"Sweetie, bath time in three minutes."
"One minute 'til bath time!"

At this point you escort (or carry!) your child into the bathroom while announcing, "Bath time!"

When it's time to get out of the tub, follow the same pattern:

"We're going to get out and put pajamas on in five minutes."
"Sweetie, time to get out and put on pajamas in three minutes."
"One minute 'til pajama time!"

At this point you gather your child out of the tub while announcing, "Pajama time!"

As you are putting on pajamas, tell your child what comes next, "After pajamas we'll brush teeth, then read books, then go to sleep."

You can use the 5-3-1 counting technique when it comes time for you to turn off the light and again when you leave the room. If you use this tool several times throughout the day, too, you'll find that your little one will be cooperating with all kinds of tasks!

Create a Bedtime Chart

The verbal reminders keep you and your child on track, but adding a bedtime chart, as described in detail on page 114, can be the most effective way to teach your child the steps involved in your bedtime routine. You'll illustrate all the steps, including the evening snack, brushing teeth, nursing, back rubs, reading, and whatever else is involved in your nightly getting-ready-for-bed routine. Include the specifics about when you will leave the bedroom. You may even want to include a picture of what *you* will be doing after you leave—sitting at your desk, cleaning up the house, or going to your own bed. If your child knows what you will be doing and understands that you'll be close by if he needs you, he may be more willing to let you leave without a fuss.

Put Siblings Together

If you have two or more children over eighteen months old, and if they welcome the idea, you can switch your toddler's bedtime alliance from you to his sibling. Many cultures routinely use this technique as a natural way of helping children learn to sleep without an adult nearby, and many families discover the ease and beauty of this arrangement quite naturally.

An effective routine involves tucking both children into bed with stories and cuddles and then leaving them to snuggle and whisper until they drift off to sleep. A word of caution! If this is new to your children, they may find playtime more fun than sleep time. To prevent adding an hour or more of listening to yourself say, "Shhh! Go to sleep now!" you may want to stay with them a little longer. Read to them, play soft music, or tell them a story in the dark so that when you leave the room, they are relaxed and sleepy and will actually *sleep*.

Night Waking: When Will My Child Sleep Through the Night?

Our three-year-old son still wakes up two or three times every night and needs one of us to settle him back to sleep. I read that children are supposed to sleep through the night by the time they are three or four months old! Is there something wrong with our son? Or have we created problems because of the way we've handled his sleep?

The only problem here is the perpetuation of the myth that children should sleep independently through the night from the time they are a few months old. The first obstacle here is that, technically speaking, it is impossible for a child to sleep "through the night" at any age. You already know this from what you learned in Part I about sleep cycles: all human beings wake up five or more times each night, particularly when shifting from one stage of sleep to another.

The issue, then, is not for a child to sleep all night without waking up but for a child to be able to fall back to sleep—totally on his own—each time he does awake. This means that most parents, who wouldn't leave their child alone for ten minutes during the day, would like their little one to be totally independent for about twelve hours, from 7 P.M. until 7 A.M.—a mighty high order for a young child. The fact is that many children don't comfortably achieve this level of autonomy until they are almost ready for kindergarten.

The National Sleep Foundation has published a nearly two-hundred-page study based on interviews with 1,473 adults who have young children in their households. This report, the 2004 *Sleep in America* poll that I've mentioned previously, provides an enlightening picture of children's sleep. The data clearly demonstrate that night-waking toddlers and preschoolers are not unusual; on the contrary, they are perfectly normal. In response to the question about how many times the child woke up and needed help or attention from an adult on a typical night, here's how the answers panned out:

Toddlers

4 percent	Three or more times per night
5 percent	Twice per night
38 percent	Once per night
47 percent	**Total of toddlers who wake *at least* once per night and need an adult's help to return to sleep**

Preschoolers

2 percent	Three or more times per night
3 percent	Twice per night
31 percent	Once per night
36 percent	**Total of preschoolers who wake *at least* once per night and need an adult's help to return to sleep**

Of the 245 families I surveyed for this book, 47 percent said their child wakes up during the night and requires a parent's attention before returning to sleep. Just after I reviewed all this information, I discovered the following confusing and contradictory statement in a clinical pediatric sleep book: "Nightwaking in young children is one of the most common problems that parents face. By six months of age, most babies are physiologically capable of sleeping throughout the night. However, up to 50% continue to awaken during the night." I'm really baffled by something, and you may be too. If up to 50 percent of the population does any particular thing, I don't see how it could be considered anything but *normal*. Dr. Penelope Leach, a British child psychologist and world-renowned parenting expert, says, "It's nonsense to say that children who wake a lot and need their parents have a disorder. I think it does a great disservice to parents." She goes on to say, "There is a general belief that if you are kind but firm no night-time fusses should ever happen. It is a myth."

What Does All This Mean?

What all this means is that it is perfectly natural, absolutely normal, and totally expected for your toddler or preschooler to wake up in the night and need your help to fall back to sleep. Sleeping all through the night, every night, without needing a parent's assistance is like learning to walk or talk or drink from a cup—all kids get there, but they do so at their own speed, a little at a time, and in their own unique way.

I promise I won't leave you dangling here, though. Just because something is normal doesn't mean you have to simply live with it until things change on their own. You can do many things to prod the natural process along a little more quickly. After all, to encourage your child to walk, you hold him by the hand; to help him learn to talk, you communicate with him all day long; and to teach him to use a cup, you begin with a child-safe, nonspill, two-handled sipper cup. The same philosophy holds true with night waking. Part of your child's night-waking situation is related to age, personality, and biology, but part of it is affected by many controllable factors that can be modified, step-by-step, in a gentle nudge toward autonomy.

First, I'll identify and review the myriad reasons why your child wakes you up. Then, I'll suggest a number of solutions for you to choose from so you can encourage your child's nighttime independence, which, in turn, will gain you the uninterrupted sleep that you crave.

Keep in mind that because so many possible things contribute to night waking and other sleep behaviors, it's often necessary to enact a complete sleep plan—not just one small piece of the sleep puzzle—to achieve the type of nighttime and daytime sleep that you are hoping for. So if you haven't yet done it, take the time to read through Part I of this book and create a written sleep plan. Then include some of the following ideas.

Figuring Out Why Your Child Wakes You Up During the Night

When I began researching the possible reasons why toddlers and preschoolers wake their parents up during the night, I was amazed at the almost endless possibilities. I began to believe that *any* young children who actually do manage to sleep all night on their own are the true *miracles*.

Identifying your child's particular reasons and motivations can be helpful, although some are easier to discover than others. If you can come up with some logical possibilities, you can set a plan to help your child sleep without needing your continued nightly interventions. I want to remind you, however, that almost 50 percent of toddlers and 36 percent of preschoolers do wake up and call for an adult at least once per night, so set reasonable goals for the little person in your house.

The following are the most common reasons that toddlers and preschoolers need a parent's attention during the night; see if any of these might describe your child. I'll include a few specific tips after each one and additional general ideas in the section that follows.

He Has to Go Potty or Has a Wet Diaper

If your child wakes every morning with a soggy diaper, it's possible that his wet, cold diaper or the sting of urine keeps him from sleeping soundly. Even if a wet diaper has never bothered him before, this may become an issue as he gets older.

If your child is potty-trained and pees a bucketful when he first gets up in the morning, a full bladder possibly is preventing him from easily falling back to sleep upon a brief awakening. If your child sleepwalks, sleep talks, or has night terrors, these are also clues that a full bladder may be an issue for him, as a few sleep specialists have found a possible link between these conditions.

Try limiting fluids during the two hours before bedtime. If your child wears diapers to bed, make sure they have extra nighttime absorbency and coat his bottom with ointment. If your child uses the toilet, make sure you take him to the bathroom several times during your bedtime routine, including as a last step before getting into bed. If your child is newly potty-trained, don't rush bedtime dryness. It's perfectly fine for him to rely on nighttime diapers or disposable training pants until he remains dry all night on his own. Worry about wetting the bed can keep a child from restful sleep (see page 259).

She Has Nightmares or Night Fears

If your child wakes up crying or gets very clingy after waking, then goes back to sleep easily with some comforting, it is possible that bad dreams, nightmares, or fears are the culprit. She may even mumble comments that lead you to think that she's had a bad dream or that something is scaring her when she wakes up at night.

Just as your mind wanders when you get in bed at night, young children may have scary thoughts that enter their minds after the lights are out and the house is quiet. These aren't quite nightmares, but they are frightening nonetheless. You can read about nightmares on page 205 and nighttime fears on page 229 and learn some solutions.

If your child is having disturbing thoughts, you might be able to figure out where they are originating. Often they come from television shows, books, overheard adult conversations, or misinterpretation of older siblings' play activities. It may surprise you to know that some traditional children's prayers may contribute to worries instead of peace, such as those that refer to death or dying. For example, the well-known

> Now I lay me down to sleep,
> I pray the Lord my soul to keep.
> If I should die before I wake,
> I pray the Lord my soul to take.

Such prayers can create unease or fearsome thoughts just before bed.

Some children's stories and movies contain scenes that may be disturbing or frightening to young children. Keep in mind that children interpret things differently than adults do, so you'll need to watch your child carefully for clues that he thinks something is scary.

If any of the preceding occurrences is the case for your child, some daily routine adjustments, your reassurances, and the planting of positive thoughts and images can be enough to help her back to sleep.

A pleasant reassuring nighttime prayer that evokes feelings of peace and safety may be in order, such as the one in Tip 8 on page 100 or this version of the old standard, created by Terry Kluytmans:

> Now I lay me down to sleep,
> I pray the Lord my soul to keep,
> Guard me while I sleep tonight,
> And wake me safe at dawn's first light.
> God bless Mommy; Daddy, too,
> And help me to always be true to you.
> Amen.
> *Copyright © 2002 by Terry Kluytmans. Used with permission.*

Pleasant songs or verses before bed can plant happy thoughts into your child's head. Several options come to mind, such as "Angels Watching Over Me," "This Little Light of Mine," "Mama's Lullaby," "Sleepytime," or "Come Dreams." You can find the lyrics to many children's songs at http://kididdles.com, or you can even make up a comforting song or poem of your own to end the day.

Make it a point to pay close attention to the things that might settle unpleasantly in your child's mind during the day and pop up at bedtime. Ending the bedtime routine with pleasant bedtime books, stories, or songs can be helpful in warding off nighttime fears and nightmares.

His Nap Schedule Is Off

An inconsistent daily nap schedule, insufficient daytime sleep, or a daily nap that runs too long or too late can increase your child's night-waking problems. Research shows that many children up to the age of four or five still need a daily nap, and without it they will have more nighttime disturbances, including night wakings, nightmares, and insomnia.

Check the nap table on page 12 for the average number of nap-time hours that most children need, and see how your child's daily naps match up. Then read over the section on solving daytime sleep problems that begins on page 241.

Her Bedtime Is Too Late, or She's Not Getting Enough Nighttime Sleep

Very often when children's bedtimes are too late or if they don't get in enough bedtime hours, they exist in a state of chronic sleep deprivation. This condition isn't always easily identified; it shows itself in ways such as impatience, dawdling, fussiness, or temper tantrums. Ironically, sleep deprivation doesn't usually make children sleep like a rock; rather, it makes their sleep less peaceful and causes them to wake much more often throughout the night. Even worse, it will exacerbate any sleep conditions such as nightmares, night terrors, tooth grinding, and insomnia.

Take another look at the sleep table on page 12 and read over Parts I and II of this book. Healthy sleep isn't achieved by focusing on any one solution but rather by focusing on your child's whole sleep situation.

His Bedtime Environment Isn't Conducive to Good Sleep

Too hot, too cold, too lumpy, too scratchy, too loud, too quiet . . . the list goes on. Some children are far more sensitive to their sleep environment than others, just as some adults are. These sensitive children easily can be awakened if anything in their sleep environment isn't perfect, and once awake, they don't fall back to sleep easily.

To see if you've missed something that may be interfering with your child's ability to be comfortable all night long, revisit the checklist and information on page 65 relating to creating a cozy sleep environment. To uncover any conditions that need correction, pay attention to your child's complaints or requests. You may find that a pair of soft socks to prevent cold feet, a room temperature change of a few degrees warmer or cooler, a different type of pajama, or a blanket of a different fabric will increase your child's ability to fall back to sleep during the night.

She Is Hungry or Eating the Wrong Foods Before Bed

Children don't grow at the same pace from birth through adolescence. They have growth spurts when they seem to shoot up several inches all at once. It is during these times that a child suddenly needs more food. To complicate matters, active toddlers and preschoolers don't easily identify the signs of hunger. So they may not adequately fuel their growth during the day, and hunger appears when they are finally still and quiet.

In addition to simple hunger, some foods are more conducive to a restful night's sleep than others. Food allergies can cause disturbed sleep, so consider eliminating from his diet any foods he may be sensitive to.

You can read about the best timing for snacks and best types of prebedtime foods in Tip 6 on page 79. More information about allergies and sleep is covered on page 335.

He's Mastering New Milestones

If your child's night waking has suddenly become worse, consider if he is also in the process of mastering exciting new skills, such as learning to walk, run, jump, read, or use a computer. These become an all-encompassing passion and seem to hover in a child's

mind and body, day and night. So when he has a partial awakening, he suddenly becomes fully alert—ready and willing to begin
practicing his newfound activity.

You can help your little one in this situation by maintaining
equilibrium in his days. Provide your child with a balance of time
spent learning and practicing new skills, downtime for old favorite
activities, and a bit of nothing—quiet play without pressure. Also,
avoid letting him get involved in a new activity right before
bedtime.

He Has a Touch of Separation Anxiety

Separation anxiety is very common during the toddler and preschool years. All children go through this phase; it's just more pronounced in some children than others. Even children who don't
display the obvious traits of separation anxiety dislike being separated from the adults whom they are attached to. It's a sensible
fear: children who feel safe and secure when their caregivers are
close by may feel unsettled when they wake up alone in the dark
of night.

Some children develop more separation anxiety after life
changes, such as starting day care, weaning from the breast or bottle, or moving from a crib to a bed. A parent's life changes can
affect a child's sense of security, as well, such as when parents separate or marry, Daddy gets a new job, or when Mommy becomes
pregnant, has a new baby, or returns to work. Sleep disruptions are
a natural response during times of transition.

Maintaining a stable, consistent bedtime routine is an important component to overcoming separation anxiety. In addition,
helping your child to have a midnight plan for night waking can
give him confidence when he does wake up. The plan might
involve coming to a parent's bed, taking a sip of water, cuddling a
stuffed animal, or thinking happy thoughts. It may help to encour-

age your child's attachment to a specific toy or special blanket; these are called security objects, or lovies, and they can keep your child company when you aren't there. Reassure your child when he goes to bed each night that you are just down the hallway and that you'll see him as soon as he wakes up in the morning. Sometimes a prebedtime discussion of what is planned for the morning can help encourage a peaceful night's sleep.

She's Teething

Anyone who tries to convince you that teething won't keep a child awake has never had a toothache nor looked inside a toddler's mouth at her big, purple, swollen gums. It's reasonable to suspect that teething pain can indeed prevent a child from sleeping soundly. You'll find the common signs of teething and an assortment of suggestions for soothing teething discomforts on page 305.

His Temperament Makes Him a Light Sleeper

I'm always amused when a parent of one child, who happens to be an all-night sleeper, claims to have all the answers to great sleep. I have four children, and all four had vastly different sleep personalities as babies, and they still do. Ask any parent of multiple children about the differences in their sleep patterns, and you'll hear varied stories. Think about yourself, your spouse, your parents, your siblings and your friends. Do you all have exactly the same sleep behaviors? Of course not, and neither do young children. The bottom line is that personality traits affect how a human being sleeps.

A child who is especially sensitive, persistent, timid, intense, or high-need will likely have more night wakings than an easygoing child. These children will require a more sensitive approach to their night wakings.

In addition, stages of development can affect a child's night-waking patterns. There are times when any toddler or preschooler will be more clingy, fearful, or needy than usual, which can definitely affect his sleep patterns. Consider your child's personality when deciding on solutions to night waking.

Children with special needs, newly adopted children, or children suffering from illness will often experience sleep difficulties. For these little ones, it is important to pay attention to the factors that help bring restful sleep and to create and follow a thoughtful bedtime and sleep routine. (For additional tips turn to the sections pertaining to each of these situations.)

He Has Insomnia

If your child takes a long time to fall asleep most nights, even when he's tired, and if he is awake for long periods when he gets up in the night, he may have insomnia (an inability to sleep despite being tired).

Many ideas throughout this book can help a child who has difficulty falling asleep, since oftentimes this is related to poor sleep hygiene (sleep-related habits), inappropriate or inconsistent bedtimes, lack of napping hours, overtiredness, sleep associations, and chronic sleep deprivation. All of these issues are addressed when a good sleep routine is in place. When you set a sleep plan for your child and follow all the steps, you should find your child welcoming sleep much more easily.

Another possible reason for insomnia can be found in a child's diet. Sodas and chocolate containing caffeine are common sleep-preventers. Foods high in sugar, artificial colorings and preservatives, and foods high in protein or simple carbohydrates have been known to keep children from falling asleep easily when consumed too close to bedtime. Replace these with foods that promote sleep.

Complete lists of food dos and don'ts can be found in Tip 6 on page 79.

Children with allergies, asthma, ear infections, reflux, or other health conditions can suffer insomnia as well. So if you can iden-tify these issues and work to solve them, it will likely improve your child's sleep.

She Has an Undiagnosed Sleep Disorder

A major percentage of children's sleep disorders go undiagnosed and untreated. Sleep disorders, which are medically or physically based disturbances of sleep, comprise a broad range of problems. Even a partial list adds up to over fifty different conditions. If your little one has any unidentified sleep problems, these will prevent her from sleeping well—no matter how many other solutions you diligently apply.

Take a look at the list of symptoms on page 383 that may indi-cate a sleep disorder. If your child displays any of these signs, it would be a good idea to talk to a sleep specialist for an assessment. In addition, if you've conscientiously followed the tips in this book for a month or more but have not experienced improved sleep, you may be fighting against a sleep disorder, and a visit to a sleep clinic may uncover the problem. (See Could It Be a Sleep Disorder? on page 382.)

He Has Allergies or Asthma

Children who suffer from a chronic nighttime cough, stuffy nose, noisy sleep, or labored breathing may have allergies or asthma. You may be able to identify symptoms during the day, as well, such as labored breathing after running or aggressive play. He may also get a runny nose, sneeze, or cough when around animals, outdoors near plants and flowers, when around dust and dirt, in a room with cigarette smoke, or when out in cold weather.

Allergies and asthma are two of the most common childhood diseases. Since both of these conditions cause excess mucous secretion and swelling of nasal tissues, they can make it difficult for your child to breathe when lying down, which in turn disturbs the quality of your child's sleep. Some of the most common foods that can cause sleep-disturbing symptoms in allergic children are dairy products, eggs, nuts, and wheat. If you suspect that your child may have one of these conditions, it's wise to talk to your health care professional. (Also see related chapter Allergies, Asthma, and Gastroesophageal Reflux Disease [GERD] on page 335.)

If your child has already been diagnosed with allergies or asthma and is taking regular medication, talk with your pharmacist about the possible side effects of the medication. Sometimes such medications cause drowsiness, but other times they can cause wakefulness.

She Has Tummy Problems

If your little one chokes or coughs while sleeping, or goes from totally asleep to wide awake and crying, perhaps there is a medical reason for her waking. Children can sometimes suffer from uncomfortable feelings but be unable to explain or describe these. Reflux (gastroesophageal reflux disease, or GERD) may be the culprit. The section with information about reflux and how to handle it is on page 335.

Something New Is Happening in His Life

A new baby sibling in the house; moving; parents' divorce; a new day care; vacations; Mommy returning to work; weaning from breastfeeding, the bottle, or the pacifier; and a visit from out-of-town grandparents are just a few events that can affect a young child's sleeping patterns. Sleeping patterns are disrupted for three main reasons: (1) the excitement or stress involved, (2) the fact that all routines go out the window, and (3) your own emotional upheaval, which is absorbed by your child.

Commonly, a child's sleep is disrupted by a temporary change in his daily routine, but afterward the temporary change becomes a permanent habit. It's beneficial, therefore, to identify the situations that may be affecting your child's sleep and take conscientious steps to help him make adjustments without allowing his normal routine to totally disappear.

Patience, love, and a little extra attention can work wonders. After a disruption, get back on track by writing down your bedtime routine and sleep plan and following it every night. The good news is that if changes are recent, it shouldn't take very long to get back to normal.

He Has Strong Sleep-Onset Associations

If your little one is waking you up four or more times each night, it may be that he *cannot* fall back to sleep alone and therefore needs your presence almost every time he has a brief night awakening. He needs you to re-create the situation that he feels is necessary for falling back to sleep; this is called a sleep-onset association. He may have been doing things the same way since he was a newborn, which is likely in the case of a child who breastfeeds or bottle-feeds to sleep each time he wakes up. Or he may have habituated to this need over time or because of a specific situation. Perhaps your child was sick or you were away on vacation, and you abruptly changed your nightly rituals and hovered over him or slept next to him all night long. No matter how long it has been going on or how it all started, your presence has become his major sleep cue.

This issue is a big one. Often it is the most challenging situation to change, but it can be done. Many of the following solutions can help your child develop new sleep associations so that he's comfortable falling back to sleep without his current sleep aid—*you*.

If your child needs to breastfeed to fall back to sleep, read through The Nighttime Nursling on page 165. This is often the most complicated association to change, so the specific ideas will provide the guidance you'll need. If your child starts out the night in his own bed but then travels to yours, read The Night Visitor on page 217. (Also check the chapter "Mommy Stay!": Needing a Parent's Help to Fall Asleep.)

Solutions, Ideas, and Thoughts to Consider

Now that I've covered many of the reasons that children wake up during the night, you can see the possibilities are endless. Your child may even have multiple reasons for night waking, in addition to age, biology, and maturity. It's important to remember that all human beings have periods of light sleep and brief awakenings during the night, so the actual night waking is not the problem. This reality, plus the amazing list of possible solutions, will explain why a one-size-fits-all or cry-to-sleep plan doesn't make sense, and why it very often doesn't work.

So all children have night wakings, but if your child is disturbing *your* sleep every time he wakes up, then that is the real issue. A place to start is to figure out your child's reasons for night waking. Then you need to look for—and apply—the best solutions to help him learn how to turn over and settle back to sleep on his own whenever he wakes up.

In addition to subject-specific solutions mentioned in the previous list of possibilities, the following tips can help in many different cases. Look these over and add any likely solutions to your overall sleep plan.

Create a New Bedtime Setting

Your child's sleep environment may be a key component to falling asleep at bedtime and again at every night waking. Take a look at how your child falls asleep at bedtime. What happens during the fifteen or twenty minutes as he is falling asleep? What does the room look like, feel like, and sound like? This setting is important to how easily your child falls asleep.

Some children can fall asleep under one set of conditions, yet sleep through the night under different conditions. This is another one of those child-rearing mysteries. For many children, though, when sleeping conditions change between when he goes to bed and when he wakes in the night, he may feel unsettled and have a harder time falling asleep.

Once you've identified that the two situations are different, try to figure out how to make them more alike. For example, if it is light outside when your child goes to bed but totally dark when he wakes in the night, you can do several things. Cover the windows with insulated shades, curtains, or even cardboard, and then use a very small night-light during the end of the bedtime routine. If the house is very noisy at bedtime, add some white noise that can mask these sounds at bedtime, and even all night long for the light sleeper. (Think of the comforting sound of a fan or a recording of ocean waves.)

Here's a checklist to help you figure out what things are different in each setting and what are the same. Some things you can change at bedtime; for others, you'll need to make a middle-of-the-night adjustment:

Condition	At bedtime	Middle of the night	How can I make them the same?
Is it light, dark, or in between?			
Is it warm or cool?			
What noises can your child hear?			
What toys are in bed?			
Is the window open or closed? Are doors (to closet, hallway) open or closed?			
Does your child have a pacifier or bottle?			
Does your child breastfeed while falling asleep?			
Does your child fall asleep in your arms but wake up in the crib?			
Other:			

If you create a sleep-inducing setting for when your child first falls asleep at bedtime and make it similar for subsequent midnight wakings, this may help your child fall back to sleep on his own during the night.

Keep in mind that the bedtime setting is only one aspect of your child's total sleep plan. You'll find the most benefit from organizing a complete daytime and nighttime sleep strategy.

Monitor Your Nighttime Responses

When your child wakes up in the middle of the night, it is a time to offer comfort and help him resettle to sleep. It is *not* a time for turning on lights, talking, eating, watching TV, or singing songs. It's also not a time for anger, threats, or pleading, which won't solve night waking and can actually make it worse.

In the middle of the night you should be reassuring and offer comfort, but you should also be totally, exceptionally, excruciatingly *boring*. Take care of your child with as little conversation and motion as possible—almost as if you are tending to him in your sleep. (This should be easy, as you'll likely *be* half-asleep!)

The key is to get your child to lie down, close his eyes, and go back to sleep as quickly and with as little fuss as possible. You want to maintain the expectation that nighttime is for staying in bed sleeping and nothing else.

Let Your Sleeping Presence Do the Job

Older toddlers and preschoolers who wake in the night sometimes simply need the presence of a parent, and even a *sleeping* parent will do the trick. If you suspect this might work for your little one, try the following idea: Place a sleeping bag, futon, or mattress on the floor near your own bed. Explain to your child that you understand how he sometimes wants to be near you in the middle of the night, but when he wakes you up it makes you unhappy and grumpy. Show him his new sleeping place, and invite him to move there if he wakes in the night and needs company.

Do a few practice runs each night before bed so he can feel exactly how this works. These rehearsals will also plant a seed so that when he wakes in the night and is half-asleep, he'll still be likely to do exactly as he practiced before bed.

Be There . . . but Not Quite

When your child wakes in the night and you go to her, what happens then? If you spend time nursing, providing a bottle, rocking, lying with her, or any other activity, and you keep up this assistance until your child is totally asleep, you are only continuing your child's need to have you help her fall back to sleep. There is a way for you to provide nighttime comfort and prevent tears, yet take steps to help her learn how to fall back to sleep on her own.

When you go to her in the night, begin by doing what you usually do—but briefly. Once she is settled, separate yourself physically from your child for a minute, but stay in the room. Don't make a big announcement that this is what you're doing, since you would likely hear complaints! Instead, settle your child, and then find something you must do in the room: close a window, put the laundry in the hamper, or fold the diapers. Yes, it's a bit odd to be about these tasks in the middle of the night, but your child doesn't know that. As you go about your business, you can hum quietly or *shhh* to your child. Many will accept your comforting presence and fall back to sleep while you are puttering around. This is a major step to learning how to fall asleep without the physical assistance of a parent, and accomplishing it can lead to fewer calls for you in the night.

You might try putting a chair or futon in your child's room. Then when he calls to you, settle him and tell him it's time to go to sleep. Sit in the chair or lie on the futon until he drifts off.

Provide Your Child with Some Company

Many young children simply don't like the feeling of being alone when they wake up in the middle of the night. Naturally, they search out their preferred company: their parents. It may help to provide your child with some nighttime company. One of the following might suit your child:

• **A special stuffed animal**—or a whole zoo of stuffed animals. It helps if they have names and are assigned the job of keeping your child company during the night. Some children adopt a specific toy as a lovey and find comfort with it for years, others change lovies from time to time, and others are happy with any number of bedtime buddies.

• **A tape recorder or CD player** with an audiobook, relaxing music, or white noise. Set this up bedside to provide middle-of-the-night company. (No TV though. That has been proven to create additional bedtime and sleep problems!) Teach your child how to turn it on if he wakes up.

• **A bowl of fish** or an aquarium. This has the added benefit of soothing white noise from the water filter system and a soft glow of color from the tank light (not too bright though).

• **A little pet** that can sleep near your child. The best choices are low-maintenance ones, since your child is nowhere near old enough to take care of his own pet and you're probably too tired to do it yourself. A turtle or frog can make an easy-care roommate for your child. (Avoid nocturnal pets like hamsters that run on a squeaky exercise wheel all night. And don't put a dog or cat in bed with a baby or with a child who may have allergies or asthma.)

• **A sibling.** If you have more than one child, you might consider creating a sibling bed. One caveat: don't put a newborn in bed with an older sibling. For safety's sake, wait until the baby is about eighteen months old. Twins and higher-order multiples are often happiest and most at peace when sleeping with a sibling. You may need to stick around and read or tell stories until your children are settled and sleepy so that this doesn't turn into an evening play session. Many siblings find great joy in sleeping with each other, and it may help cement early friendships.

Garrett, three years old, and Kirby, eleven years old

Invite Your Child to Create Solutions

Many parents suffer through years of endless night waking, yet they never even think to include their child in the process of finding a solution! Older toddlers and preschoolers can often contribute valuable ideas to the sleep plan, and if they are involved with creating solutions, they may be more likely to cooperate with the plan. Here's a blueprint for problem-solving together:

1. Choose a quiet, uninterrupted time to talk with your child (during the day—not right before bed!).
2. Explain the problem in unemotional terms, such as, "When you wake me up when it's nighttime, I don't get good sleep, and then I don't feel happy. I want us both to be happy, so I want you to help me think of some ideas." Don't present this as a negative thing or as punishment but rather as "the two of us trying to figure something out together."
3. Explain what you would like, "I want you to sleep in your bed all night long and let Mommy sleep in her bed all night long."

4. Ask your child for ideas, "What would help you sleep in your bed all night?" (Have an open mind and be prepared for some odd answers! You'd be surprised—if a child comes up with something, then it makes sense to him and it may just work.)
5. Discuss the ideas together, and make a list of possible solutions.
6. Include some of these ideas in your overall sleep plan.

Role-Play a Nighttime Waking Solution

Your child likely has a pattern for how he acts when he wakes in the night—it may be calling out to you, crying for help, or crawling out of bed to find you. When he has a partial awakening, he automatically does what he has always done. Therefore, if you want to change his behavior, it may help to set a plan and then have a few dress rehearsals before he goes to bed each night, until the new routine becomes natural.

The best way to do this is to make it interesting and fun. You can begin by pretending to be your child and playacting a midnight waking. Then let him demonstrate the sequence of events.

You might also choose to tell a story with your child as the main character to remind him of what he should do. It might sound something like this:

> Tyler wakes up and looks out the window. He sees that it is dark outside. He listens. It's very quiet because everybody is sleeping. Tyler finds his teddy bear and puts it on his pillow. He finds his sippy cup of water and takes a drink. Then he pulls the covers all the way up to his chin. It's warm and cozy in his bed and he closes his eyes. Pretty soon he is sleeping and dreaming about taking a ride on a horse. He knows that in the morning Mommy will come and get him.

If you are making a big change in what you expect your child to do when he wakes up, don't expect that one night of instruction will do the trick. You'll likely need to tell this story every night for weeks until it becomes a consistent reality.

Patience, Patience! (And Then a Little More Patience)

Night waking is the most difficult sleep issue to deal with because we parents so desperately need a solid night's sleep to have the energy to raise these children who are keeping us awake all night. It's likely that the night-waking issues you are dealing with have been in place for a long time, perhaps even since your child was born. You aren't alone, remember, this is normal. If there was any such thing as a one-night sleep solution, believe me, every parent in the world would know about it and all other sleep ideas would cease to exist!

In order to encourage your night-waking child to let *you* sleep all night, you'll need to set up your plan and actually follow it. Not just once, but night after night until everyone in your house is sleeping well. Reading through a hundred good ideas won't change a thing if you don't implement them.

The other thing to keep in mind is that sleep success comes in bursts. There will be good nights, followed by sleepless nights, followed by more good nights. There will be setbacks that cause more night waking, such as teething, illness, growth spurts, vacations, and developmental and emotional milestones. The road to sleep success isn't a straight line—it's more like a dance: two steps forward, one step back, and even a few sidesteps in between. The good news is that eventually you will end up where you want to go: with you and your child sleeping all night long.

The Nighttime Nursling

I love breastfeeding my toddler during the day and right before bed, too. But having him wake me up in the middle of the night to nurse is becoming very difficult to deal with. He's eighteen months old, and he still wakes up four or five times a night to nurse! My sleep has been disrupted for far too long, and I crave a full night's sleep. Also, he won't sleep past dawn unless he's latched on—not feeding, mind you, just pacifying. I absolutely don't want him to cry himself to sleep now, any more than I did when he was a newborn. Are there ways to night-wean him without tears?

This situation is extraordinarily common among breastfeeding mothers who don't believe that babies should be left to cry to sleep. It's a beautiful testament to the fact that you care deeply about your child's feelings, and I applaud you for being such a sensitive and loving mother. I've also been in your position and know *exactly* how you feel—frustrated, confused, sometimes angry, and desperate for an uninterrupted night's sleep! At twelve months old my son Coleton was a frequent night-nurser. He woke to breastfeed every hour and a half, all night long, every night—and that was the ultimate motivation for me to write the first *No-Cry Sleep Solution* book.

The breastfeeding-to-sleep association is one of the most complicated and difficult sleep situations to change for a jumbled-up assortment of reasons. I'll go through those reasons for you, and perhaps this will help you understand your situation a little better. After each point, I'll include some rational reasons that will help you past your roadblocks to eliminating nighttime breastfeeding.

Then I'll provide you with a menu of solutions to choose from that will help your child sleep all night without breastfeeding.

• **The power of the milk.** Breastfeeding is nature's most perfect sleep aid, it can make an active child relax and put a sleepy child out cold. It doesn't always work this way with a toddler, but even if it doesn't, it is part of the history of this strong sleep association.

As you feed your child, you receive the benefits of "mothering" hormones, also referred to as "the love hormones," called prolactin and oxytocin. In addition to stimulating your maternal instincts, these hormones help you relax, often to the point of falling asleep yourself. Such a powerful substance—one that helps both mother and child fall asleep—is easy to get used to and very hard to give up.

The most difficult adjustment is the time of transition from frequent night-nursing to all-night sleeping. It does take commitment, effort, and time to make the change. Once you've created new routines that aren't based on nursing-to-sleep, you'll both be nodding off without it just fine.

• **The multipurpose benefit of nursing.** I breastfed my first-born just moments after her birth and weaned my fourth child at the age of three—happily logging over nine years of breastfeeding experience. My husband, Robert, fondly called the process "The Secret Weapon." He learned early on about the power of nursing to calm, quiet, nurture, . . . and fix just about anything wrong with a child. I'm certain you have learned this as well. Breastfeeding easily becomes the automatic response to calming your child— daytime or nighttime. Because you've relied on breastfeeding up until now, it is hard to change gears and adopt new ways of responding to your child in the middle of the night.

You can continue to use The Secret Weapon during the day, if you'd like, for as long as you wish. You'll just need to learn and adopt some new techniques for soothing your child in the middle of the night, and apply some ideas to help him fall back to sleep without breastfeeding.

• **The reluctance to substitute.** If you're still nursing your toddler or preschooler, you've already had a long and prosperous breastfeeding relationship with your child. If your little one is still nursing to sleep, it may be an easy and peaceful process. Even if it's no longer easy or peaceful, it is definitely a routine set in stone. When you think of making a change or if you've *tried* to make a change, you quickly learn that your child isn't willing to give up this wonderful custom very easily. Therefore, you've discovered that the choice is between a quick, easy, gentle path to sleep or a major, drawn-out, tear-filled battle. So you choose . . . quick, easy, and gentle. And without a clear solution, why wouldn't you?

If you organize a specific plan and follow your set route, you can make changes. Yes, the transition may be tiring and challenging since you're changing established patterns that have been in place for so long. You will have to put more effort and creativity into handling your little one's night wakings, but just for a short time. You will emerge on the other side with both of you sleeping all night long and looking forward to morning cuddles, or maybe even a morning nursing session, after a well-rested night.

• **The num-nums are your child's lovey.** We've all heard about the value of a child having a lovey, technically called a transitional object. This is something your child finds comfort in, something that makes him feel secure in a fast-moving world. Many breastfeeding toddlers and preschoolers have adopted Mommy's breasts as lovies. And even if they have a stuffed animal or blankie that is a lovey—it's often a pair: teddie *and* breast or blankie *and* breast. (Or sometimes it's even more complex: the pair is Mommy's hair *and* breast, or Mommy's hand *and* breast.)

Young children want their lovies anytime they feel a bit uncertain or uncomfortable, and that includes waking up in the dark night. Perhaps somewhere inside (or maybe even right up there on the surface) you feel proud that you hold such a place of importance in this little person's life. Each time that little hand reaches out for you or you are presented with a glowing, milky smile of love and gratitude, you realize how important breastfeeding is to your child, and it fills you with a very special feeling of love and pride.

As a mother of three autonomous teenagers and an independent preschooler, I relish memories of the time when each of them was my little nursling. Although those times pass, the good news is that over the years you still remain the center of your child's world—the definition just changes along the way. Each milestone redefines your relationship, but the connection between you just grows stronger. A loving and bonded relationship doesn't have to include all-night breastfeeding.

- **It's the way it has always been done.** Ever since the day of her birth, you've used breastfeeding as a key component in helping your child fall asleep. You both know how it works, it's simple, and it's effective. Making a change is like learning a new language—for both of you. The way you interact before sleep time and the routines involved have been instinctively completed, as they have for time eternal between mothers and babies. Often, the *only* key component to your child's bedtime routine, and night-waking routine, has been nursing—nothing else is critical to the process and nothing else will work to help your child fall asleep. Your little one has a very strong nursing/sleep association, and he may believe that he *needs* to nurse to fall asleep, since he has rarely done it any other way. Eliminating breastfeeding from your sleep routine requires that you make conscious changes and complicate your sleep routine in order to help your child learn how to fall asleep without nursing—all at the time of night when you're simply too tired to do so.

Children are creatures of routine and habit, and it doesn't take long to create new habits. With a plan, consistency, and patience, you'll soon be rewarded with new routines that don't involve waking up to nurse your child back to sleep. When you are motivated enough to make changes, you'll pluck up your courage and do what's necessary—even though it means making your own sleep-deprived state worse for a short time. The reward of uninterrupted, all-night sleep is worth it.

- **The sacred process phenomenon.** You're a dedicated mother, and you love your child more than life itself. In this love, you desire to raise a good child and be the best parent that you can be. You find it necessary and *right* to create certain limits: you won't let your child run into the street, eat candy for dinner, put play-dough in the DVD player, or hit the baby. That's all part of your job as a mother. When it comes to breastfeeding, however, you find it very hard to say no. After all, this is a very special, bonding, and important act that's also good for your child's health and growth. Breastfeeding is a noble act, and breastfeeding is love. And how do you say no to love? So very often, the challenge of feeling wrong about saying no can get in the way of making any sort of change, even though your child is no longer a tiny baby yet continues to wake you every hour wanting to nurse and you're desperate for a full night's sleep.

It is perfectly OK for your toddler or preschooler to sleep all night without breastfeeding. Really! Millions upon millions of children have done so, and millions more will. Your child isn't an infant anymore, and he or she won't suffer hunger or loneliness without frequent nighttime attention from you. A good plan that involves a loving bedtime routine and a delightful morning snuggle can maintain that beautiful connection that you have created between you. Furthermore, you just may be a more patient and loving mother all day long if you're getting a good night's sleep, and I'm sure your little one will enjoy having a happier, well-rested mommy.

• **Fearing the end of breastfeeding.** Sometimes active toddlers and preschoolers have so much going on during the day that they nurse very little and their sessions are brief. Breastfeeding is following its natural course from every hour or two as a newborn to once or twice a day. Some nursing mothers in this case may dread giving up nighttime nursing since they fear it may signal total weaning soon afterward.

I avoid using the term *night-weaning*, because for many mothers it denotes the end of breastfeeding in total and gets in the way of solving nighttime nursing issues. While this may be true for some children who are ready to wean, many, many, *many* children give up night-nursing but continue daytime nursing for a long time thereafter. (All of my children night-weaned long before daytime weaning. My Coleton stopped nighttime nursing at thirteen months, but didn't completely wean until after his third birthday.) Whether you want to wean your child completely is a separate decision from giving up nighttime feedings.

The Menu of Solutions

All babies are different and all mommies are different, too. There is no one perfect answer that works for every mother-baby pair. A list of ideas follows for you to review and choose from to create your own plan for reducing or eliminating your child's night nursing.

I suggest that you read through all of these ideas and choose a few that sound right for you. Make a plan. Then pick a day to begin, and stick with your plan for several weeks before you give up or revise it. Remember, you are changing patterns that are firmly in place and this isn't an easy thing to do. You may find that it will be one step forward, two steps back. But if you continue this dance, you'll end up exactly where you want to be.

Keep your eye on a date perhaps thirty or more days from now—circle it on the calendar—and anticipate that you'll be celebrating sleep success at that time. Doing this will help you through this challenging transition period and give you the strength to keep to your plan.

So here we go. On to the list of solutions!

Pantley's Gentle Removal Plan

Your little one falls asleep at bedtime breastfeeding, and then he wakes in the night to breastfeed again until he is totally back to sleep. He follows this pattern each time he wakes up. The problem here is that when he experiences those normal wake-ups between sleep cycles he becomes confused and disoriented, looking for his sleep aid. In order for his very strong sleep association to change, he needs to learn how to fall asleep without the sensation of nursing so that he doesn't look to re-create that sleep condition when he wakes in the night.

In order to take the steps to change your child's sucking-to-sleep association, you must complicate night wakings for a week or even a month. But in the long run you can wean your child from using your breast as his only nighttime association. I wish it were simpler, but you must be prepared to disrupt your own nights for a while to make some important, worthwhile long-term changes.

How to Use Pantley's Gentle Removal for Toddlers and Preschoolers

A helpful first step is to create a phrase that means, "We're all done nursing." You'll want to first use this during the day at the end of each nursing session. As you finish nursing and are moving your child off your lap and closing up your clothing, repeat your phrase two or three times. Choose your own phrase, based on your personality and your child's age, but it could be something like, "All done. Milk is all done. Bye-bye, milk." This becomes a cue phrase to close your nursing sessions and will be helpful in the middle of the night or too early in the morning, when you would like your child to stop nursing and go to sleep.

When your child wakes up in the night and wants to nurse, go ahead and nurse him as you normally have. Remember that a toddler or preschooler is most likely waking not because he is hungry but because he wants comfort and considers nursing as his method of falling back to sleep. So what you'll do, instead of letting him *fall asleep* at the breast, is to let him nurse for only a few minutes until his sucking slows and he is relaxed and sleepy.

Make sure your child is done "eating" (when she is not actively sucking and swallowing, but just pacifying). Then you'll want to take your nursling off the breast. There are several ways to do this, depending on what works for you.

- Break the seal with your finger, and gently remove the nipple from her mouth.
- Use a quicker, more confident break with your finger. If you are sitting and nursing her, then immediately move her up to your chest and hold her snugly while you swing, sway, rock, pat, shh, or otherwise comfort her.
- If you are lying beside her, use the quick, confident release, and then shift your breasts away from her face (perhaps turn on your tummy somewhat) while patting, rubbing, or doing whatever soothes her.

Don't use your closing phrase just yet! Often, especially at first, your child will be confused and want to continue nursing, because that's what she has always done. Try to shift your breast away from her. You may be able to very gently hold her mouth closed with your finger under her chin, or apply pressure or pat her chin just under her lip (this helps to ease her from sucking to stillness), and at the same time rock or sway with her and say, "Shhh. Go to sleep now." If she struggles or fusses and you foresee a battle, go ahead and let her nurse a bit more, since you don't want her to become totally awake and start crying, but repeat the removal process as often as necessary until she finally falls asleep.

How long between removals? Every child is different, but about ten to thirty seconds between removals usually works. If your child is a young toddler and has slept five or more hours, she may be hungry and need a longer session. You'll be able to tell this if she is sucking strongly and swallowing regularly, so wait a few minutes until she slows her pace. You'll not want to remove in the middle of a letdown, either, unless you're prepared to hold your hand over your breast to stop the milk flow.

It may take two, three, five, or even more attempts, but eventually your child will accept being off the breast and will accept the loss of the nipple, get comfortable, and begin to fall asleep without the nipple in her mouth. *This* is when you say your closing phrase! (Quietly!) This way you create a connection between the closing phrase and her actually being *finished* nursing.

When you've done this a number of times over a period of days, you should find that the removals are much easier, and your little one's awakenings are less frequent. You can then begin to use your

Mother-Speak

"We got to calling this the Big PPO (Pantley-Pull-Off). At first Joshua would see it coming and grab my nipple tighter in anticipation—ouch! But you said to stick with it, and I did. Now he anticipates the PPO and actually lets go and turns and rolls over on his side to go to sleep! I am truly amazed."

—Shannon, mother of nineteen-month-old Joshua

closing phrase earlier in the process and begin to be more persistent in ending the nursing session.

As Pantley's Gentle Removal Plan begins to work, it's a good idea to pull off sooner and sooner in the process, and one day your child will surprise you by pulling off on her own. But to get there, you must have consistency on your part.

At first, your gentle removal might look something like this:

Your child wakes up and begins to nurse vigorously.
Her eyes close, and her sucking rate slows.
You gently remove your nipple.
Your nursling moves her open mouth toward you, looking to nurse.
You try rocking and hugging, but she'll have none of that!
You put her back to the breast.
Count: one thousand, two thousand, three thousand, . . . ten thousand.*
You gently remove your nipple.
She moves her open mouth toward you.
You try stalling, shushing, and patting, but no dice.
You put her back to the breast.
Count: one thousand, two thousand, three thousand, . . .*
You gently remove your nipple.
Your sleepy child moves her mouth a little, and you gently hold her mouth closed by pressing lightly on her chin.
She doesn't resist; she is nearly asleep.
You say your closing phrase.
You move your child away from you in bed, or place your child in her own bed, and pat her bottom to settle her.
She goes to sleep.

---

*The counting is really more for you, to give you a gauge to measure your time and a way to keep yourself calm during your repeated attempts. You can be flexible as you figure out what time spacing works best for you and your child.

Repeat the gentle removal process every night until your little one learns that she can fall asleep without nursing. If your child is a relatively good napper or if you're dedicated to making a more rapid change, you can use the technique for putting her to sleep at naptime, too. If your child doesn't nap well or if you have the patience, don't trouble yourself with trying too hard to use the removal technique during the day for naps, since you both may end up frustrated. Remember that good naps mean better nighttime sleep—and better nighttime sleep means better naps. It's a circle. Once you get your child sleeping better at night, you can then work on the naptime sleep. As soon as you solve the nighttime association, however, and create a daily nap routine, the naptime sleep may solve itself. (You might read through the chapter on naptime problems on page 241.)

Patience with Your Child, Patience with Yourself

At any time if you feel too frustrated to continue with the PPO, just let your little one nurse to sleep so that you can sleep too, and try again the next time he wakes up. Unless you have a deadline, such as wanting to get pregnant or planning to return to work, don't feel you must succeed quickly. This process may take some time. Be patient. Since the goal is to avoid crying, this is not a one-day solution (as if there *were* such a thing!). But within the next thirty days, as you gently break this strong sleep association, you should see a major reduction in the number of your child's night wakings, because he won't need to breastfeed each time he moves through his sleep cycles.

Remember, too, that all the solutions in this book are like pieces to a big sleep puzzle. Make sure you are applying all the other information you've learned about your child's sleep from other parts of this book. If your sleep plan is complete, you will see your child's sleep improving more quickly. So make sure you have a proper bedtime routine, correctly time your child's naps

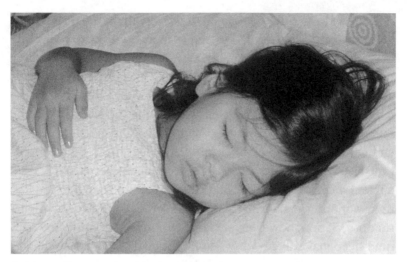

Adriane, three years old

and bedtime, and take advantage of white noise, sleepy-time music, and a sleep-conducive environment.

Create a New Bedtime Routine

Often, the way your child falls asleep at bedtime will affect the rest of his awakenings for the night. This is because of the sleep association that has been established. It seems that however your child falls asleep for the night is how he expects to remain all night long. You can help reduce the amount of times you must tend to your child if you create a falling-asleep ritual that can nearly be duplicated in the middle of the night without your presence. Notice that I didn't say this would stop the actual night wakings! If you remember from the very beginning of this book, it is perfectly normal for all human beings to wake up several times during the night, particularly between sleep cycles. The goal is for your child to fall asleep easily *by himself* when this happens.

If you can, try to modify your child's bedtime routine so that at the very end he is lying by himself on his bed, without nursing. You can be on the bed six inches away, on a chair near the bed, or standing at the door, and in many cases this will be the only way to prevent your child from getting upset and becoming totally awake. Whatever routine you choose, stay consistent with it every night. There's no sin in parenting your child to sleep every night at bedtime, even until he starts first grade or beyond. The putting-to-sleep ritual can be a loving and peaceful end to every day. And for many parents, if your child then sleeps all night, it doesn't matter if you have to stay with him until he falls asleep at bedtime.

The point here is that you'll want to avoid having your child fall asleep *at the breast* for the first falling asleep of the night, and this is where the gentle removal process is helpful.

If you have a current routine that finishes each night with your child falling asleep at the breast, you may want to revamp your entire prebedtime routine so that you finish the schedule in a new way. Choose to finish your routine with something that your child enjoys and that relaxes her. You may want to use massage or cuddling as your final step. If you add soft music, white noise, or an audiobook, it can make the drifting off to sleep very pleasant.

The Storytelling Ritual

With older toddlers and preschoolers, a great approach to aid in weaning from breastfeeding is the storytelling ritual. Introduce an interesting new routine for your evenings. Allow your child to breastfeed as usual, but don't talk during the process. Then have your child lie next to you in the bed in the dark and tell a story. If your child enjoys a sippy cup of water or sucking on a pacifier or teething toy during the story, that's fine. The key is to have him lie in bed without nursing.

The stories that appeal to many children feature them as the main character. You can tell a story about his real day, reliving his jaunt to the park, or tell a story about tomorrow's scheduled events. You can make it a fantasy and tell a story about your child building a boat and floating out to meet many interesting fish and friends in the sea. You'll find that you don't have to be incredibly creative to tell a satisfying story. And often, your child will become attached to a certain theme and want to hear the same story over and over and over. (*Ahem. There once was a little boy named Coleton who built a very big boat and sailed out to sea . . .*)

The key is that the story comes *after breastfeeding* and never during! Once you've done this a few times, your child will begin to look forward to the night's story. The advantage to finishing the bedtime routine with a verbal story in the dark is that your child is apt to fall asleep during the tale, as opposed to during a picture-book reading, which requires the lights on and eyes open.

Set Time Perimeters

If you've been on call for your nursling all night long, you don't necessarily have to go "cold turkey" and stop all breastfeeding. It may help to set a chunk of time when "the milk sleeps." (Use whatever phrase your family uses to indicate breastfeeding.) Explain to your child that when it's bedtime you need to sleep, your milk needs to sleep, and if you wake up too much, you get grumpy and don't feel happy. Ask for his help so you can sleep all night long. Even a young toddler can get the feeling behind your words. This can help the process move along more smoothly; since you're not doing something to him, you're enlisting his help so you can both sleep better.

Begin by taking a good look at your child's current night-waking pattern, as well as your own sleep needs. Set a period of time when you will say no to breastfeeding, such as from midnight to 6:00 A.M. During that time, if your child wakes to breastfeed, tell him "the milk is sleeping" or a similar description that he can understand. Hold him, pat him, let Daddy or your partner rock him, but persist in the idea that the milk is asleep.

The first few times you do this may be quite difficult. (OK, truth be told, it may be very, very difficult.) But if you are consistent, after a few days of this your child will begin to understand and the fussing will dissipate. When that happens, you can then expand the milk-sleeping time by an hour in either direction and continue to make adjustments until you reach a point that you are happy with.

Remember to use a collection of other ideas from this book rather than just choosing this one idea alone.

Use Light and Dark as Nursing Cues

An idea similar to the previous one invites your child in on the process of knowing when it's OK to nurse and when he must wait. The easiest cue for your little one to understand is light and dark. For this to be most effective, first teach your child the difference between light and dark if he doesn't already understand the difference. (Take her in a bathroom and play a game—lights out: "Dark!" lights on: "Light!" Read books about opposites. Comment on the time of day as you look out the window.)

Make sure that your child's windows are covered and no lights are coming into the room from the hallway during the hours that you set for sleeping. (A night-light is fine if he likes it.) At bedtime, explain your expectations to your child clearly. For example, you might tell her: "We nurse when it's light. We sleep when it's dark." There are a number of children's books about sleep. You might get some of these and point out that everyone sleeps when it's dark. Or follow the steps to write your own book in Bedtime Battles on page 117. Read these books as part of your bedtime routine.

Another variation is to set a white-noise alarm or your clock radio to an easy-listening music station, to go off at the earliest time you will allow nursing. Tell your child that if it's quiet, she should go to sleep. If the music is on, she can wake you to nurse. Whenever your child wakes up during the night, repeat your expectations. For example, you would say, "Shhhh. Night night. We nurse when it's light. We sleep in the dark." Or "We have to wait until the music is on." Tell her it's time to go to sleep. You can then hold her, rock her, hum to her, rub her back, whisper words of comfort, put your cheek against hers, give her a pacifier, or anything that helps her or you. (Any of these techniques are much easier to wean from than breastfeeding to sleep.)

While you're doing any of these soothing techniques, avoid being in the position you have used for breastfeeding. For example, sit up if you usually lie down, avoid sitting in the chair where you usually breastfeed, and don't hold your child cradled in the nursing position. This can be a challenge when you're tired, but keep your eye on the goal—sleep!

It may also help your child if you offer "something" instead of nursing. For example, have a cup of water near the bed and ask if she would like a sip, or offer a pacifier or teething toy if your child has one that he uses at other times of the day. You may also want to teach your child to wait a few minutes during the day when he wants to nurse. If he can learn to wait during the day, it may give him the practice he needs to be able to wait at night.

A Place for Everything, and Everything in Its Place

Very often we breastfeeding moms begin a routine of nursing our child to sleep in a particular place, such as in bed. Our routine becomes cemented into our child's sleep-time process. After months, or years, the association between the location (the bed) and the action (the breastfeeding) becomes so tightly connected that it's hard for your child to have one without the other. Sometimes changing the location of the prebedtime breastfeeding to someplace entirely disconnected to sleep can eliminate the middle-of-the-night feedings.

Choose a new and comfortable place for your evening nursing session to take place. This should be different from your sleep-time location, such as downstairs on the family room sofa. Tell your little one that it will be your new nursing place. Set up a new ritual where you nurse on the sofa and then go off to bed. It's perfectly fine to turn out the light and stay with your child until he falls asleep or is content when you leave the room. You can give a massage, hum a repetitive tune, tell him a story, or use a relaxation exercise from page 94. It may take some persistence the first few nights, but don't give in and nurse in the bedroom! If your child cries and becomes upset, take him downstairs to the sofa for a very brief nursing session and then return to the nonnursing bedroom.

If you'd like to avoid another six months of frequent night nursing, it is very important that you stay firm for the first time he goes to sleep at night so that you set a pattern for the entire night to follow. If your child wakes up to nurse during the night, take him back downstairs to the sofa. Breastfeed him until he is sleepy. Carry him back up, and return to your nonnursing soothing techniques. The first few days of your new routine may be a challenge because you're changing habits that are firmly in place. But stick with it for ten days to two weeks, and you'll almost certainly see good results happen.

Adding Some Motivation

For an older toddler or preschooler, you may want to add a little incentive to this process to encourage your child to go along with

Mother-Speak

"I'll admit that I avoided using the gift-wrapped prize concept because I wasn't comfortable with it. However, after six months of struggling to get my three-year-old to go to sleep without nursing, I finally decided to give it a try. Would you believe it! She loved waking up to a prize! It was the key to our success. Thanks for suggesting I do the same thing for potty-training—it's working for that too!"

—Ling, mother of three-year-old Xiu Mei

the new routine. Regardless of what you've thought about giving children prizes in the past, you may find yourself revising your opinion. (Likely this won't be the first time you'll do so in your parenting career.) This idea was voted Most Popular among the children I surveyed.

This is what you do: Purchase twenty or thirty small prizes and wrap them in wrapping paper. Set them up in the hallway outside the bedroom and tell your child that when she waits to nurse until morning she can have a prize. In the morning you can make a big production about what a wonderful job she did and make the prize opening part of your morning routine. Once the prizes have all been opened, your new routine will be established. If your child wants more prizes, ask her if she wants you to rewrap all her original prizes. Surprisingly, most children think that's a grand idea, since the excitement is in opening a gift, not necessarily in what's inside the wrapping paper!

An alternative prize program is to put up a chart or calendar and allow your child to put up a sticker for each day she has waited until morning to nurse, with a bonus prize for every five to ten stickers earned.

Enlist the Help of Another Adult

If your husband, your partner, or another of your baby's caregivers can help your child back to sleep, this may make it easier on both you and your child when you make the move away from nighttime breastfeeding. You can begin the process by having your partner put your child down for a nap a few times or involve him in the regular bedtime routine for a few nights, and then let him take over the prebedtime routine for a night or two. Or you can just jump right into the middle-of-the-night adjustments—any way can work, as long as you set a plan that you both agree to.

If your partner has already been a big part of the naptime or bedtime routine and you have his blessing, you might even be so bold as to schedule a Mommy's night out and let your partner have the house to himself. This can work especially well with an older child who may buy in to the novelty of a special night with just Daddy. If preceded by some fun or a special movie or treat, it may turn out to be a very pleasant night for them. And don't worry, you'll only be a phone call away if you're needed!

If Daddy hasn't been a part of the bedtime routine, you can take a few days or so to introduce his presence. Choose soothing bedtime music or white noise to accompany your bedtime routine (if you don't already do this). Begin by having your partner sit beside you and talk, sing, hum, or tell a story—not totally distracting, just a gentle presence—during the nursing-to-sleep routine. After a night or two, he can even pat, touch, or hold your little one's hand. Think of this as a special family bonding time, which it is.

The next step is to nurse your child and then let Daddy finish off the falling to sleep process with a back rub, patting, or cuddling, using that special bedtime music or white noise as a familiar thread. Mommy, you can stay or leave the room, depending on what works best for your child and you. After a few more days,

Mother-Speak

"We agreed that Daniel would take over the midnight wakings with Savannah for ten days. I listened in by the door on the third night and heard him singing a wacky good-night song. He used a boring monotone voice to sing good night to every single toy in her room. It worked! She actually fell asleep without nursing."

—Annette, mother of nineteen-month-old Savannah

see if your partner can go through the bedtime routine without your presence. This entire step-by-step process of change can take a few days or a few weeks depending on your child's personality, how motivated you are to make a change, how patient you both are, and whether you have a "deadline" impending (an upcoming mom-away trip or the impending birth of a sibling, for example).

Make sure that in advance of the switch in the bedtime routine you and your partner discuss the details of how this will work, both at bedtime and in the middle of the night. Will your partner go to your child as soon as he wakes up? How will your partner help your child go back to sleep—back rubs, pats, white noise? What will you do if your child starts to cry? It's important that you both agree on how you'll handle this, otherwise Daddy will be doing his best and feel he's doing well, but you'll hear crying and come running into the room just as he feels he's making progress! So decide in advance: how much fussing or crying will you allow to happen in your partner's arms before The Secret Weapon is invited to come to the rescue? A good idea is to put yourself in a different room with the door closed so you can't hear what's going on between father and child. After all, daddies are known to come up with some very unique ways to calm their little ones and help them go back to sleep.

It is really best if you let your partner decide when to come to you for assistance. If you convince yourself that you really can trust your partner, then you can even go back to sleep and tell him to wake you if he needs you. Keep in mind that Dr. William Sears, the ultimate father of attachment parenting theory and father of eight, says that "Crying and fussing in the arms of a loving parent is not the same as crying it out." While you don't want a hysterical child in the arms of a frustrated father, a bit of complaining in Daddy's loving arms won't harm either one of them.

Try this suggestion for at least a week before you judge its effectiveness. Many families report that the first few nights are the hardest, but then it gets progressively better. There are times when this plan doesn't work well, particularly if you have always done the bedtime routine yourself. The change to a different person— no matter how beloved—may be just too much for your child to handle, and the two of them won't last five minutes before your child screams for Mommy, after which both of them become extremely upset. However, this does work for many families. They report that even during the challenging part of the process, their child remains his usual happy and energetic self during the daytime, so if your partner is patient and willing, this is worth a try!

Setting a Plan

Once you've read through all the ideas in this section and the one that follows, put together your specific plan for how you are going to handle your child's desire to breastfeed during the night. It helps if you write out your steps.

You may want to follow the instructions for making a bedtime chart from page 114 to help your child understand and cooperate

Mother-Speak

"I found it virtually impossible to soothe my daughter back to sleep without the breast. She would just get agitated and angry. Our answer was to have Daddy go to her when she woke up and resettle her. The first few nights she was quite irritated that it was Daddy and not Mommy coming to her beck and call. But by the end of the week, she was totally in love with her Daddy. My husband still says that helping to night-wean her (though he was sleep deprived at the time) was one of the most important ways he has ever bonded with his little girl. I noticed that closeness in their relationship immediately and it still hasn't gone away, even though we're long past that time."

—**Deirdre, mother of nineteen-month-old Violet**

with your new routine. This will make your routine more predictable and add an element of fun as well.

Pick the number of days that you are going to follow your plan in total—ten to fourteen is usually sufficient to see at least enough success (if not a complete change!) to motivate you to stay your path. Plot your days on a calendar, and arrange to take naps during the day if you are extra tired and if you can manage it.

A reminder to be patient and forgiving: if at any point during the night either you, your partner, or your child is too upset to follow the plan, go ahead and nurse her back to sleep without guilt. There is no reason to push yourself or your child to the limit. Just try again with the next night waking or the night after. As the mother of three teenagers, I feel it's my duty to remind you that in the grand scheme of your lifetime this is just a teeny, tiny blip of time. So take a deep breath—and a nap if you can—and try again the next night. Most of all, remember those four important words, *"This too shall pass."*

How to Continue to Co-Sleep—Without All-Night Nursing

We thoroughly enjoy having our daughter in bed with us, and we aren't ready to move her to her own bed. The problem is that I am not getting enough sleep because of her all-night, on-demand nursing sessions. Can we co-sleep and actually sleep?

Nothing is quite as special as the silent sweetness of your precious little one snuggled up to you during the night. Mothers and fathers alike tell me that this is one of the greatest times of joy in parenting, and my husband and I have to agree. One common drawback is that nursing mothers of frequent night-waking children get to a point where they begin to suffer from interrupted sleep, and they may even begin to have feelings of frustration and anger at being repeatedly awakened from a deep sleep. With some breastfeeding co-sleepers there's no way they will sleep next to Mommy without nursing. They've simply always enjoyed the pleasure and can't understand why in the world you'd ask them to stop. Other children, though, *can* learn to actually *sleep* next to Mommy all night without having to breastfeed through the night. If this is your goal, here are a few ideas to help you along.

Wait a Minute!

Many breastfeeding co-sleeping mothers have responded instinctually to their children's nighttime needs from the moment of birth. Anytime their little one makes a noise—even as subtle as a sniff or a sigh—Mommy automatically puts the child to breast. The beauty of this process is that both the child and Mommy sleep better, since neither fully wakes at any point during the night. The problem is that after a year or two or *more* of this process, Mommy begins to resent the frequent prods to wake and nurse. The surprise news for many mothers is that they don't need to do this. Sometimes when you wake to attach your child, believe it or not, he is still asleep! Children make lots of noises in their sleep: they moan, grunt, snore, snort, whimper, cry, laugh, and even nurse *in their sleep*. These sounds don't mean they need to breastfeed, because they may not even be awake or they may be just partially awake and shifting between sleep cycles.

An important step to helping your child sleep without breast-feeding is to determine the difference between sleeping noises and awake noises. When your child makes a noise in the night: stop, listen, wait. As you listen attentively to her noises, you may be surprised to hear her fall back to sleep, and you'll learn that half of your nighttime nursing sessions have been performed while your child was sleeping. So withhold for a few moments your automatic reaction to respond to your child and listen attentively instead. She may just surprise you and fall back to sleep on her own.

Shorten Your Nighttime Nursing Times

When your child was younger, it was important to her development that you fed her adequately when she awoke in the night. You may have the habit of falling asleep yourself during breast-feeding, so your child stays latched onto the breast even after she has fallen asleep. Now that she's over a year old (or is that two years?), nighttime feedings are no longer about food. They are purely for comfort or due to a sleep-association habit. Therefore, there is no need for your child to have lengthy middle-of-the-night nursing sessions. You can help your little one learn to fall asleep and stay asleep without this aid by shortening your nighttime nursing intervals.

When you are sure your child is awake and looking to nurse, go ahead and nurse him for a short time. Stay awake! And as soon as he slows his pace from the gulping, drinking mode to the slow fluttery comfort nursing, you can gently disengage him while patting him or rubbing him. (See Pantley's Gentle Removal Plan described on page 171.)

Sometimes you can put your child's hand on your breast, or on your chest or arm, during the removal, since many will accept this touch as a substitute for nursing. It seems to keep you "connected," and he knows that the milk is nearby if he needs it.

Another interesting option is to make the latch a little less comfortable and less convenient for your child. Instead of lying tummy-to-tummy with your child cradled in your arm, shift yourself slightly onto your back so that your nursling has to work a bit to keep the nipple in his mouth. Often he'll decide it's too much effort, and he'll let go and go to sleep. In addition, after nursing sleep on your stomach or cover your breasts completely, so that the nummies aren't easily accessible to your partially awake nursling.

After using these techniques with my son Coleton, he began to disengage *himself*, turn over with his back to me, and fall asleep! It was wonderful. Perhaps only a co-sleeping and breastfeeding mommy can understand just how sweet her baby's backside can be at this time. In fact, Coleton did this until he was almost two years old. He nursed until he was comfortable, then rolled away from me and went to sleep. I left him in bed with his brother David in our "sleeping room" and was free to join my husband in our own bed for child-free sleep and couple time.

Move the Milk

Here is another idea especially for co-sleepers. After breastfeeding, scoot yourself away from your child. If he is snuggled right up against you, he will awaken and want to nurse more often—sometimes, as I mentioned earlier, even in his sleep. If your little one is used to feeling you against him, then you may want to try a tactile replacement. A small stuffed animal is perfect for the job. Simply place the toy next to your child's body or legs (away from his face) when you move away, so that he feels something against him.

For those persistent night nursers, you may even want to change your sleeping arrangement for a few weeks until you get the frequent night waking under control. During the transition, you can nurse your child on one bed; once he is asleep, you can move to another. It can be in another room or only five feet away, but moving the milk can prevent additional awakenings.

I must tell you, though, that some very persistent breastfeeding and co-sleeping night wakers have a "Mommy radar" and may continue their numerous wakings until Mommy and child sleep in different rooms. If you try all of my other ideas and find that your little one is still waking frequently, you'll need to make that ultimate decision: what's more important right now, co-sleeping or just plain sleeping? I cannot answer that question for you, and there is no *right* answer. You'll need to examine the needs of every member of your family to determine just what path you should take. Even if you decide to move your child to a different sleeping spot, remember that when he is sleeping solidly through the night, you can welcome him back into your bed anytime.

When the time comes that you're ready to move your child to her own bed, you may want to read the sections about moving from the family bed on page 269 and visits to the parent's bed on page 217.

The Early Bird:
Waking Up Too Early

I don't need an alarm clock. Every day my daughter wakes up early—usually before 6:00. Is there any way to get her to sleep longer in the morning, or is she just an early bird?

It is true that some children seem to be natural early birds, but only about 10 to 15 percent actually have a biological tendency to be a complete lark. Another small percentage is somewhat lark-ish, but most early-rising children are simply waking up early for outside reasons that affect their rising time, and these can be changed.

You may be able to tell if your little one is *really* a lark if she does any of the following:

- Wakes up on her own and is cheerful and chatty
- Is most active and energetic in the late morning to early afternoon
- Sleeps soundly
- Gets tired after dinner
- Goes to bed early and easily
- Wakes up early no matter what time she goes to bed

If this describes your child, you may indeed have a little lark on your hands. Even so, you might be able to squeeze a bit more sleep time in the morning if you make some changes in your child's routines by applying the ideas that follow.

If your early riser does not fit the previous description, she's likely not a natural-born lark and you'll have good luck encouraging a later wake-up time once you start to use the following ideas.

First Things First

One of the common reasons for early waking is simply that your child has had enough sleep! Take a good look at Table 1.2 on page 12 and add up your child's night and nap hours of sleep. If your two-year-old is napping for two hours and then getting an average amount of hours of sleep at nighttime, that would be eleven night sleep hours. If she is going to bed at 7:00 P.M., guess what? Eleven hours later . . . it's 6:00 A.M.! (Remember, too, that *early* has a different definition for everyone; many people arise at 5:00 A.M. or even before that, without considering it too early.)

Even if your child is getting less than the sleep hours in the table, she may be one of those rare children who needs a bit less sleep than the average. In either case you can't expect her to sleep longer in the morning simply because *you* went to bed at midnight or were up all night with her baby brother and you're still tired. (Oh, but if it only worked that way!)

If this is the case in your house, you have two options. Gradually move her bedtime later by about ten to fifteen minutes until she's going to bed an hour later and (you hope!) waking an hour later in the morning. If you've already read the first part of this book, you know that an earlier bedtime is often best for a child and sometimes a bedtime change won't affect awakening time, but you certainly can experiment with this to see if you can find a happy medium that works for both of you.

The other choice, of course, is to make your own bedtime earlier so that an earlier wake-up time works for you. This may be nicer than you think, since most larks are cheerful in the morning and grumpy in the late evening. So by adjusting your family hours, you'll have more time in that happy place together.

Other Reasons Why Your Child May Be Waking Up Early

If you've added up your child's sleep hours and determined that an excess of sleep isn't the cause of early awakening, you should be able to add more sleep time in the early morning. Before getting into the general tips for encouraging longer sleep, it may help to figure out why your child wakes up early and how to address those issues. Here are a few things that might be waking her up:

- **Light.** Daylight, streetlights, or house lights can all cause a light sleeper to wake up.
  Solution: Cover the windows, keep the room dark.
- **Noise.** Some children are easily roused when they hear voices, traffic, pets, plumbing sounds, or neighbors.
  Solution: Use a radio tuned to a classical music or talk-show station and set on low volume, or a white-noise machine to mask outside noises. You can set it like an alarm to go off on a quiet volume about an hour before your child's typical awakening time so that other noises don't rouse her. (Don't worry—if you are using white noise or keeping the volume low it won't wake her.) Another option, if you can, is changing your child's sleeping place to a quieter room.
- **Nature calls?** Perhaps her diaper or training pants are wet, or she has to use the bathroom.
  Solution: Give your child less liquid in the hour or two before bed. Provide several prebedtime potty visits. Use diaper

Mother-Speak

"I put a piece of cardboard over the window and set a clock-radio to early morning classical music. Sebastian is sleeping about an hour later in the morning than he was—and it hasn't affected his bedtime at all!"

—Candice, mother of three-year-old Sebastian

doublers or extra-thick nighttime diapers. If she's completely potty-trained, teach her how to use the bathroom by herself during the night and leave a night-light on in the hallway. If she hasn't tried this before, she may not have even realized that she can do this on her own.

• **Comfort.** Her covers have fallen off, the house has cooled down, and she's chilly, or the heat has come on and she's too hot.

Solution: Adjust the heat level of the house, put a fan on her dresser (keeping it and all cords out of reach), or change what she wears to bed or the types of blankets on her bed.

• **Hunger.** Her tummy rumblings wake her.

Solution: Give her a low-sugar, high-carbohydrate snack before bedtime. Provide her with a bowl of crackers and a cup of water on her nightstand.

• **Habit.** She has been waking up early for a long time, and now her internal clock alarm goes off at that time.

Solution: Gradually adjust her night and nap sleep schedule until she is sleeping and waking at a better time.

• **Nap routine.** She's napping too early, too late, too often, or too long.

Solution: Reorganize her nap schedule according to the information on page 51.

More Tips for Encouraging Longer Sleep

Very often an early-waking child does so out of habit, and it may take a few weeks of consistent changes before you see a new wake-up time emerge. Be patient and use the following tips in conjunction with the previous list and the general ideas in the first part of this book:

• Apply the concepts covered on page 55, and reset your child's biological clock. Do this by keeping the hour before bedtime dimly lit, sleeping time dark, and breakfast time brightly lit.

• Keep your child's room dark during all the hours you want her to sleep. Use blinds, curtains, or even a blanket or big pieces of cardboard to keep out unwanted light. Do your prebedtime reading by the dimmest light possible, and finish the routine with storytelling in the dark.

• Schedule playtime in the afternoon or early evening outside whenever you can. If you can't get outside, keep the play area brightly lit. You may even want to invest in a natural sunlight lamp, which emits a clear sunlike glow.

• Try treating the early-morning awakening as if it were 2:00 A.M. and respond to your child as you do with a night waking. If the windows are covered and the room is dark, your child may accept that it's the middle of the night and not the morning.

• Children who wake early often nap early, too, usually going for a nap within an hour or two of waking up. This is actually the end of their nighttime sleep! Try holding off the morning nap by fifteen to thirty minutes every day until it falls an hour or two hours later in the day than it is now. After a week or two, you should see a new pattern emerge.

• Hold off breakfast for thirty minutes to an hour after your child wakes up. She may have set her "hunger alert" to go off at 6:00 A.M. By holding off breakfast in the morning, you may be able to reset the time she gets hungry. If she can't wait that long, try a small snack, like a few crackers, and delay a full breakfast for a bit.

• Maintain a consistent bedtime and awakening time seven days a week. Changing the schedule each weekend will likely prevent you from finding success at getting a reasonable wake-up time during the week.

What to Do If Your Lark Continues to Wake Up Early

If you've tried these ideas and kept to them for a few weeks, but find that your little rooster continues to wake up early, you may want to accept that it's her natural waking time and approach the problem differently. Here are some tips:

• Every night after your child goes to sleep, put a box of toys next to her bed. Rotate these so that there's always something new and interesting in the box. Tell her that when she wakes up, she can check her box and play with whatever she finds in there. Be creative, but make sure the toys are safe, and of course, nothing noisy! (If your child is still sleeping in a crib, you can leave toys at the foot of the crib.)

• Set a clock radio to a pleasant music station, and have it turn on at your acceptable wake-up time. Tell your child that she can't leave her bedroom to wake you up until she hears the music.

• Leave a sippy cup of water and a snack, such as crackers, on her bedside so that when she wakes up she will have something to eat. (No choking hazards.)

• Make a recording of your child's favorite songs or stories, and show her how to operate the machine. Let her listen to her special music when she wakes up.

Alexandra, four years old

• Invite her into your room or your bed. Tell her that if she wakes up, she can come quietly into your room. Let her climb in bed and snuggle with you, or create a little resting area with a sleeping bag on the floor for her. You might even create a fort, such as using a blanket over a card table, and call it her morning nest. Put a few toys and books inside and see if she'll play quietly for a while before waking you.

• Shhh. Don't tell anybody I gave you this idea, but as a last resort it can be a lifesaver: Set up the DVD player with her favorite movie, and teach her how to push the play button. Leave a sippy cup of water and a bowl of dry cereal for snacking. This will buy you an extra hour of shut-eye.

• Childproof, childproof, childproof! Make sure that your entire house is safe for your early riser so that if she's wandering around while you're still asleep she won't get herself into trouble.

• Practice. Once you've established some ideas for what you'd like to have happen in the morning, let your child show you exactly what she'll do when she gets up. By role-playing a few times, she'll be comfortable doing as you wish when she wakes up so early in the morning—playing with her toys, climbing in bed with you, playing in her fort, or listening to her music.

Will My Lark *Ever* Sleep Later?

Oh, yes. Your lark *will* begin sleeping later in the morning . . . once she starts school and is required to wake up at 6:00 A.M. Frustrating, but true! As children get older, many of them go through an owl stage—finding it hard to fall asleep at a reasonable bedtime, but easy to sleep until noon. (Look for my next book—on school-age sleep issues.)

Tooth Grinding: Chewing and Clenching During Sleep

Our four-year-old daughter often joins us in our bed during the night. She sometimes wakes me up with loud noises as she grinds her teeth together. To be honest, it's a pretty creepy sound to wake up to! Why does she do this? Can she hurt her teeth doing it? Is there any way to get her to stop?

The harsh sound of a child grinding her teeth in the night can be eerie, but in most cases the sound is the only problem for you to be concerned about. It's a common condition, called bruxism (BRUK-si-zm), and almost a third of all children grind or clench their teeth while sleeping; the majority of grinders are under five years old.

What Are the Signs of Bruxism?

In many cases, like yours, a parent or sibling will hear a child grinding her teeth in the night. Other symptoms of bruxism are a sore jaw, loose teeth, tooth sensitivity, or morning headaches. An older child may complain of these symptoms. Some children who suck their fingers, bite their nails, or chew on the inside of their cheeks also grind their teeth at night.

Why Do Children Grind Their Teeth?

The exact reason why children grind their teeth isn't known, but there are some widely held theories about bruxism. Any one of these may be the reason that your child is what professionals would call a "bruxer."

• New teeth might be the motive for grinding. Your child may be acting in response to the feel of new teeth in her mouth. Some children whose upper and lower teeth aren't quite aligned properly may grind in an unconscious effort to make the teeth come together correctly.

• Other sleep disturbances sometimes involve tooth grinding. Children who snore (page 339) or have sleep apnea (page 340) may also be teeth grinders.

• Dehydration may be a cause. A few studies discovered that children who don't drink enough water—not milk, juice, or soda, but *water*—have a higher incidence of tooth grinding.

• Intestinal irritations or food allergies may be a culprit. Children with food allergies, nutritional deficiencies, or intestinal infections such as pinworms may grind their teeth.

• Nighttime pain can cause grinding. If your child has a painful bout of teething or an earache, it may result in tooth grinding as a natural attempt to ease the soreness.

• A vitamin deficiency might exacerbate grinding. On occasion a child's grinding can be connected to a deficiency of vitamin B or calcium. Boosting the amount of dairy products in your child's diet or providing her with vitamins, as recommended by your health care provider, may help.

• Stress or anxiety can instigate bruxism. Some children release the stress of the day with nightly teeth grinding. This doesn't necessarily mean that your child has excessive stress in her life; rather, it's just her way of dealing with everyday anxieties.

Unusual events, such as a change in day-care arrangements, the birth of a sibling, a move to a new home, or the parents' divorce may increase the amount of grinding that occurs.

In some cases you may be able to pinpoint the reason your child is grinding her teeth, but frequently it's hard to know exactly why she's doing it. Whether you can or can't determine the reason, any of the treatments that follow may help reduce, or even eliminate, the grinding.

Is There Any Way to Prevent the Grinding?

A number of ideas and remedies are suggested for stopping tooth grinding. Since your child is unaware that she's grinding at night, there isn't any point in talking to her about it. Doing so could even make things worse, since you'll create stress about it. The following ideas are simple and healthy interventions, so it's worth trying some of them to see if you can reduce your child's nightly grinding.

- Create a relaxing bedtime routine that includes a warm bath, tranquil music, peaceful reading, or a massage just before sleep to reduce any nighttime stress. The routine itself can also create a feeling of security that may reduce the grinding if it is stress-related.
- If you wake up to hear your child grinding, gently hold or massage her jaw while she sleeps. This won't solve the problem, but it may be enough to stop her for the moment. Don't wake her up to make her stop, because she's unaware of the grinding and waking her will just disrupt her sleep cycle.
- Take your child to your health care provider for a checkup, and mention your concerns about the tooth grinding. If any infec-

tions, earaches, or other health problems are discovered, medication can be prescribed to remedy the problem.

• Teach your child how to relax for sleep. Tell her that she can
use these methods if she wakes up during the night and has trouble falling back to sleep. You can read about some specific relaxation techniques on page 94.

• Identify any stressful issues in your child's life and see if you
can work to relieve the tension. If your child is feeling anxious
about the impending birth of a sibling, for instance, reading a few
books together on the topic, shopping for baby toys together, or
talking about what's to come may ease her fears and reduce some
of the worry.

Are There Any Possible Problems to Watch For?

In most cases of toddler or preschool bruxers, there is no damage
happening to their teeth. To make sure this is the case with your
child, mention the grinding to your health care provider at your
next regular visit. In some cases, a dentist is the only one who can
tell you if your child's grinding is creating a problem with her teeth
or her jaw development. If you know that your child is grinding
on a regular basis, it's a good idea to have your dentist take a look.

What Will the Dentist Do If Bruxism Is Causing Problems?

A dentist can examine your child's teeth for signs of excessive
wear, cracks, chipping, or jaw problems. He can also determine if
the alignment of your child's teeth needs addressing. In many

Jackie, three years old

cases, he may just want to inspect your child's teeth several times a year to monitor their growth and watch for any changes. Most often, baby teeth don't last long enough to suffer any real damage from grinding.

If your dentist feels that the grinding is creating problems for your child's teeth or jaw development, he may be able to file the teeth to make them align more correctly. For older children, it's possible that he'll suggest a custom-made mouth guard to be worn during sleep. This is a plastic mouthpiece similar to those worn by athletes. Don't try to self-prescribe this solution. Work with your dentist, since an ill-fitted mouthpiece could come loose and cause your child to choke. Most dentists will hold off on a mouth guard if your child is a toddler or young preschooler.

Will My Child Always Grind Her Teeth?

A number of children will stop grinding when all their baby teeth are in, and many will stop once their full set of permanent teeth come in. Some children continue the practice, and some children who don't grind when they're little begin to do so when they are of school age. Some studies show that as many as 90 percent of people grind or clench their teeth at some point in their lives, but only about 5 percent of adults grind their teeth hard enough to warrant treatment.

Bad Dreams, Nightmares, and Night Terrors

In our playgroup, we've been talking about our children's bad dreams. It seems like all the kids in the group have them at one time or another. Some have them more intensely or more often than others, but they all have them. Why do children have bad dreams, and what's the best way to deal with these?

The value of sharing stories with other parents is that you learn something very reassuring: no matter what situation you're dealing with, other parents are having the same experience. As you have discovered in this case, all children have bad dreams. Dreaming is the time when the brain sorts through the day's events and emotions. Children spend substantially more time in the dreaming stage of sleep than adults do, so they have many more dreams—both good and bad. The intensity of toddler and preschooler dreams mirrors the intensity with which these little people live, so dreams can be surreal exaggerations of real life. In addition, a young child's vibrant imagination, curiosity, and creativity are evident even during sleep. In light of all these reasons, it's easy to understand why all children have bad dreams and why research shows that episodes of nightmares are at their peak during the ages from three to six.

How Are Nightmares Different from Bad Dreams?

Everyone dreams, and dreams can be good, neutral, or bad. A nightmare is a bad dream that results in a partial or full awakening. The child, coming fresh from the dream, remembers what she was dreaming about and retains the emotions of fear or anxiety that were the theme of the nightmare. So, in a sense, a nightmare actually becomes a nightmare when a child wakes up and consciously thinks about the dream she just had.

What Should You Do About Nightmares?

As adults, when we wake up from a dream in bed and in the dark, no matter how vivid it was we immediately identify the experience as a dream. A young child, on the other hand, hasn't quite mastered the understanding of life versus dream, reality versus fantasy, real versus pretend. When your child wakes with a nightmare, he will likely be confused. For young children, telling them, "It was just a dream" doesn't quite explain what they just experienced. They don't have the wisdom yet to understand the fantasy aspect of dreams; after all, most of them believe that the Tooth Fairy, Santa Claus, and Big Bird are real. Keeping this in mind, it only seems fair to comfort children in the same way we comfort them when they face a tangible fear or danger, since the emotions they feel are likely the same.

The following are things you can do if your child wakes with a nightmare:

- The most important thing you can do when your toddler or preschooler has a nightmare is be there and offer comfort, just as you would in any other situation when your child is feeling afraid or hurt.

- Stay with your child until she feels relaxed and ready to go to sleep. If she's reluctant to have you leave her side, go ahead and stay with her until she is actually sleeping.
- Stay calm. Your attitude will convey to your child that what's happening is normal and that all is well.
- Reassure your child that he's safe and that it's OK to go back to sleep.

Should You Let Your Child Come to Your Bed?

By far, the easiest way to offer comfort and get your child—and yourself!—back to sleep quickly is just to scoop her up and bring her to your bed. Or if she has a toddler bed or floor mattress, lie down beside her until she (and possibly you) fall back to sleep. If this works for you, then you've found a simple solution.

Unfortunately, though, easiest is not always the right answer. The decision on this topic depends on your family's feelings about co-sleeping and where you are in your own child's sleep plan. If you're not comfortable with bringing your child to your bed, if you are in the middle of a plan to move your child from the family bed to his own bed, or if you've just recently done so, you may want to avoid bringing him back to your bed, even after a nightmare. Doing so may create a situation where your child will suddenly start having "nightmares" just as soon as she goes to bed. (Which is quite peculiar, since nightmares usually occur during the second half of the night or early morning. Just goes to show you how bright and creative your child is.)

If you choose not to bring your child to your bed, you still have plenty of other ways to offer comfort until your child is settled and ready to go back to sleep. You can sit beside him, take him to a rocking chair for a cuddle, or set him up with a snuggly blanket, some soft music, a night-light, and a favorite lovey toy to snuggle.

Should You Talk to Your Child About the Nightmares?

Let your child set the pace for discussion about nightmares. In the morning he may or may not remember what happened, and even if he remembers, he may or may not be thinking about it much. If he brings it up and does want to talk about it, let him explain what happened. Keep in mind, however, that it may be a very disjointed story. You can listen with interest, and then tell your own version of the story: give the nightmare a resolution or a happy ending. Pick out the main points, which may often involve a monster or an animal, and help your child come up with a great way to finish the story. The monster or animal might run away or become friendly. If you have an older child who seems to want to delve deeper into the topic, you can have him draw a picture of the nightmare. Then make a production about drawing a second picture that shows a resolution, or get rid of the nightmare once it's on paper—crumple it up and throw it away. This technique is often helpful in reducing future episodes of nightmares.

What Are Night Terrors?

Night terrors are completely different from nightmares or bad dreams. These mysterious episodes are also referred to as *sleep ter-*

rors, since they can occur during daytime naps as well as night-time sleep. Any parent who has witnessed a child in the process of a night terror will understand completely why it has the name—it can be terrifying for the parent to observe. During a night ter-ror, your child will wake suddenly, and she may let out a panicky scream or a fearful cry. Her eyes will likely be opened and her pupils dilated, but she won't be seeing. She may hyperventilate, thrash around, or talk or yell in a confused incoherent manner. She may be sweating, her face may be flushed, or her heart might be beating rapidly. She may jump out of bed or even run around the room. She'll act as if she's being chased or threatened, or she may appear to be terrified by a horrible nightmare.

Actually, your child is not frightened, not awake, and not dreaming. She's sound asleep and in a zone between two sleep cycles, somewhat stuck for a few minutes. When the sleep terror passes, she'll resume the cycle before it was interrupted. The child having a night terror is not having a nightmare, is unaware of what's happening, and won't remember the episode in the morn-ing. So the *terror* part of night terrors is named not for the child but for the parent who watches the disturbing scene.

Now that you understand what night terrors are all about, it should take some of your fear and concern away. While it may still be difficult and unsettling to watch your child during an episode, you can rest assured that your child is neither awake nor frightened.

What Should You Do About Night Terrors?

This is the hard part. A parent's natural response upon seeing the child acting terrified is to hold him and comfort him, to which he would respond by calming down. During a night terror, however, your child is not awake nor aware of your presence. You may try to hold him, but trying to hold a thrashing child during a night terror usually results in his pushing you away or fighting you off—making the whole thing even more frightening for you. In this case, you can try a gentle pat or touch along with a series of comforting words and *shhh, shhh* sounds, but realistically these might be more to give you a sense of doing something to help rather than achieve any real purpose.

If your child gets out of bed, you can try to lead him back. If he's sitting up, you can try to guide him to lie back down. There is no value in waking your child up; in fact, trying to wake him may just prolong the episode.

Your goals are to keep your child safe by preventing him from falling out of bed, down the stairs, or banging into furniture and to get him back to bed after the night terror has run its course.

Should You Talk About the Night Terrors?

Given that your child isn't aware of what's happening during the episode, since he most likely has no memory of it and can't control the night terrors, there's no reason to talk to him about what's happening. Actually, doing so may just upset him and cause him to worry or fear bedtime.

While you shouldn't talk to your child about the night terrors, do remember to talk to a grandparent or baby-sitter who may tend to your child during naptime or sleep time. If your child has older siblings, talk to them as well. Let them know a little about night terrors, and reassure them that what happens during a night terror is normal. Tell them exactly what might happen and how to handle the situation. Take care that little ears aren't overhearing the conversation, since your child might hear bits and pieces and make assumptions about what he hears. This could cause him to become confused or scared.

Is It a Bad Dream, a Nightmare, or a Night Terror?

The chart on the next page is a quick reference for figuring out what's going on with your child when nighttime frights appear.

How Can You Prevent Your Child from Having Nightmares and Night Terrors?

To a certain extent you can't really prevent your child from having nightmares or night terrors. However, some things have been found to reduce the number of episodes or the severity of the episodes. Even if you can't prevent these, some of the following tips will help your child learn how to deal with nightmares or the feelings of fear and uncertainty if he wakes up after a bad dream:

- Monitor the movies and television that your child watches, during the day as well as in the evening, since scary images can show up in your child's nightmares. Pay attention to not only the shows she watches but also whatever is on the screen when she's in the room. Just because it's a program created for children doesn't make it safe: many cartoons and children's shows are filled with images of violence. So choose carefully what you allow your child to watch. Keep in mind that young children can be scared by things that adults might find amusing. Watch your child's reaction, more than what's on the screen, for a true indication of his response.
- Avoid books that have pictures or stories that disturb your child. Again, watch your child for cues to her feelings, as toddlers and preschoolers can find the oddest things frightening. For exam-

	Bad dream	Nightmare	Night terror
When does it happen?	Anytime during REM sleep	Anytime, but commonly the second half of the night or early morning	The first few hours of the night's sleep
During what stage of sleep does it occur?	REM (dreaming sleep)	REM (dreaming sleep)	Non-REM sleep
How many children are affected?	100%	80%–90%	6%–15%
What age is affected most often?	All ages, because dreaming occurs even before birth	All ages (Some experts believe that nightmares begin at about a year old, but others feel they may start a few weeks after birth.)	Usually between 3 and 12 years old, occasionally as young as 6 months (Only about 1% of people have night terrors through adulthood.)
Is it hereditary?	N/A	No	Yes

How does a child act?	Usually there is no way to tell if a child is having a bad dream; bad dreams occur during normal sleep. Sometimes a child grimaces, moans, or moves about during a bad dream, but he is not awake.	A child wakes up frightened after the nightmare and sometimes cries.	A child's eyes often are open, but he is not awake. He may cry, scream, or hyperventilate. He may sit up or even get out of bed.
How will a child respond to comforting?	He won't know that the parent is there, because he's still sleeping.	She will seek out or call for a parent, want to be held and comforted, and relax when reassured.	He may push the parent away, fight against being restrained, and act strangely.
How long will the episode last?	REM sleep periods (and therefore dreams) typically last from 5 to 45 minutes.	Nightmares are brief, but the settling period afterward can take some time.	Night terrors typically last only a few minutes, but they can last for as long as 30 minutes.
How and when will the child fall back to sleep?	If a child is awakened during a dream, he'll usually fall back to sleep quickly after brief comforting.	The child may stay awake until her fears are gone, and she may need a parent's help to go back to sleep.	The child will easily return to quiet sleep once the episode passes.
Will a child remember what happened?	The child will sometimes remember parts of a dream.	The child will frequently remember sections or the overall mood of the nightmare.	Usually the child has no memory of what happened.

ple, many toddlers are afraid of clowns, trolls, human-looking dolls, or distorted images of real things.

• A child who is overtired or sleep deprived will have more episodes of nightmares or night terrors. If your child is plagued by night problems, the first step is to check out your child's sleep hours according to the table on page 12. Then read over the tips in Part I of this book to create a consistent bedtime plan.

• An erratic sleep schedule can contribute to sleep terrors and possibly to nightmares as well. Aim to have your child in bed at the same time every night and see if this reduces these nighttime problems.

• Make sure you follow a calm and peaceful routine the hour before bedtime. This will ensure that your child falls asleep while feeling happy and safe.

• If your child is taking medication, ask a pharmacist or your health care professional whether the medication could be disturbing your child's sleep.

• Children with special needs or those with ongoing medical ailments may have more frequent or severe nightmares or night terrors. If your child has any special health conditions, discuss this possibility with your health care provider, or chat with parents of children with similar health circumstances to share ideas.

• For some children, a heavy meal before bed may bring on nightmares or night terrors. If your child currently eats a big meal before bedtime, experiment with an earlier dinnertime and provide your child with a light snack an hour or two before bedtime.

• Some children have more night terrors if they are new to nighttime dryness and go to sleep with a full bladder. Remember to have your child use the potty just before she gets into bed, even if she "just went" or "doesn't have to." Encouraging her to go potty one last time before getting into bed may help prevent night terrors. Examine your child's life situation to see if stressful conditions may be promoting nightmares. Stress from situations like the parents' divorce or marriage, a move to a new home, the birth of a new sibling, or the death of a family member or pet can manifest themselves into nightmares. If you can pinpoint a problem and find ways to reassure your child that he is safe, it may help reduce the intensity or frequency of nightmares.

• Some children find that hanging up a sign in their bedroom is reassuring. Make one that says, "Good Dreams Only" or "No Bad Dreams Allowed," and decorate it with happy pictures. Hang it in your child's room or on her door.

• Some children find comfort in hanging a dream catcher above their bed or on their window. This Native American ornament made of webbing, beads, and feathers "catches" the bad dreams and lets the good dreams flow through.

• Your child may be uncertain about whether what happens in a dream is real or imaginary. During the day you can begin teaching your child the difference between "real" and "pretend." Point out things in a movie or on television, and discuss whether they are real or not. Point out how she can "see" a picture in her head when you tell her a story and how this is sort of like a dream that happens when she's sleeping. An older child may be taught how to finish a bad dream by adding a good ending to it.

Is There a Time to Call a Professional?

Don't ever hesitate to call a professional if you have concerns about your child's sleep. A professional can help you in a variety of ways. These include techniques that can be used to control episodes of sleep terrors or nightmares without the use of medication.

You should discuss your child's situation with your health care professional or a pediatric sleep specialist if any of the following occur:

- Your child has frequent, intense nightmares.
- Your child has night terrors three or more times per week.
- Your child is afraid to go to bed because of a fear of nightmares.
- Your child sleepwalks or runs in her sleep during episodes, putting herself in possible danger.
- You have questions that this book hasn't answered or your instincts tell you that something isn't right.
- You have tried all the tips provided here but your child is still having problems with nightmares or night terrors.

The Night Visitor: Trips to the Parent's Bed

Our four-year-old falls asleep easily in his own bed, but inevitably somewhere around 2:00 A.M. we hear a little pat-pat-pat down the hallway. He climbs up in our bed and snuggles in for the rest of the night. We admit to each other that we love our little guy cuddled up with us, but we feel a little embarrassed about it. My in-laws say that he's getting too old for this and he belongs in his own bed. I do sometimes think it would be nice to have an uninterrupted night, but when I don't let him get in our bed, he gets very upset and I just end up sleeping with him in his bed. What should we do?

Just like most parenting situations, there is no one right answer to this question: the answer is different for every family. I will, however, help you figure out *your* right answer. To begin with, rest assured that you are not alone. It's perfectly natural for a toddler or preschooler to seek out his parents for middle-of-the-night comfort and security—it's a sign of his trust and his deep love for you. And it's perfectly normal for parents to provide that comfort and security by bringing their child into their bed or by lying with him in his own bed. An ongoing parentcenter.com poll on this topic has garnered 13,586 votes as of this writing. The question is *"How do you handle middle-of-the-night visits from your child?"* (ages two to eight). The results confirm that your house isn't the only one that echoes with those little pat-pat-pats in the middle of the night: 41 percent responded, "I let her crawl into my bed" and another 4 percent said, "I let her sleep in a sleeping bag on the floor near my bed." Thirteen percent said, "I take her back to her room and lie down with her until she goes back to sleep." Twenty-six percent said, "It depends on the situation."

It's very common for toddlers and preschoolers to seek out their parents when waking in the night, and as you see, it's very common for parents to respond by welcoming their little traveler into their bed or lying with him in his own. So there's no reason for you to feel embarrassed. What's happening at your house is perfectly normal and you're obviously in good company.

There are many gentle ways to encourage your child to stay in his bed all night, but before I introduce those ideas, it's best if you evaluate your situation. Spend a day and think about your answers to these questions, and discuss them with your partner:

- Are you, your partner, and your child all getting a good night's sleep?
- If no one else in the world knew or cared about what you're doing, would you be happy with the routine you have now?
- Do you think you'll be content if you have the same routine six months from now? A year from now?
- Are your child's visits to your bed interfering with the level of intimacy between the two of you, or are you still finding plenty of time to meet each other's needs for physical closeness?
- If you are a single parent, is your child's need to have you with him in bed preventing you from spending your evenings or early mornings doing things that you need or want to do?
- Are you considering making a change because *you* want a change and because it's right for your family—or is it to appease a friend, relative, or someone else?
- Did you used to enjoy your child's middle-of-the-night visits but find yourself liking it less over time and you're unsure of how to make a change?

- If tonight your child suddenly began to sleep all night in his own bed, how would you feel: overjoyed, happy, a bit sad, very sad, or depressed?
- What specifically about your child's night visits bothers you? Is it that he wakes you up? That it prevents you from uninterrupted couple time? Are you concerned that others are worried about it? Do you want to get pregnant again or are you already expecting and don't want an overcrowded bed once the new baby arrives? Explore your own reasons for wanting to make a change.
- Why does your child visit you in the night? Is it simply a habit? Or are fears, nightmares, separation anxiety, bedwetting, allergies, teething, reflux, or other problems causing her to wake up and search you out? (Read up on these issues in other parts of this book and deal with them as part of your overall sleep plan.)

The first step is to take a day or so to ponder these questions and to examine your real feelings about the situation. Often ambivalence and frustration result from not taking the time to identify what you really feel and not having a clear goal and purpose to your actions. Once you have a better understanding of your thoughts and your partner's thoughts, choose one of these goals (or create your own):

- We're going to continue as we are, without guilt or concern, for _____ months. At that time we will reevaluate the situation and make a new decision.
- We're in no rush but would like to begin making a change. We're going to make gradual changes and anticipate that within _____ months our child will be sleeping all night in his own bed.
- We want to make a change right now, as soon as possible, so we will commit to a specific plan and follow it every night.

Don't Send Mixed Messages

If you've shared your bed with your cuddly and sweet-smelling toddler or preschooler, whether from birth or just recently, I can almost guarantee that even though you've decided to move her out, a little part of you doesn't want to let her go. This is natural given the preciousness of the experience of sharing your bed with your child. If you really do want your child to sleep in her own bed, however, you'll need to keep these emotions in check. Don't make the mistakes that these test families did during the moving process. (The names have been changed to protect the guilty from embarrassment.)

- Sharon reported that by using the ideas in their sleep plan, they were having great success getting their toddler, Kayla, to sleep in her own bed. "She did so for a whole week and I was getting very excited! Tonight, as she was getting ready to get into *her* bed, my husband, as a reward for her doing this, invited her back into our room! So, needless to say, we are back at square one with more resistance."

- Monica's husband was the culprit in their house, too. She says, "We are going slowly but making progress, and our goal is to have our son moved before the new baby arrives. Thomas is spending every second or third night in his own bed. But I have just realized that on mornings when Frank wakes to find Thomas next to him, there is a great cuddle-fest with Frank going on and on about how he loves snuggling with his little 'Thomas-Bear' during the night. He asks, 'Who cuddled with Daddy all night?' and 'Are you my little snuggler?' Daddy's joy is so obvious that it is a clear invitation for Thomas to continue to sleep with him!"

- "I can't believe what I did!" Marisa's new message came just a week after she e-mailed to tell me that Gracie was making far fewer visits to her mommy's bed during the night. "I woke up last night and realized that Gracie was spending yet another night in her own bed. I missed her next to me so much that I went into her room and climbed in bed with her! Now tonight we're heading up to get ready for bed, and sure enough, she's asking me to sleep in her bed with her again! I think I've just created a whole new problem! Please help!"

When I shared these stories with the mom of a fourteen-year-old boy, she just laughed. "You have no idea!" she exclaimed. "My own son slept on a sleeping bag in our room once or twice a week until he was twelve. Then we went on a monthlong vacation. When we returned he just stopped coming into our room. A month passed, and one night I was stunned to hear my husband (a very independent he-man sort of guy, by the way) say to our son, 'Hey, Nathan, you want to camp in our room tonight?' When I stood gaping at him, his only response was a shrug and, 'I've missed him.'"

What was your instinctive response to my friend's story? Did you shudder to think you could have your child sleeping nearby for so many years to come? Or was your first response one of joy for this close-knit family? There isn't a right answer, you know. Either response is normal. If any of these situations strike a chord with you or shake up your image of what you really want to do right now, I suggest you back up a few pages. Reread the beginning of this section and take another day or so to examine your genuine feelings and your family's needs. Realize, too, that this isn't an all-or-nothing state of affairs. It isn't always necessary to have a 100 percent rule against children in your bed; you may want to find a compromise that fits your unique family situation, such as allowing morning snuggles, post-nightmare visits, or pajama parties on the weekends.

It Is OK to Make a Change, You Know!

For those of you who are still with me—those of you who have decided that it's time to move your little cuddler out of your bed and say good-bye to those nighttime pokes from little elbows and toes—let me reassure you that it's perfectly fine to make this change. There is no one right age or time or situation to adhere to; it's just a matter of parental choice. If you're ready, you're ready. Your child is obviously well loved and secure, and those feelings won't change when you use a sensitive, loving method to keep her sleeping in her own bed all night long.

What to Do Next

There are a number of ways to keep your little one in his own bed all night. Since every child and every situation are different, each family will approach this situation in a unique way. What follows is a menu of ideas for you to choose from. Pick one, two, or more that sound right for you, and give them an honest try. Keep in mind that your child is happy and would most likely be content to keep things as they are until he's five to ten years old. So if you want to avoid tears, struggle, and anger, then don't expect things to happen in a night or two. Be patient and keep to your plan. Over the next few weeks or months (depending on your time goal), you will see success.

How quickly this happens depends on your child's personality and how motivated you are to move things along. Very often the process is erratic: your child will spend one night sleeping alone, then arrive in your bed the next two, but after that not show up for two or three nights, and soon a week will go by without a visit. If you have no "deadline," then it's easiest to move along at this pace. If, however, you have a reason to rush the process, such as the upcoming birth of a new sibling, or if your nightly sleep is being disrupted, then be more persistent in your actions and you should have quicker results.

The Solutions

What follows is a list of ideas that have worked for other families like yours. You can choose from these or combine bits and pieces to create a totally unique solution. Be patient with yourself and your child as you proceed.

From Bed to Floor to Out the Door

If you don't mind your child coming into your *room* during the night, but would like to keep him out of your *bed*, then set up a sleeping place for him in your bedroom. This place can be as simple as a futon and blanket on the floor to as complex as a den made out of a card table draped with a sheet, housing a sleeping bag and pillow.

Set up your child's sleeping place and show it to him during the day. Present it with a flourish and a happy attitude. You might announce that he's a big boy now and can choose where he wants to sleep: either in his bed or his special sleeping place. (Offering a choice is always good!) Ask that if he comes into your room, he should "please be as quiet as a mouse" and go right to sleep in his special place. It's a good idea to rehearse this a few times during the day and once again right before bedtime. These practice sessions will help him remember what to do during the night; otherwise, he'll just do as he has always done.

During the night, if he forgets and climbs in bed with you, just help him down to his little place and remind him that that's where he needs to be. It's perfectly fine to lie with him until he falls asleep at first. It will help him get used to this new routine. Over time, it will then be easier to take the next step and encourage him to stay in his own bed, since he'll be giving up only a pad on the floor—instead of the family bed—for his own cozy bed.

The Morning Snuggle

This idea shifts your child's visit from the midnight hours to a more acceptable early morning time. Many parents enjoy this plan as well, since they don't have to give up snuggling their little one entirely but can enjoy it *after* they've had a good night's sleep.

Create a special signal that tells her when she is welcome to come into bed with you. There are various cues that young children can understand. You can choose one depending on your child's age and level of understanding. One idea is to tell her she can come in "when it's light outside." This works if daylight appears at the right time for you. Another is to set a music or white-noise alarm to go off quietly at an acceptable time. Explain, "If the music is playing, you can come to our bed. If it's quiet, then please go back to sleep until the music plays." Yet another is to make a picture to place on your bedroom door—one side shows people sleeping, the other shows people awake. (Magazine photos work, or you can take digital photos of yourself awake and pretending to sleep.) When you go to bed at night, hang the sleeping side up. Flip the photo over to the "awake" side when the acceptable time for morning cuddles arrives.

The Weekend Promise

With this approach, you begin by explaining to your child that you want her to sleep in her bed all night. Tell her that when she stays in her bed all week, then she can sleep with you on the week-

Andy and Isobel, two years old

end or on Sunday. Post a calendar and let her stick a star on each day that she sleeps all night without waking you. Put a special design on the weekend days.

This idea works perfectly for some children who relish their weekend sleepovers in the big bed. Others, though, find it too difficult to separate *yes* nights from *no* nights. If you think it may work with your little one, give it a try.

If you decide to use this approach and she attempts a visit during the week, return her to her own bed by using the Rubber Band Bounce, which follows in this section.

The Special Big-Kid Bedroom

Some children can be enticed to stay in their room if you choose a special date for the event of their move into their own bed—

such as a birthday or a made-up "Big-Kid Day." Leading up to the big day, you can rearrange the bedroom, buy new bed linens, decorate the walls with happy pictures or posters, and put glow-in-the-dark stars on the ceiling. (Don't make too many big changes to the room, though. If it's entirely unfamiliar, it may not be inviting come bedtime.)

For a few weeks or months leading to the event, talk about what a big girl or big boy he'll be, and make sleeping in his bed all night a milestone occurrence. When the big day arrives, have a cake and a few presents, if you wish—sleep-related items such as a new book and a stuffed animal are good choices. Take a picture of your child in his new big-kid room, then cross your fingers! If he still ends up in your room (and there's a good chance he will), use the Rubber Band Bounce that follows and take him back to his room.

The Rubber Band Bounce

This is a good idea for a family who wants to make a quick change to their middle-of-the-night routine and for a parent who's willing to get out of bed repeatedly for a week or so. When you're consistent, this plan often has excellent results after a week or two.

Just before your bedtime routine begins, explain briefly why you want her to stay in her bed. Say, for example, "When you come in my room during the night, you wake me up and then I'm grumpy." Tell her that you want her to stay in her bed all night long. Begin the night with a pleasant, peaceful go-to-bed routine. Finish it with your child in her bed. Anytime she gets up—*every time* she gets out of bed—calmly, peacefully, and lovingly put her back to bed. Kiss her, hug her, rub her back. Even sit or lie next to her until she falls back to sleep, if necessary.

Don't talk much, don't turn on any lights, and choose a key phrase to repeat to her a few times, such as, "It's night-night time now. Mommy loves you. Please stay in your bed and have sweet dreams."

You may have to repeat this ten times the first few nights, but with real consistency you should see this process reduce nighttime visits quickly. In order for this to work, you need to be calm, boring, loving, and *very* consistent.

Create New Sleep Associations

Take a look at your child's bedtime routine. How does he fall asleep at night? In Part I of this book we talked about sleep associations and brief awakenings between sleep stages. If your child is falling asleep with you by his side and then wakes between cycles to find you gone, it's possible that *you* are the sleep aid he needs to be able to fall back to sleep easily. If he learns how to fall asleep without you, he may then sleep all night without leaving his bed. If this is the case, incorporate into your sleep plan some of the suggestions from page 123, "Mommy, Stay!": Needing a Parent's Help to Fall Asleep.

Gift-Wrapped Motivation

My sleep survey uncovered the fact that most preschoolers can be highly motivated to make changes when offered a prize (which, I'm sure, if you have a preschooler, is no great surprise to you). There are several approaches you can use.

The sticker approach has been a popular choice. Purchase a calendar, and put it in a visible place on the wall. Allow your child to put a sticker on the calendar each morning after he stays in his own bed. A nice twist is to have two kinds of stickers—big special ones for successful nights and smaller stickers for nights when he "tries."

Your child's goal is to attain a certain number of big stickers—which can be whatever number you want it to be, but shouldn't be so many that your child loses interest during the wait. You may want to start off with a small number—say, three stickers, and work your way up to ten or so. When the magic number of stickers is on the chart, your child gets a prize. This can be a trip out for an ice-cream cone, a coveted toy, or a special privilege.

An alternative is to create a "Prize Chain," which can be very successful with preschoolers for goals as varied as bedtime issues to potty training. Here's what you do: Buy twenty to thirty little prizes, such as small plastic animals, a deck of cards, play jewelry, crayons, or stickers. Wrap each prize individually in brightly colored wrapping paper. Lay the prizes all along the hallway just outside her bedroom door. Tell her that any night that she stays in her bed all night—until morning—she gets a prize.

Look at or, even better, count the prizes and remind her of the plan every night before she goes to bed, but don't force the issue. It may take her a week or even longer to really "get it." Even after she truly understands how to win, she may get a prize one night and then join you in bed for the next three. Don't worry, she'll then earn another prize, skip a night or two, and so on.

What do you do when you're out of prizes? In your serious adult mind you may find this extremely odd, but most preschoolers are very happy to have you rewrap *all the same prizes* a second time around! Usually, at the end of the second round the prizes lose their importance, but it doesn't matter because by then your child's new routine is set in place.

How long the process of change will take depends on how strong your child's need is to be with you during the night. She may well feel that you are a much better prize than any toy you could offer, and isn't it glorious to be loved so much?

Nighttime Fears: Monsters, the Dark, and Things That Go Bump in the Night

Our daughter has become afraid of the dark. She says that she thinks monsters are going to get her. This makes bedtime particularly unsettling. How should we deal with her fears?

It's perfectly normal for a toddler or preschooler to imagine monsters or other things that generate a fear of the dark—it's one of the most common childhood fears. Actually, an emerging fear of the dark tells you that your child is growing, developing, and getting smarter. When your daughter was a baby, she didn't know that things existed when she couldn't see them; she lived purely in the moment. Now she knows that the dark covers up things she can't see and that things happen even if she is not there to witness them. She still has a lot of growing up to do, however, to understand how the world truly works. She has a ways to go before she can clearly distinguish between *real* and *imagined*. It will be many years before she reconciles the true dangers of the world with how they relate to her everyday existence and her level of safety and security. It's all about the process of growing wiser with each year of life.

What Messages Are You Sending?

Young children may seem too distracted to notice us adults much, but make no mistake: they are always watching, listening, taking it all in, and looking for clues as to how the outside world should be interpreted. They rely on signals from adults, particularly those closest to them, to tell them if their fears are logical. Your response to your child's concerns will tell her whether she truly has something to fear or if everything is safe and sound. The key to handling your child's fears of imagined things, such as monsters in the dark, is not only to *say* that things are OK but to *act* as though they are. If you make a big deal about her fear and if you keep looking under the bed or checking the closet to reassure her that everything is OK, your daughter may begin to wonder why you continue to look—are you expecting to find something?

While you don't want to overreact to your child's fear of the dark, you do want to be sensitive to your child's feelings. Understand that, while the object of your child's fear is not real, your child's fear is. The feelings of fear that she has are valid and the situation calls for a diplomatic and sensitive approach.

Can You Explain Away the Fears?

Even if you explain things in great detail to your child and even if you assure him that he's safe, he may still be scared. When my son Coleton was three years old, he developed a nighttime fear of the sound of airplanes flying overhead. One day, while getting ready for bed we heard the inevitable sound. I'm sure all my previous comments came to his mind as he looked up at me and said, "I know they can't hurt me, but they still scare me." It was a remarkably simple way to explain that while my reassurances were important to him, my presence was still very much needed.

Solutions to Choose From

The following section outlines a variety of ideas that have worked for other parents of young children. As you look these over, you'll be sure to find several that sound promising for your own child. Go ahead and try one or two, or combine the ideas into your own custom-made monster-fighting strategy. No matter what solutions you choose, the underlying message should always be one of confidence that there really are no monsters and that your child is perfectly safe in the dark and in her bed. No matter what individual steps you take to address your little one's fears, send the message that you know he is safe, you are there for him, and everything is just fine. Eventually, with your help, his fears will pass.

What's Real and What's Pretend?

This is a good time to teach your child how to discern between valid and imagined fears by helping him learn the difference between real and fantasy. This isn't a onetime lesson but a process that takes place over many conversations. You might discuss the differences between a rabbit you see at the zoo, Bugs Bunny, a stuffed bunny, and a rabbit he imagines in his mind. You can talk about the pictures he creates in his head as you read a book to him or when you tell him a story. You can contrast the difference between real things, like a dolphin, and imaginary things, like a mermaid. You can make a game of it: "Can a stuffed bunny eat your soup?" "Can a real bunny talk?" "Can you walk on the ceiling?" Show him that imagining something can't make it so.

Examine the fantasy creatures that you have introduced your child to, such as the Easter Bunny and the Tooth Fairy. A child who willingly accepts and believes these to be real may have more reason to believe in monsters, goblins, and the bogeyman as well. The amusing and entertaining make-believe characters don't have to be banished from your home, but they are one aspect of night-time fears that you'll need to consider as you work your way through your child's uncertainties.

Practical Tactics

Find ways to help your child confront and overcome his fears. Some helpful tactics follow:

- If dark shadows are creating suspicious shapes in the night, spend some time together finding spooky shapes or making shadows in your child's darkened room. Make a game of guessing what they really are, and then turn on the light to see what the shapes really are.
- You might give your child a flashlight to keep at his bedside to use if he wakes up. Lighting the hallway to your room or the bathroom with a night-light is helpful if he leaves his bed during the night. Keeping the closet and bedroom doors open (or closed) can help; ask your child which she'd like better.
- Giving your child one, two, or a whole zoo of stuffed animals to sleep with might help her feel safer. Many children are comforted by stuffed animals or special blankets. These security objects can help your child feel less alone.
- Allow your child to fall asleep with a night-light or even a regular lamp on if she wants to. Let your child drift off to sleep with the light on, and turn it off before you retire. Most kids love Christmas lights, so hanging a string of green or blue bulbs (not bright or flashing) in his bedroom may help him drift off to sleep in the soothing glow.
- Leaving relaxing music playing or white-noise sounds running can be helpful to some children. The familiar sound is

easier to fall asleep to than the quiet house with its strange creaks and other noises.

- An older child who suspects that intruders can come into the house may be reassured if you explain how the house is protected. Showing him how the dead bolts, window locks, or burglar alarm work may be helpful.
- Some children may be reassured if you explain the sounds of the night: the heater coming on, branches hitting the house in the wind, someone flushing a toilet. If strange sounds are explained, they lose their ability to frighten a child.

Introduce Your Child to Happy Monsters

A number of children's movies and books feature fun and lovable monsters. Let your child spend some time with "Sesame Street," *Shrek*, or *Monsters, Inc.* Getting to know Cookie Monster, Shrek, and Sully may give him a new vision of what his imaginary monsters are really like. Choose these movies or books with care, though, and preview them before showing them to your child. Many feature bad monsters as well as good, and the villains may frighten your child.

Get a Pet

If you're open to the idea, put a small pet like a lizard, turtle, or even a fish tank in your child's room. Having this pet for company might be enough for him to no longer feel alone. A warning for you from this mom-of-many-family-pets: keep in mind that a toddler or preschooler cannot take care of his own pet, so all the pet care will be your responsibility. Also, don't choose nocturnal animals who are noisy at night or those that might bite or scratch your child.

Take the Mystery Out of the Dark

To make the dark less mysterious, plan a few fun nighttime activities. Building a campfire and having a marshmallow roast is a great nighttime event. Taking a stargazing walk or looking for night birds also can be fun. Having a candlelight dinner or building a tent in the family room and telling stories (not scary ones!) by flashlight are often well received by even the most sensitive child. Any of these ideas will help your child make friends with the darkness so that when it's dark at bedtime, it won't seem so foreign.

Monitor Scary Input

Avoid having your child watch scary TV shows and movies or read books that contain things that scare her. This rule applies to any time of the day, as children have good memories and can remember at bedtime something they saw that morning. Observe your child for clues as to what frightens her; what she may view as "scary" may not be scary to you. Keep in mind that anytime your child is nearby, he could be viewing what's on the screen. For example, if you watch the news while your child is in the room, his little eyes and ears will be tuned to the unpleasant scenes that are often shown. His lack of total understanding can magnify the intensity of these scenes and they will pop up in his mind at bedtime.

Imaginary Beasts, Imaginary Solutions

Since the creatures that scare your child are a figment of her imagination, you may be able to banish them with an imaginary solution—a spray bottle of monster remover (water) and a magic wand are the two most common tools used. The key to this solution, in my opinion, is to let your child know that the monsters are pretend and the weapons are pretend, too. Without this caveat, you may unintentionally make matters worse—your child may be thinking, "Yikes! Even *Mommy* thinks that the monsters are real and the only protection I have is this measly squirt bottle!" Many creative children, though, catch on to the idea and create their own sense of safety through this process.

Create a Poster

Children who are becoming interested in letters, reading, and words may find comfort in putting something down on paper. You may want to help your child create a sign to hang on the bedroom door. Some children will feel better with a simple statement of ownership, "This is Sarah's happy bedroom." Others may want to deal with the problem and state, "No Monsters in This Room!" Whichever one your child chooses, make sure that the sign is a pleasant one. Decorate it with flowers, rainbows, and other happy objects. An anti-monster billboard showing the dreaded beast in detail can be a frightening reminder when seen right before bed every night.

Read Some Books

Since nighttime fears are universal, quite a number of children's books have been written on the topic. It may help to read these— during the day. Avoid them right before bed, though, and read them yourself before you share them with your child. Some of the elaborate pictures in these books simply put a face on the "things" in your child's imagination, making the fear more intense.

Ask!

Try asking your child what will make him feel better. When he says, "I'm scared," keep it simple as you ask, "What will make you

236 CUSTOMIZED SOLUTIONS FOR YOUR FAMILY

feel better?" He may have an interesting and unique approach to his problem, and no matter how odd it may sound, try to be accommodating. One little boy said that he wanted to sleep with his head on the bottom of the bed and his feet on his pillow; a little girl wanted the red light of the smoke detector covered up, since it looked like a "bad eye watching me sleep." These solutions made sense to the children who came up with them and helped them overcome their fears.

Allow Your Child to Explore His Feelings

Some children will obsess about a fear for several days or even weeks. When airplane sounds were the root of Coleton's nighttime fear, he became very interested in reading books about airplanes, finding pictures of airplanes on the Internet, talking to Daddy about how airplanes make such big sounds, searching the sky for planes, and playing with toy airplanes. After a few weeks of this, he seemed to master his understanding of them, and the fear of their noise in the night gradually faded away. This is a very normal process, as a child's internal drive to overcome his fear guides his curiosity and his thought processes.

The Foolproof Way for Getting Rid of Monsters Under the Bed

Many young children are afraid that something lurks in the dark void under the bed. Many older preschoolers and even grade-schoolers take flying leaps onto the mattress to avoid being grabbed by what waits beneath. The very best solution may be simply to eliminate the "beneath"— put the mattress (or mattress and box springs) directly onto the floor and pack away the bed frame for a year or two. After all, there can't be anything under the bed if there is no under-the-bed!

In a similar vein, some children may find it comforting to have a bed skirt around the bed, creating the illusion that there is no dark space under the mattress.

The Power of Prayer

If your faith is an important part of your family's life and your child's faith has been growing since birth, you have a powerful weapon against any nighttime fear. Teach your child a comforting prayer to recite anytime she feels afraid. Teach her how to rely on her faith in times of worry and to know that she is being watched over and is safe day and night. You may want to put a reassuring religious figurine, such as an angel, near your child's bed or hang a calming picture or verse on the wall.

Create a Peaceful, Pleasant Bedtime Routine

Oh, yes, that again! Many bedtime problems, including nighttime fears, can be waylaid with a specific, regular, and comforting bedtime routine. (See page 59.) You may want to include a session of happy thoughts just before lights-out time: remembering the fun highlights of the day or thinking of upcoming fun events. This can direct your child's before-sleep thoughts to more pleasant things.

Be There for Your Child

If your child is scared in the night—whether it's a monster, the dark, an airplane, or a dripping faucet—the most important thing is to be there for her and help reassure her until she feels safe and secure. Depending on your sleep-time goals for your child, you may want to go to her when she is scared at night or invite her to come to your room when she is afraid. You can put a sleeping bag on the floor next to your bed or simply invite her to climb in with you.

Reassure your child that she is perfectly safe, but then tell her that sometimes little children do get scared at night and that's normal. Explain what she should do if she's scared during the night. Having a plan in advance can help her, sometimes so much that the fear goes away.

When Does Fear of the Dark Go Away?

If you think about it, nearly all scary scenes in movies occur in the dark. An evil beast following someone on a bright sunny afternoon just doesn't evoke the same sense of terror as the same scene shown in shadowy darkness. Therefore, it's obvious that even as adults we have our apprehensions about the dark, though we manage to overcome them by our understanding that any true threat of harm is an unlikelihood.

With help from the courageous adults in their lives, the majority of children manage to control their fears so that they can feel comfortable as they fall asleep at night. Be prepared though: as children grow and learn more about the world, nighttime fears may reappear in other forms. At that time, revisit this section and reapply the solutions.

Is There a Time to Be Concerned?

Most children work through their fears with a parent's help. Talk to your health care provider or a family counselor if any of the following occur:

- Your child seems to become more and more afraid over time.
- The fears carry over into the day, and she obsesses about them for more than a week or two.
- No solution or approach seems to help lessen his fears.
- The fear becomes excessive.
- She demonstrates other behavior issues that you are concerned about, such as daytime anxiety, regression of skills, or signs of stress.

Naptime Problems: "I Don't Want to Sleep!"

My two-year-old daughter refuses to nap, but then she gets cranky later in the day. Does a two-year-old need a nap, or should I just put her to bed earlier at night? If she should be napping every day, how do I get her to take one?

Napping is an important component of a child's healthy mental and physical growth. A daily nap refreshes a child so she can maintain her energy, focus, and ability to learn for the rest of the day. A nap reduces the body's level of cortisol, which is a stress hormone, helping a child to feel calmer. Think of a nap as a time to empty out the morning's stresses and allow a child to begin the afternoon with a clean slate. Some studies even show that young children who nap every day are more flexible and adaptable, have longer attention spans, and are less fussy than those who don't nap.

The majority of children who miss naps don't make up the lost hours at night. Even those who do manage to sleep more at night still must deal with the long time span between morning and bedtime. In addition, nap sleep is different from night sleep in its configuration of sleep cycles and in its effect on a child's health and behavior, so extra night sleep doesn't always achieve the best results. While napping can help make up for lost nighttime sleep, extra night sleep can't recover the benefits of a missed nap.

No exact number of nap hours or naptimes can be dictated for all children of a certain age, because all children have slightly different sleep needs, just as all adults do. A majority of children have similar nap requirements, however, and they need nearly the same amount of *total* sleep hours each day. So depending on their night sleep, parents can pretty much guess how much naptime their children need. There are a few exceptions, of course (that seems to be the rule when it comes to raising children). These exceptional children, however, are few and far between, and under perfect conditions, nearly all non-napping toddlers and many non-napping preschoolers will adapt to a routine daily nap.

Naps and Night Sleep

There is a definite correlation between the length and the quality of daytime naps and night sleep. Conversely, night sleep affects naps, so it can be a vicious circle. Many children who are not getting adequate night and nap sleep will often wake up early and then, an hour or so later, appear to need a nap. Ironically, children who don't nap well don't sleep well at night either. So if you can improve your child's daily nap schedule, he may well sleep longer at night.

Improving your child's daily nap routine can help him feel happier, grow better, be less fussy, and sleep better at night. (And add to that, having a little time for yourself can also help *you* to be less cranky.)

How Can You Tell If Your Child Needs a Nap?

Young children approach life with gusto. They have so much to learn and so much to do that if it were up to them, they wouldn't sleep—day or night—until they simply fell over. Leaving the decision to nap up to your child, then, is like allowing her to choose between vegetables or ice cream for dinner. Just as ice cream would win hands down, your little one is unlikely to choose *sleep* over *awake*. This leaves the decision entirely up to the grown-ups in the house.

If you watch carefully and know what to look for, you will be able to tell if your child needs a nap. There are two lists that follow. The first helps you determine if your child needs a daily nap. The second will tell you that your child is weaning from taking a nap every day but on some days will still need to sleep.

Signs That Your Child Needs a Daily Nap
- Wakes up in a good mood, but gets whiny and cranky as the day progresses
- Has more patience early in the day, but is more easily aggravated later on
- Cries more often and more easily in the afternoon and evening than she does early in the day
- His coordination deteriorates over the course of the day: he begins falling down more, can't manage a puzzle as well, has trouble pulling up his pants or tying his shoes
- Has an afternoon or early evening slump, but gets a second wind later in the day
- Shows signs of being tired, such as yawning, rubbing eyes, or looking slightly glazed, in the afternoon or early evening
- Becomes wired or hyperactive later in the day and won't settle down easily
- Often falls asleep in the car or when watching a movie
- Has a difficult time waking up in the morning, or wakes up grumpy and stays that way for a while

One More Significant Indication That Your Child Still Needs a Daily Nap
- *You* desperately need that daily break from child-tending so you can do adult things and recharge your own battery.

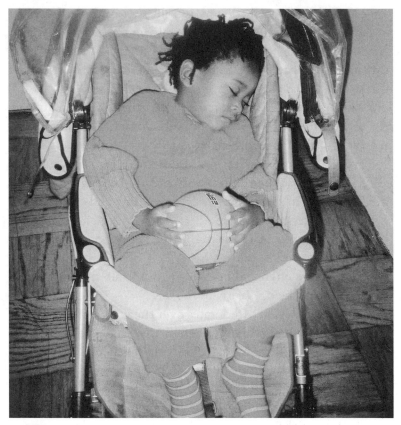

Zion, two years old

Signs That Your Child Is Weaning from Daily Naps but Still Needs One on Some Days
- Usually has a consistent personality from morning until bedtime, but on very active days tends to become fussy in the evening
- Is generally in good spirits but is overly grumpy or whiny on busy days

- On days when he naps, he takes a long time to fall asleep at night or goes to bed much later than usual
- Lies in bed a long time before falling asleep at naptime or never falls asleep at all when put down for a nap
- Usually goes to bed at a reasonable time and sleeps well all night long

How Much Naptime Does Your Child Need?

If you've reviewed the preceding lists and suspect that your child needs a nap, the next step is to review the table of typical sleep hours on page 12. Once again, children differ in their sleep needs. Some naturally need less or more than shown on the table—but it is a general guide that applies to most children. Keep in mind, though, that even if your child's sleep hours add up to the right amount, his or her behavior tells you more than any chart possibly could. When in doubt, always try for a nap, since even a period of quiet time can help a child feel more refreshed.

When Should Your Child Nap?

The timing of your child's naps is very important, since a nap that occurs too late in the day will prevent your child from being tired when bedtime approaches. Consequently he'll take longer to fall asleep at night, and he may then sleep later in the morning. This can disrupt the following day's nap- and bedtime schedule, which can often begin a long pattern of disrupted sleep.

Researchers have also discovered that certain times of the day coincide with the biological clock; these optimum periods balance sleep and wake time to affect nap sleep and nighttime sleep in the most positive way.

Generally, the best naptimes are as follows:

- If your child takes two naps: midmorning (around 9:00 to 11:00) and early afternoon (around 12:00 to 2:30)
- If your child takes one nap: early afternoon (around 12:00 to 2:30) after lunch

How Long Should a Nap Be?

The goal for the day's nap is to allow your child to get adequate rest and rejuvenation to fuel the rest of the day. A nap that is less than thirty minutes in length typically doesn't accomplish this objective. A short catnap can take the edge off, but because it's not long enough to complete a sleep cycle, it may just make your child fussier in the long run. Of course, there are those exceptions again (they do happen), that small percentage of toddlers or preschoolers who can function beautifully on a twenty-minute nap. But don't assume this to be the case with your child, unless his daily naps and nighttime sleep are consistent and he appears well rested throughout the day. (Conversely, brief naps are best for adults.)

The optimal length of naps varies by age and among children, but the best naps are usually one to three hours in length. The previous sleep table can give you a good rule of thumb for your child.

If your child tends toward short naps, don't give in and assume that it's all the naptime she needs. Try some of these tips for increasing the length of her naps:

- Give your child lunch or a snack about a half hour before naptime. Include carbohydrate-rich foods, such as whole-wheat toast and cheese, or other options shown in Tip 6 on page 82.

- Don't give too many fluids in the hour before naptime, and make sure your child uses the potty or has on a fresh diaper for naptime.
- Make certain the sleeping room is dark. Daylight coming in the window can rouse your child before naptime is over.
- Play soothing music or white noise during the entire nap. If your child partially wakes up mid-nap, the gentle sounds may help him fall right back to sleep.
- Make sure your child is comfortable. He shouldn't get too cold or too hot. His sleeping attire should be cozy; either put pajamas on him or take off his pants and let him sleep in a diaper or underpants. Whether you leave socks on or off depends on your child and the temperature of the room, but do whatever works best for him. Make use of an air conditioner, heater, fan, or humidifier to keep the air temperature consistent and comfortable.
- Check to see if discomfort from teething, allergies, asthma, ear infection, or other health-related issues is preventing your child from taking longer naps. If you suspect any of these, a visit to your health care professional is in order.
- Pay attention to the typical length of your child's short naps. About five or ten minutes *before* the usual awakening time, plant yourself outside the bedroom door and listen carefully for signs of movement. (Use the time to read a book, knit, practice yoga, or do another peaceful, pleasant activity. Or go ahead, be practical and fold laundry or pay your bills.) The minute your child starts to move around or make noise, go in quickly. You'll likely find him in a sleepy, just-about-to-wake-up state. Use whatever technique helps him fall back to sleep, such as breastfeeding, rubbing, patting, or just

lying next to him. If you've caught him quickly enough and he's still tired, he'll fall back to sleep. After a week or so of these interventions, your short napper should be taking a much longer snooze without any help from you.

Watch for Signs of Tiredness

Tired children fall asleep easily, and your child will give you signals that he is ready for a nap. If he isn't tired, he'll resist sleep, but if you miss his signals, he can easily become *overtired* and will then be unable to fall asleep when you finally do put him to bed.

If you watch your child's signs for a week or two, you should be able to create a good nap schedule based on his personal daily biological rhythm. Use the time you pick as a guideline, and then use his tired signals as the main cue for naptime. If you spot the signals, don't begin a lengthy prenaptime routine—just get your tired little one off to bed!

Your child may demonstrate one or more of these signs that tell you he is tired and ready to nap—*now*:

- Reducing his level of activity
- Becoming more quiet
- Losing interest in playtime
- Rubbing his eyes
- Looking glazed or unfocused
- Having a more relaxed jaw, chin, and mouth (droopy looking)
- Becoming whiny and cranky
- Fussing or crying
- Losing patience with toys or activities
- Having tantrums
- Yawning
- Lying down or slumping in his seat

- Watching television or a movie with a blank expression
- Caressing a lovey or blanket
- Asking for a pacifier, for a bottle, or to nurse

The Nap Routine

Once you have created a nap schedule that works with your child's daily periods of alertness and tiredness, follow a simple but specific nap routine. Your child will be most comfortable if there is a predictable pattern to his day, since toddlers and preschoolers thrive on consistency. He may come to predict when his naptime approaches and willingly cooperate with you. For example, he may begin to recognize that after lunch and storytime comes naptime. In addition, if you include relaxing activities in your nap routine, such as massage, rocking, white noise, or soft music, or a bottle or breastfeeding session, it can help to prepare your child for sleep.

How Nap Routines Change

Children's sleep patterns change over time, so don't think that the routine you set up today will be the same one you'll use a year from now. Young toddlers will shift from two daily naps to one; older toddlers and preschoolers will eventually stop taking naps altogether. These changes don't happen in a day. There are often weeks or months of transition where naps become sporadic. During these periods of change, it becomes more important to read your child's tired signs and work with his daily moods to gauge his need for naps, taking advantage of "quiet times" to allow your child to rest, even if he doesn't fall asleep.

On days when your child doesn't nap, it's OK to put him to bed a little bit early. Just don't dramatically change his bedtime by an hour or more, or you will risk affecting the next day's schedule and starting a weeklong disruption to his sleep pattern.

If your child has a wonderful nap schedule, then suddenly starts rebelling, you should suspect that she isn't feeling well (check for an ear infection, teething problems, or allergies) or a transition is in the works. Take a look at your child's nap and night sleep according to the sleep table, take another look at both lists of nap signs (pages 243–245), and evaluate the situation to see if a change is required to better match her new sleep needs.

Tips for the Reluctant Napper

If your child hasn't been a very good napper and you're working to create a nap routine, the following ideas may help you encourage her to actually sleep when you think she should sleep. This list isn't meant to be followed in its entirety, however. Just choose those ideas that sound like they may work for your child, and include them in your daily nap routine.

• Use consistent lullaby music or white noise during naps. You can use a bubbling fish tank, a fan or heater (taking care that it gets neither too hot nor too cold), a recording of nature sounds, or a white-noise clock. This creates a very strong sleep cue that brings on relaxation. It also blocks out household or outside noises that may wake him up and reduce the length of his naptime.

• If you have a young toddler, bring your stroller in the house and walk her around until she falls asleep. Even simply rolling the stroller back and forth over a "lump" like a doorway threshold can work. If your child sleeps only a short time and starts to wake, you can often walk or bounce her back to sleep. Once she gets used to taking a daily nap, you can make the transition to her bed.

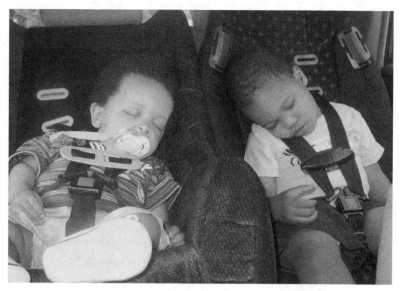

Michon, ten months old, and Avery, twenty-two months old

If you're looking for a way to incorporate some exercise into your own day, take the stroller outside at naptime each day and take a walk. You'll feel great, and your little one will get in the day's nap.

• Make sure the room is dark during sleep. Cover the windows in any way you can— even with a piece of cardboard or aluminum foil. Some children are very sensitive to light, and it prevents them from falling asleep or wakes them up after a short period of sleep.

• Some children are so intent on having fun and learning about the world that they hate to stop even for a minute! If your child gets upset with just the *mention* of naptime, change your approach. Instead of announcing "Naptime," say, "It's quiet time," or say nothing at all and read a few books, listen to a peaceful tape, turn on your white noise, give a bottle, or nurse her. If your little one is tired, she'll surely fall asleep. If not, the quiet time will work wonders to take the edge off, for both of you.

• Lie down with your child in a dark room. Play quiet music, an audiobook, or white noise, and relax and close your own eyes. Once she's sleeping soundly, you can get up. That is, if you're not sleeping too! If you *do* fall asleep, it's because your body needs that sleep. Research has shown that a short midday siesta is healthy for adults. Enjoy the nap!

• Instead of choosing a children's audiobook, choose one for yourself. The melodious voice on most audiobooks will be soothing to your child while you catch up on your own reading for pleasure or business.

• Instead of making the dreaded naptime announcement, offer your child a series of choices that lead her in your intended direction:

> Do you want to read two books or three? Do you want to choose them?
> Do you want to listen to music or birdsong today?
> Would you like to rest on your bed or Mommy's bed?
> Which stuffed animal do you want to cuddle today?

Older toddlers and preschoolers love having choices, and they are more likely to cooperate if they are invited to make the decisions themselves.

• Avoid letting your child get involved in a fun activity right before naptime. If your child is beginning to build a wonderful castle of blocks, is starting a new puzzle, or has just opened a new tub of play dough, she'll be very reluctant to leave her project and take a nap. Save the good stuff for when she wakes up.

• Give your child something to look forward to after naptime. Promise something for "when you get up from your rest." It could be a walk to the park, a game of Candyland, starting that new puzzle or tub of play dough, or having a cookie and milk. Tell your child what you'll be doing as he sleeps, and make it sound very boring, such as "I'll be doing my paperwork while you sleep." Saying this lets your child know he won't be missing anything exciting and that the fun things will happen when he wakes up.

• Set a timer. Tell your little one you'd like him to "rest quietly" for at least twenty minutes. Tell him you'll set a timer and he can get up if he wants to when he hears it ring. This can be the kitchen oven timer or a clock radio. Have him watch you set the timer, or help him do it himself. If he falls asleep, remember to turn off the timer so that it doesn't wake him.

Another way to use this idea is to set the sleep feature on a clock radio for sixty minutes (or the length of your child's nap). Choose a soft music or all-talk station. Tell your child that she can get up when the music (or talking) stops.

• If you've tried for fifteen or twenty minutes to get your child to nap and she is still wide awake, then she's not tired enough to sleep. Let her get up and play for an hour or so. Tire her out with activity; then when she shows signs of being tired, try again for a nap—if it's early enough in the day. If it's too late for a nap, then aim for a slightly earlier bedtime that night.

Napping Away on the Go

When my fourth child, Coleton, joined our family, his siblings were eight, ten, and twelve. We had a busy schedule filled with school and sports activities. To even *attempt* to be home every single day at naptime would have been pointless. Instead, I discovered the following tips for napping on the go:

• If your little one falls asleep in the car, take advantage of this blessing. Try to arrange car trips to occur at naptime. Give your child a snack and a clean diaper or potty visit before you leave the house, recline his car seat back (if it has that option) or bolster his head with a child's travel pillow, and take off his shoes. (If you're buying a new car seat, look for one with deep side wings for in-car sleeping.)

• Give him his blankie or lovey and play quiet music or an audiobook. Keep your own reading material or paperwork in the car so you can allow his nap to continue once you've parked. (NEVER, EVER, EVER leave your sleeping child alone in the car. It could be dangerous.)

• Invest in a few nap mats or roll-up stadium blankets (used for outdoor sports). These are easy to keep in the car. If you are at an older child's function or a friend's home, this can be placed on the ground or floor for a portable nap pad.

• Keep your stroller in the car for another portable bed option. Many sleep-resistant babies can be lulled to sleep in the fresh air during a stroller ride.

• Modify your child's sleep times to match your schedule if there's a slight difference. For example, if your child is ready to nap at 1:00, but you have to pick up your older child every day from school at 1:30, then shift the day's events to make a car nap work for you. Schedule playtime and lunchtime so that 1:30 becomes the new naptime.

Spring Forward, Fall Back: Dealing with Daylight Saving Time

We're about to change our clocks ahead for daylight saving time. I know it's only an hour, and it may be my imagination, but the change seems to upset our routine for weeks. When it comes to my children's nap- and bedtimes, what's the best way to deal with the time change?

It's not your imagination, and you're not the only one to struggle with the sleep change that accompanies daylight saving time. About 70 percent of people find that their sleep schedule is off for a while after the time adjustment. Studies show that there's an average increase of 7 to 10 percent in the number of traffic accidents on the day following the time change when people lose that one precious hour of sleep!

"The one-hour time changes in spring and fall can be disruptive to people's sleep cycles," says Richard L. Gelula, National Sleep Foundation's chief executive officer. "The return to standard time and the supposed 'gain' of an hour of sleep (which often doesn't happen) can have negative consequences, as does the potential 'loss' of an hour of sleep in the spring," he adds.

The resetting of watches disrupts everyone's physical rhythm; you can't push a button to change your biological clock. If you remember from the discussion in Part I on this topic, a sleep deficit of even one hour can have a dramatic effect on sleep and wakefulness. Another reason that the daylight saving time shift greatly

affects us and our children is that many people are already feeling
the effects of daily sleep deprivation. Any small upset to the sleep
schedule thus has an exaggerated effect.

Lessening the Impact of the Daylight Saving Time Changes

It can help simply to know that it's normal to take a few days to a
week or even longer to adjust to the time change. Even if you use
the suggestions that follow, have a little patience with yourself and
your children until your biological rhythms catch up with the
clock on the wall. Here are a few things that can help you make
a quicker adjustment:

- Take advantage of the power of light and dark to reset your
  body clocks. Keep the house dimly lit in the hour before bedtime, and use bright lights for the first hour after you wake
  up in the morning.
- If you have to put your child to bed an hour earlier, before
  he's actually tired, extend your prebedtime reading time.
  Reading in bed can help a child calm down and feel drowsy.
- Follow as many of the ideas in Part I of this book as you can.
  Paying attention to details like naptimes, afternoon exercise,
  and choices of food in the evening are all small ways to help
  your child feel tired at bedtime.
- Just because the clocks officially change at 2:00 A.M. doesn't
  mean you have to change yours at that time. Since most people don't get up in the middle of the night, many change
  their clocks first thing in the morning. But this can jolt your
  system when you realize you're suddenly one hour off. So
  instead, change your clocks mid-afternoon *before* the time
  actually changes. That way you'll have made part of the

adjustment to the new time before it actually comes into effect. You'll have adjusted your child's nap and evening meal to the clock, which will help the bedtime adjustment flow more smoothly.

If the Time Change Wreaks Havoc in Your Home

If you and your child are having lots of bedtime problems already, and the change in time makes things much worse, see if you can split the hour difference into fifteen-minute increments for four days up to the actual time change. If you have many appointments or older children to pick up from school and sports activities, you can't actually change your clock. But since most toddlers and preschoolers can't tell time, you can simply write down the bedtimes for the week in advance and just begin your bedtime routine at the adjusted time each night. The following tables show examples for both the shift to daylight saving time (DST) and the switch back to standard (STD) time.

If you are going to be "springing forward" on Sunday at 2:00 A.M. (becomes 3:00 A.M.), and your child's usual bedtime is 7:30 P.M., he will be going to bed one hour later. To break that down into fifteen-minute increments, your week's bedtime schedule would look like this:

Day	Bedtime per the time on the clock
Wednesday	7:30 (STD time)
Thursday	7:15
Friday	7:00
Saturday	6:45
Sunday	6:30 (STD time)/7:30 (new DST time)

If you're going to be "falling back" on Sunday at 2:00 A.M. (becomes 1:00 A.M.) and your child's usual bedtime is 7:30 P.M., he will be going to bed one hour earlier. To break that down into fifteen-minute increments, your week's bedtime schedule would look like this:

Day	Bedtime per the time on the clock
Wednesday	7:30 (DST time)
Thursday	7:45
Friday	8:00
Saturday	8:15
Sunday	8:30 (DST time)/7:30 (new STD time)

Do You Have to Keep the Same Bedtime Year Round?

Before you automatically make the bedtime hour change, take your family's needs into account. Some families, particularly those with older children who are in school, are happy to modify bedtime to be later during the summer vacation months. If this suits you, then modify bedtime and awakening time to be one hour later during the spring and summer. Do what works best for you!

A Safety Reminder

Many fire departments encourage people to change the batteries in their smoke detectors when they change their clocks. The majority of home fires occur at night when people are sleeping. Working smoke detectors more than double a person's chances of surviving a home fire, so keep your child and your entire family safe by changing your alarm batteries along with your clocks.

Bed-Wetting

My four-year-old has been potty trained during the day for a long time, but he still wets the bed almost every night. Is there something wrong? Why can't he master this part of training, and what can we do about it?

The development of nighttime urinary control is a biological process. As children grow and develop, so does their ability to control their bladder. There is a wide range of normal for when this nighttime control occurs. Bed-wetting, called enuresis (en-yur-EE-sis), is common among young children. Since almost 50 percent of all three-year-olds and up to 40 percent of four-year-olds wet the bed several times a week, it is considered normal behavior at this age. Additionally, 20 to 25 percent of five-year-old children and 10 to 15 percent of six-year-olds don't stay dry every night. In addition, many young children who are dry at night for a long period of time begin to wet the bed again, sometimes after a time of change in their life or stress. (If your child suddenly has a change in nighttime or daytime bladder habits, it's a good idea to check with your health care provider to make sure your child doesn't have an infection or other health issue.) By the age of nine, only 5 percent of children wet the bed, and most of those children do it only once a month. As children get older, fewer and fewer have bed-wetting accidents. In the majority of cases, the problem goes away even when parents don't use any special treatment for the condition.

The most common reasons for bed-wetting are biological. Your child's kidneys aren't sending a signal to his brain when he's asleep, his bladder hasn't grown large enough to contain a full night's supply of urine, his bladder overproduces urine at night, or he sleeps so deeply he doesn't wake up to go to the bathroom. As children grow, all of these conditions are self-correcting.

Bed-wetting is also hereditary, so if one or both parents were bed-wetters, a child has a greater chance of doing the same. Diabetes, food sensitivities (specifically to caffeine, dairy products, fruit, and chocolate), some medications, or other health conditions can contribute to nighttime bladder-control issues. Bed-wetting also can be a symptom of a sleep disorder, so if your child has other signs (see page 383), you may want to investigate this possibility.

How to Help Your Child Stay Dry

While at this age it's not necessary to work on nighttime dryness, you can help a child who *wants* to stay dry at night by doing the following:

- Limit liquids for an hour or two before bedtime. You don't need to cut out liquids entirely, though. Limiting liquids only reduces the amount of nighttime urine; it doesn't stop the reasons for bed-wetting.
- Make several prebedtime trips to the bathroom—one at the beginning of your bedtime routine and once again at the very end, just before lights out.
- Avoid using absorbent training pants, and use a special mattress cover instead. Absorbent pants or diapers can delay the normal development process, because a child can't feel when urination occurs.
- Make sure that your child uses the potty often (about every two hours) during the day. This encourages normal bladder function and can help with nighttime dryness.

- Use positive reinforcement with a sticker chart to help her monitor her success.
- Keep a night-light on for a clear path to the bathroom, and give your child permission to use the bathroom during the night if he needs to. Just the subconscious message may help.
- Avoid placing any blame on the child, and don't make her feel guilty or ashamed. Let her know that it's normal and will take time to change.

It Is a Learning Process

No child chooses to wake up cold and wet. Bed-wetting almost never happens because a child is lazy or disobedient. It's just like learning to walk or learning to talk—there's a wide range of normal and no reason to rush the process.

For a bed-wetting toddler or preschooler the best solution is the most simple one: allow your child to sleep in a diaper, padded training pants, disposable absorbent underpants, or use a special mattress cover until he begins to stay dry all night.

According to the National Kidney Foundation, you only need to talk to a doctor about bed-wetting if your child is six or seven years of age or older, or if there are other symptoms of a sleep disorder. With older children, a specialist can help direct parents as to the use of bed alarms, bladder-training exercises, diet changes, therapy, or medication.

There are plenty of things we parents must worry about and strive to change, but usually during the toddler and preschooler years, this isn't one of those things. All you have to do is be patient. In time it's very likely your child will be dry at night without your having to be involved in a solution at all.

Sleepwalking and Sleep Talking

Our son sometimes walks around the house in his sleep. He also frequently talks in his sleep—mainly muttering things we can't understand. Is this a problem that we need to do something about? Will he outgrow it?

Sleepwalking is a common sleep quirk for toddlers and preschoolers, and nearly a third of children will have at least one sleepwalking episode. Boys are more likely to sleepwalk than girls. Sleepwalking tends to run in families, so you may find that your parents or your spouse's parents have a few humorous stories to embarrass you with. Very often these stories have to do with a sleepwalker using a very odd object as a toilet—often a trash can or a box in the closet.

Sleepwalking usually happens in the beginning of the night, between one and three hours after your child has gone to sleep. Usually, a sleepwalking child opens his eyes, gets out of bed, and wanders a bit disoriented around the house. He's in a state between sleeping and wakefulness and not at all aware that he's even out of bed! If you talk to him the next morning about his sleepwalking, he won't remember it at all. So it's better not to bring it up when he's awake, as it might even make him confused, worried, or scared.

What to Do When You Find Your Child Sleepwalking

If you wake to find your child walking around the house, gently carry him or lead him back to bed. You don't have to talk to him, other than a few comforting words, since he won't really be hearing you. Most often, your child will simply fall right back to sleep once he's resettled in bed.

Sleepwalking isn't a sign of any emotional or physical problem, and most children simply outgrow it. The worry for parents is that their child will wander outside, fall down stairs, or trip over something and get hurt, since sleepwalkers aren't aware of exactly where they are or where they are going. If you have a little sleepwalker, you should take these precautions:

- Attach a bell to the bedroom door or a motion detector in front of his doorway so that you are alerted to the fact he's up and out of bed. If you're a deep sleeper and won't hear a bell or an alarm, you can put a child safety gate in his bedroom doorway. A gated doorway, as awful as that may sound, could prevent your little one from wandering around the house without your knowledge and getting hurt.
- A co-sleeping family can put the sleepwalker between two parents or between a parent and a wall so that you're alerted when she tries to climb out of bed.
- Avoid putting a child who sleepwalks to sleep in a high bed or on the top of a bunk bed (particularly if he's wearing Superman pajamas).
- Keep all outside doors and windows locked. (Put a note up to remind yourself to check these nightly.)
- Use window guards (metal grids that snap into the window) on upper-floor windows. (This is an important idea whether or not you have a sleepwalker.)

- If your household burglar alarm has a setting that creates a beep anytime a door or window is opened, then take advantage of this handy (albeit annoying) feature.
- Install child safety gates at the tops of stairs.
- Make sure your childproofing is complete throughout the house: lock up toxic solutions or dangerous objects, secure cords, and cover outlets.
- Avoid having toys and clutter on your child's bedroom floor. (OK, maybe this isn't reasonable. At least make sure you remove sharp or hard objects.)
- Avoid giving your child excess fluids in the hour before bedtime. Have your child use the toilet every night right before she gets in bed so that a full bladder doesn't have her up and looking for a place to go potty!

Should You Try to Stop the Sleepwalking?

Most often there's no reason to try to stop your child from sleepwalking. However, if your child is making this a regular habit and you have concerns about your little, happy wanderer's safety, you can try a simple intervention that might reestablish a natural sleep cycle.

The first step is to keep track of the typical time when your child gets out of bed; specifically, how long after he goes to sleep does he get up? After you've done this for a week or so you should see a pattern. Once you find out what his typical timing is, you can wake him up about ten to fifteen minutes before he usually begins walking around. Take him to the bathroom, give him a hug, and tuck him back into bed. Follow this routine for a week, and then let him sleep without disruption and see if his sleepwalking stops. If this doesn't stop his sleepwalking, then talk to your health care provider about your concerns.

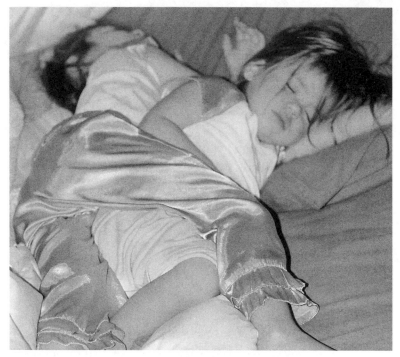

Delaney, four years old, and Lauren, two years old

I know that this isn't something most parents who are already working on sleep-related issues are willing to try! So I want to say again that unless your child's safety is a concern, you don't really need to do anything about sleepwalking. Most often he'll grow out of this phase without your intervention.

Sleep Talking

Sleep talking is even more common than sleepwalking, and about half of all children will have a few midnight jabbering sessions.

Sleepwalkers are very often sleep *talkers*, too. Some children might mumble or make sounds in their sleep, while others carry on entire conversations with themselves. Some sleep talkers use a quiet monotonous voice, but others can be quite loud and emotional. If you talk to a child who is talking in her sleep, she may respond but her answer will likely make little sense.

Most sleep talking is amusing, brief, and harmless. If the talking isn't bothering anyone else, you don't need to do anything about it. If your little sleep talker is loud and episodes are frequent and bothersome to other sleepers, you may want to consider some of the remedies in the next section.

Can You Stop Your Child from Sleepwalking or Sleep Talking?

The following tips may be helpful in reducing the amount of walking or talking your child does in his sleep. There is no foolproof solution, but since these ideas are based on general rules for healthy sleep, it won't hurt to try some of them.

- Some studies have found that children who are not getting enough sleep are more likely to sleepwalk or sleep talk. It's wise, therefore, to check the sleep table on page 12 to see if your little one is getting enough sleep hours and modify his bedtime if he needs more sleep. (If you haven't already noticed, this is a common reason for many sleep problems.)
- Inconsistent sleep times can contribute to sleepwalking and sleep talking, so if you haven't already made the change discussed in Part I of this book, you may want to take another look at setting a specific daily bedtime and daily awake time for your little night wanderer or night talker.

- Another possible cause of sleepwalking and sleep talking is fatigue or stress and tension. The tips that begin on page 89 discussing relaxation techniques may be worth trying.
- Because a late heavy meal can contribute to these sleep problems, avoid having your child eat a big meal before bedtime. Stick to a light snack devoid of heavy spices or sugars.
- Occasionally, sleepwalking is brought about in response to a change in the child's life, such as moving, the parents' divorce, attending a new school, or another major event. These are temporary situations, and once your child is settled in to a new routine, the sleepwalking should disappear.

Moving from the Family Bed to Independent Sleep

Our son has been sleeping with us since he was a newborn. It has been truly wonderful, but now that he's getting older, we think we should move him to his own bed. How do we know if this is the right time to move him, and how can we do it gently?

Children sharing sleep with their parents has been a natural occurrence for human beings since the beginning of time, and it is still common in many countries today. Our independent-focused society leads many people to believe that it's rare, unusual, or even weird. But here's the bottom line—lots and lots of families co-sleep. According to sleep polls, over 50 percent of parents follow some sort of co-sleeping arrangement in their home. On one hand, it's nobody's business where you choose to let your children sleep. But on the other hand, it would be wonderful if we could normalize the concept of co-sleeping so that everyone in society realizes that it's a natural and popular option for family sleep.

Regardless of how happy you've been with your co-sleeping arrangement, all things change and develop, just like weaning from the breast or bottle, moving from diapers to underpants, evolving from crawling to walking, and graduating from preschool to kindergarten. This is just one more natural part of growing up.

Some families are very willing to let their children sleep in the family bed until they're ready to move on, no matter if the child is two or ten (and that's perfectly fine!). Other families have various reasons they want their children to sleep in their own beds

Mother-Speak

"When reading *One Fish Two Fish Red Fish Blue Fish* by Dr. Seuss, we were on the page that shows two children sleeping with a big fuzzy creature and it says, 'And now good night. It is time to sleep. So we will sleep with our pet Zeep.' And Gabrielle says, 'Why are the kids sleeping with Zeep? You're supposed to sleep with your mother.'"

—**Ginger, mother of four-year-old Gabrielle**

(and that's perfectly fine, too!). Before moving on to the gentle ideas for moving a child to independent sleeping, let's make sure this is what you want to do, since many families are conflicted about making this change. Here are some questions to consider that will help you make this decision before you move forward:

- Are you, your partner, and your child all getting a good night's sleep?
- If no one else in the world knew or cared about what you're doing, would you be happy with your routine? Would you still be happy six months from now? A year from now? Do both parents have the same answer to this question?
- If you're a single parent, are you thinking of moving your child out of your bed because you think it's the right decision for you and your child, or because someone else thinks you should make the change?
- Is having your child sleep in your bed interfering with the level of intimacy between you and your partner, or are you still finding plenty of times and places to meet each other's needs for cuddling and, ummm, *sex*?

- Are you considering making a change because *you* want a change and because it's right for your family—or is it to appease a friend, relative, or your doctor?
- Are any other major events occurring in your child's life right now that are causing him stress or worry? If so, is it possible to put off a sleep change until things settle back to normal? If the change requires a sleeping adjustment (such as the impending birth of a sibling), can you take the time to make it a gradual, gentle process?
- Did you used to enjoy having your child in your bed, but find yourself liking it less over time and you're unsure of how to make a change?
- If tonight your child suddenly grabbed his pillow, took off down the hall, and began to sleep all night, every night in his own bed, how would you feel: overjoyed, happy, satisfied, a bit sad, depressed, lonely, or nostalgic but content?
- What specifically about your family-bed arrangement bothers you? Is it that your child wakes you up? That it prevents you from uninterrupted couple time? Are you concerned that others are worried about it? Do you want to get pregnant again, or are you already expecting and don't want an overcrowded bed once the new baby arrives?

Explore your own reasons for wanting to make a change. Understanding your reasons will help you decide on your plan and choose the best solutions.

Try Not to Waver

There's no doubt that sleep-time cuddles with your precious bundle have given you some of the most joy-filled times of being a parent. There's nothing quite as wonderful or as tender as your munchkin nestled next to you in your bed as you both drift off to sleep. There's no doubt that no matter how ready you are to send your child down the hall, no matter if he's one year old or five years old, a part of you will mourn the change. And that's perfectly normal. That's why I suggest that you spend time with the previous questions before you move on. It helps to sort through your feelings first and be sure that this is what you want to do, since ambivalence can defeat any plan that you try to put into action. If you feel good about this change, if you feel that the time is right, then you will convey your confidence to your child through your words and actions.

Once you've decided that this is the right time to move your child to his own bed, go forward with confidence. This doesn't mean you have to rush the process, just have your eye on the goal and keep traveling in that direction. All family-bed children eventually move on to independent sleep, and it's perfectly acceptable for you to choose the time for this to happen.

While a gradual process is easiest on your child, some people take this to the extreme and spend a year or more making minuscule changes, one at a time, all the while agonizing about the possibility of traumatizing their child. This is putting unnecessary stress on everyone in the family—including the child. Parents who have had their child in their bed won't stop showing their child incredible love and respect just because the sleeping place has changed. A well-loved family-bed child will be just as well-loved as an independent sleeper. While the exact description of *gradual* is different for each child, the transition can take anywhere from a couple of weeks to a couple of months. But unless it's what you want, this doesn't have to drag on for a year.

During the transition time, be sure to offer your child plenty of daytime hugs and cuddles. Often co-sleeping children get very used to lots of human contact and cuddles, and they may subconsciously miss it when they begin to sleep alone. You can offset this by making sure to fill your child's need for touch during the day, especially before bed (don't rush the bedtime routine!) and when she first wakes up in the morning.

When you use thoughtful, gentle methods and are patient about the switch, this can be a peaceful time of transition for all of you.

Making a Plan

Once you've confirmed that you really do want to move your child toward independent sleep and you want to do it now, take the next step: set a goal.

This isn't something that should be forced to happen in one night or even one week. If you don't have a pressing deadline to meet, setting a goal of a month or two, or even longer, will ease the tension you'll feel over making the change. A more gradual and gentle process can have your child sleeping in his own bed over time, while still feeling very loved and connected to you, both during and after the process. As I mentioned earlier, however, not having a clear goal can cause the process to drag on indefinitely.

Another thing to consider is that this isn't necessarily an all-or-nothing decision. There are degrees of co-sleeping, and you may find that a shift in how things work in your house may be what you need. Here are the various common ways that families share sleep, and one of these may provide a new option for you:

- The child shares a bed with parents every night and every day for naps.
- The child naps alone, but co-sleeps with parents at night.
- The child falls asleep in his own bed, but then comes to the parent's bed in the middle of the night.

- The child falls asleep in the parent's bed, but then is moved to his own bed when asleep.
- The child sleeps in his own room, but comes into the parent's bed for an early morning snuggle.
- The child sleeps in the parent's bedroom, but in his own separate crib or bed.
- The child sleeps in his own bed but can come to his parents' bed if he is ill, has a nightmare, is on vacation, or for other special situations.

The Menu of Solutions

This section provides a list of suggestions that have worked for other families. Scan through them and choose a few options that feel right to you. You might settle on one key idea or combine several for a custom solution.

Set up a plan for change, write it down, and follow your plan every night. Give your plan a week or two before you judge its effectiveness, since sometimes the beginning is a challenge—after all, you're changing a routine that is very pleasant for your child and may have been in place for a huge percentage of his lifetime, maybe even his whole entire lifetime.

Some children are willing to entertain the idea of moving to independent sleep, and others will do everything in their power to keep things the way they are. Either way, if you choose the right plan you can make a gentle transition. In most cases, you can expect that your child will resist any movement toward change—at first. But don't worry, using any of these methods will help you achieve your final goal eventually.

This list of ideas is extensive, and of course, you won't use them all. Just pick out a few that feel right for you and your child. One other tip: if along with these specific tips you also use the other ideas throughout the rest of this book, it will help you create a well-rounded sleep plan that will bring you to your goal more easily and more quickly.

A Little at a Time

Making the change from the family bed doesn't have to be a sudden and complete transformation, and it doesn't have to be to a traditional single bed in a child's bedroom. You can, if you choose, do it in stages. Some families find that the change happens easily if they move their child a little bit at a time.

The process involves setting up a second bed next to yours. It could be a crib, toddler bed, mattress, or futon. Begin by putting it right next to your bed. You might want to put fun, colorful, children's bedding on it and give him his own small blanket so that it's quite different and more interesting than your bed. Refer to it as his sleeping spot or his special place. When it's time to go to sleep, make sure that is where he actually falls asleep. If he usually cuddles up close beside you, which is typical for family-bed children, go ahead and join him in his little bed for a cuddle, but inch away as he begins to get comfortable, keeping contact with a hand or foot until you find that your child can sleep apart from you at night.

After a few days or a week or so, once your little one is comfortable in his bed, move it a few feet away from yours. You can still settle him in his spot, but then make sure you don't fall asleep there! Move over to your own bed. The next step is to move the bed to the other side of the room, and finally, down the hall to his own room. When you first do this, read over the ideas that begin on page 123 regarding a child needing a parent's help to fall asleep, since it's unlikely that your little post-co-sleeper will happily trot down the hall alone after a good-night kiss. But you will be well on your way to watching him become an independent sleeper.

Make a Special Family Bedtime

You may want to provide times when your child is welcome into your bed and encourage her to sleep in her own bed otherwise. You might connect this with daylight: *"When it is light outside, you can come into our bed."* Or you can set a white-noise alarm or easy-listening music station to go off at a time of morning when you're open to having a visitor in your bed. Let her know that when the music is on, it's OK to come to your room. Some families set a schedule, keeping weekends for family cuddle time and requiring everyone to stay in their own beds on weeknights.

Explain Who, What, When, and Why

This is a unique approach but one that works surprisingly well with some children: let them in on your plan. Explain why you want to make a change and how you'd like to do it. Set things up in advance so that all the parts and pieces work. Keep it simple and straightforward. An example of this would be, *"Mommy is waking up too much at night. It would help me if you could sleep in your bed until morning. I can read to you and rub your back, and then I will go sleep in my bed. We can cuddle in the morning when we both wake up."*

This isn't magic and usually won't cause an immediate change, but it does involve your child in the process. Some children respond very well to knowing exactly what you expect of them, and they feel proud to help you. You might even include some choices so that your child feels some control over the situation. For example, you might give a choice if your child would rather sleep on the floor near your bed or in his own bed. Also give him some options for the middle of the night, such as providing a sleeping bag at the foot of your bed. Once he's "on your team," it may make him more receptive to change.

Find Out If There Is a Problem

For many family-bed children, the only problem is that they've never slept alone and so it's unusual and unsettling to them. For others, though, making the change to solo sleeping brings out fears or concerns that they've never had to face.

Watch and listen to your child carefully. Do you suspect that she's afraid to be alone in the dark? That she thinks monsters reside in her room? Is she worried that you won't be there if she needs you? Does she wake with nightmares and no one is close by to comfort her? Is she worried about an impending event, such as the birth of a sibling or a move to a new house? If you can pinpoint any obstacles and address these first, you can confidently guide her to sleeping on her own. (For fears see page 229, for nightmares see page 205 for adjusting to life changes see page 347.)

Make Her Room a Special Sleeping Place

If your child has a bedroom now, it has likely been used as a playroom, nap room, spare closet, or TV room. But if your child has spent most of her night sleep in your bed, then she won't view her room as a place to spend the night. It may help to redecorate and create an inviting sleep place. If your child is old enough, get her involved in the process. Allow her to help choose new bedding, new curtains, wall decorations, or a new night-light. A fun addition to the new room is to string up blue or green Christmas lights, or place glow-in-the-dark stars and planets on the ceiling.

Think outside the box: your child's bedroom doesn't have to be boring or even like a traditional bedroom. Ask your child for input on room-creation. If she's involved, she may be more excited about sleeping there. With a little imagination you can transform her room into a bear's den, a bird's nest, a rabbit's burrow, a monkey's tree house, a dinosaur's cave, a truck garage, or an airplane hangar. If your child has a current favorite animal or toy, capitalize on this by using it as a theme for your little one's bedroom. Incorporate the bed as a focal point to your new design. You don't have to spend a fortune remodeling the room. Simple materials like cardboard boxes, construction paper, and end-roll fabric pieces can all be used along with stuffed animals and toys, and enhanced with your child's remarkable imagination.

If your child is over six years old and you're shopping for a new bed, consider a bunk bed. (Bunk beds are dangerous for younger children.) Make sure that the bed you buy meets the Bunk Bed Safety guidelines created by the Consumer Product Safety Commission (see page 377). Most kids love bunk beds and are eager to sleep in them. At first, it's smart to use guardrails along any open sides and have your child practice getting up and down during the day before you initiate it for nighttime sleep. Keep in mind he may be climbing down half-asleep in the middle of the night to use the bathroom or look for you.

A best bet for a new bed for a newly independent sleeper is a mattress on the floor. It's nice and safe (no fear of big falls) and gives your child the freedom to get up and down easily. You can even add guardrails to make it into a nice nest. The soft bolster-type guardrails are great for this.

After you've set up the wonderful new place, make your sleeping change. When it comes time for bed, lie with your child in her new environment and demonstrate your excitement about it. You may want or need to stay with her until she's asleep for the first week or two, until she's comfortable with the change. After that, remove yourself a little at a time, by either getting up for short trips, puttering around the room as she's drifting off, or sitting in a chair beside the bed as she falls asleep. (For more ideas see "Mommy, Stay!": Needing a Parent's Help to Fall Asleep on page 123.)

The Sneaky Way for the Little Guys

If you have a younger toddler, you can try this approach. Let your child fall asleep in your bed as always. As soon as she is completely asleep, carry her into her room and put her into her crib or bed. (This may work for older toddlers and preschoolers, but many are heavy for carrying, wake up too easily, or tend to get wise to what you're doing and refuse to fall asleep at all!) A less sneaky approach is described on page 226, the Rubber Band Bounce.

Have a baby monitor turned on so you can go to your child quickly if she wakes up. When she wakes, nurse her in a chair or bring her to bed to nurse. Otherwise, settle her like you normally do, but then take her back to her crib or bed when she is ready to sleep again.

If you use this technique, you can expect to be traveling the hallway between rooms for a while until the transition is complete. Many children will adjust rather quickly and will sleep longer stretches than when they were in bed with another person whose night movements caused extra awakenings. (Although some children will wake up more often looking for company.) You might even set a time that you'll stop the transfer. For example, move your child back to her crib for every awakening until 3:00 A.M., and then just keep her in bed with you after that time so you can get some sleep.

Like all of my ideas throughout this book, this is not meant to be a rigid, do-it-or-else proposition. You can work with this idea for weeks, making the change more peaceful for both you and your child. (Of course, if you want your little one moved pronto, you *could* be very persistent and move through the transition more quickly; that's entirely up to you.)

This idea will work better if your child enjoys her bed or crib. Spend a few pleasant playtimes during the day entertaining your child or reading to her while she is in her crib or bed. This will help her to be comfortable in the setting so that when she wakes there during the night, it will be familiar to her.

Start with Naptime

If your child has never been an independent sleeper, you can start the process by having her take naps in her own bed. Incorporate a pleasant prenaptime routine and make it a comforting process by playing soft music or white noise or letting her listen to an audiobook as she rests. Once she becomes comfortable napping in her bed, you can introduce it as a nighttime sleeping place as well by incorporating some of the other ideas from this section.

Create a New Bedtime Routine

Children are creatures of habit. If you go through your normal bedtime routine, but then expect the finale to occur in a different spot, it won't feel right to your child. Everything will be moving along normally, he'll be getting in the sleepy mood, when Bam! you want him to sleep in a new place. To avoid this, revamp your nightly sequence of events so they are different than usual.

To help your child be comfortable with a new routine, it may help to make a chart of all the steps involved and help him "read" the chart as you go through the evening. (See page 114 for how to make a bedtime chart.)

Go with Her . . . for a While

If you're moving your child from your bed to her own room, you can make the switch less intimidating by sleeping with her in her new bed for a while. After she gets comfortable with the new arrangement, try using the I'll-be-right-back technique: Get her settled, then get up for a short task such as going to the bathroom, getting a drink of water, putting on a pair of socks, or shutting a window. Tell her, "I'll be right back." As you do this, leave for longer periods of time each night, until she falls asleep waiting for you to return. Then you can change your phrase to, "I'll be back in the morning."

If your child is an all-night sleeper, lie with her until she falls asleep, and then move to your own bed. Keep your door open to her, in case she wakes in the night. When this happens, you have several options: you can simply invite her to crawl in bed with you, or place a mattress, sleeping bag, or futon on the floor next to your bed and tell her that if she gets lonely in the night she should lie down in her special little bed near you. Or you can carry her or walk her back to her own bed anytime she comes to you.

When you remind her that you'll be just a short distance away and let her know that she can seek you out when she needs to, it won't be quite so scary to sleep alone.

Give Her Permission to Call for You

If you prefer not to have your little one as a regular visitor, don't encourage her to come to you. Tell her to call to you instead, or give her a little bell to ring if she needs you in the night. You can also use a two-way baby monitor and let her call you if she needs you. When she does, go to her and settle her back to sleep. If she wanders to your room, scoop her up, return her to her own bed with some parenting-to-sleep help, and gently remind her that she should call you and you will come to her. Knowing that you'll come when she needs you will be very comforting to her. Over time, your trips back and forth will dwindle until she surprises you by letting you sleep all night long!

Give Her Some Company

If your child is used to sleeping with someone, it will be an odd feeling for her to be in her bedroom all alone. It can help to encourage her to bring some stuffed animals or a favorite doll to bed with her. These often become lovies (security objects) and provide her with a feeling of safety that may even extend into daytime.

Another type of "company" is the audio kind. Provide your child with a small music box (pick a mellow tune) or a radio or CD player with soft music, white noise, audiobooks, or even a recording of Mommy and Daddy singing or reading stories. Once your child knows how to use this, she can press the button if she ever feels lonely.

If inanimate company doesn't do the trick, try putting a small pet in her room, such as a turtle or a fish in a tank. Encourage her to keep her pet company at night. This alone can help some children stay put in their own beds! (As a safety precaution, don't allow dogs or cats to sleep with little children. And avoid nocturnal animals, like hamsters, that are noisy all night long.)

Let Him Go Camping . . . Sort Of

If you have a small tent and you're willing to set up a camping spot somewhere in the house, it can make a quirky but fun location for an older child to explore solo sleeping. Provide a sleeping bag, flashlight, and a few stuffed animals for company, and he may just start begging for bedtime! You can even turn his bedroom into a campground and set up the tent with a mattress or futon inside of it. Make sure it's perfectly safe. Check to be sure there aren't any dangerous points or strings. Keep the window flaps open and check the temperature inside the tent to make sure it doesn't get too warm.

Make It a Big Deal . . . or Make It a Little Deal

Some children respond well to a big celebration marking the day they become big enough to sleep alone. They might want to pick a special day to make the transformation, sometimes tying it to a birthday or other special event. The big day can be celebrated with a party, complete with cake, decorations, and presents, which often are sleep related, such as a new blanket, pillowcase, or teddy bear.

Other children don't want to even acknowledge that a change is happening. Any suggestion of picking a date will likely be met with tears or anger. For these children, no mention need be made of what's happening. Simply go about taking small steps that lead in the direction of independent sleep.

Invite the Morning Fairy into Your House

Children get very excited over the Easter Bunny, Santa Claus, and the Tooth Fairy. You can introduce one new character to this parade: the Morning Fairy.

To prepare in advance, go to the toy store or the birthday-favor section of a department store. Purchase about thirty little prizes such as plastic animals, stickers, toy cars, and children's books. Wrap each one in wrapping paper.

Explain to your child that any night he sleeps in his own bed all night long, the Morning Fairy will put a surprise by his bedroom door. Any morning that your child is successful sleeping in his own bed all night, leave a prize outside his door. After you've gone through the thirty prizes, your child will have a new routine firmly in place. You can then explain that the Morning Fairy has gone on to visit other children who are just learning to sleep in their own beds. She can make a return appearance if there are any relapses.

(I was going to call her the Hey You Did It Whooo Hooo Fairy, but my daughter Vanessa said the Morning Fairy would be better. Of course, you have my permission to name the fairy whatever you'd like.)

Create a Sibling Sleeping Room

If you have more than one child, it may be beneficial to everyone in the family to set up a place where they can sleep together. While a few children don't want to sleep with a brother or sister, many children love to share sleeping places with siblings up through elementary school. For safety sake, it's recommended that you wait until children are over eighteen months old to co-sleep with a sibling, but you can make a decision based on all your children's ages and sleep history.

People whose children sleep together very often swear that it reduces sibling rivalry and cements friendships. I know that with my four children this has been true. We've had a "sleeping room" from the beginning, which was in addition to each child's own bedroom. This room became a gathering place for sleep and I'd never know how many of my children I'd find there in the morning. Even today I sometimes find my five-year-old in bed with one of his teenage siblings—and it warms my heart in a way that nothing else can.

When you set up a sleeping room, make sure that the bed and the room are entirely child-safe. There's always the possibility that they'll get out of bed to play when you aren't aware of it.

Co-sibling sleep can help everyone. Parents get a good night's sleep, and children get someone to sleep with. If this is something unique in your house, you may have to create new routines that include your presence either in the room or nearby to *shhh* them so that they don't stay up talking and giggling. Although some parents believe that these special sessions are the most bonding times for their children, you don't want it happening until midnight.

A sibling bed arrangement can also include some "bed hopping" if they each have their own bedrooms. The kids can decide each night where they would like to sleep, taking turns being the host for the evening.

If you do use the sibling bed idea, you'll find that over time your children will begin to sleep separately—first one night, then two, and soon they'll settle into their own beds, in their own time frame. Many will continue to have "sleepovers" in each other's rooms for years after that, maintaining the special connectedness that a sibling bed creates.

Note: You may also want to read The Night Visitor (page 217) and "Mommy, Stay!": Needing a Parent's Help to Fall Asleep (page 123) for additional insight and ideas.

Time for a Big-Kid Bed: Moving Out of the Crib

How do we know when it's time to move our child from the crib to a bed? What kind of bed should we get, and what's the best way to make the transition?

When your child moves from the crib to his very own bed, it is a major milestone in his life as well as yours! Babies, of course, grow a little every day, but switching to a big bed is a very visible step in a child's move from babyhood to childhood. There is no precisely perfect time for making this move, and it is different for every child. Typically, a big-kid bed enters the picture sometime between your child's first and third birthday. The most important key to success in this endeavor is to be patient and allow your child the time to adjust to the change with as much pleasure and as little trauma as possible.

What Are the Reasons for Moving a Child from Crib to Bed?

If a child sleeps well in his crib, it's often best to wait as long as possible before making the change. If all is well, there's no reason to upset the apple cart! Switching to a bed gives a child a tremendous amount of freedom and brings new issues for parents to deal with, such as the yo-yo syndrome (into bed, out of bed, into bed, etc.) or early morning wanderings. A variety of valid reasons, however, signal that it's time to move a child from the crib. The most common are the following:

• Your child becomes more physically adept and learns how to climb. This creates the risk that she could try to climb out of the crib and hurt herself by falling out. If your child actually makes an attempted escape, that proves that it's dangerous to keep her in the crib any longer. This is the most important reason to make a quick move. Too great a number of children are injured from climbing over crib bars. You can buy yourself a little extra time by lowering the crib mattress to the bottom level and keeping potential climbing boosters, like stuffed animals and bumper pads, out of the crib. Many experts recommend moving a child out of the crib when he becomes thirty-four to thirty-six inches tall, when the height of the side rail is less than three-quarters of his height, or when the rail is up to the level of his nipples. No matter what, if you look at your growing child and find yourself wondering if she could climb out, it's safe to say she can.

• Your child outgrows the crib and begins to bang up against the bars, or he finds it difficult to get comfortable in a space that has become too small for him. Don't jump too soon on this one. Your perception may be that he's uncomfortable, but many crib-babies are so content in their little nests that they enjoy the snug space. You may want to experiment a bit by putting a toddler bed in the room along with the crib, or even ask your child outright if he's interested in getting a big-kid bed.

• Your child wants to move out of the crib and asks for a bed. This commonly happens with children who have older siblings, friends, or cousins already in big-kid beds, and the little one wants to be just like the older kids. If your child actually asks for a bed, and you feel she's old enough to handle it, then go ahead and take the leap. If you don't respond when she asks, she may change her mind and you'll miss a great window of opportunity.

• Your child is learning how to use the toilet and you would like him to be able to get up to use the bathroom if he needs to. Even if your child uses the toilet consistently during the day, it's often a long while before bedtime dryness enters the picture. It's not a bad thing to use nighttime diapers or disposable training pants for toddlers, so don't feel you must push nighttime toileting independence. (For more information, see Bed-Wetting, on page 259.) If, however, your child calls to you in the night for a bathroom trip, then it would be a good idea to introduce the freedom that a bed allows.

• A new sibling is on the way, and you would like the crib for the baby. The impending birth of a sibling is one of the most common reasons that children are moved out of the crib. While it seems like a practical choice, it's one that should be made carefully. Bringing a new baby into the family creates plenty of new emotions for a toddler. If your little one loves his crib, then ousting him to make room for the little newcomer may add unneeded stress. In this case, it's much better to buy a cradle, portable crib, or even a second crib for the new baby and let your older child handle one big change at a time in his life.

Mother-Speak

"Kyler helped us take apart the crib with his pretend tool set. He helped us move the mattress into his toddler bed. And we let him transfer his own blanket and stuffed animals. We explained that it really was his same bed, just with a different outside."

—Maya, mother of two-year-old Kyler

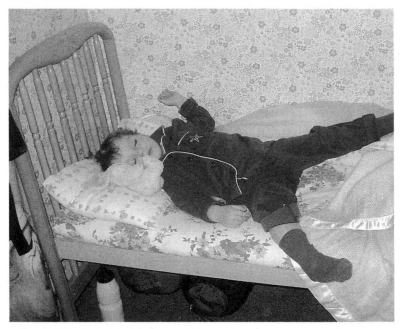

Chester, three years old

If, however, you feel that the time is right, try to make the change two months or more before the newborn arrives. You may even want to take down the crib and store it out of sight for a few weeks, or purchase new bumpers and bedding to give the crib a whole new look, so that your older child doesn't feel that "his" crib is being taken over.

Making the Move

Once you've decided that it is the right time to make the change, think through all the details before you proceed.

Are any other big events or changes coming up soon? It's best not to have this conversion coincide with other changes, such as beginning day care, weaning from a bottle, learning to use the potty, going on vacation, moving to a new home, or adjusting to the parents' separation or a new marriage. If possible, arrange the move to a big bed to occur when all other parts of your child's life are fairly stable.

Take your child's personality into consideration: How does she normally handle change? How does she take to new adventures, new toys, and new things in the house? Does she respond better to the thrill of surprises or carefully planned events? Understanding how she approaches life changes will help you decide how to introduce a new bed.

Think about the logistics of the change: type of bed, location of bed, when to remove the crib, types of bedding, and any other details involved. The following information can help you with some of these details.

What Kind of Bed Should My Child Move To?

Actually, quite a few alternatives are open to you when moving your child out of the crib. Here are the typical options:

• **Toddler bed.** A wide and wonderful assortment of toddler beds are available, and you might already have a crib that converts into a toddler bed. Toddler beds are small and low and made especially for children between the ages of one and about five. The advantage to these is their perfectly toddler-scaled proportions; some even use the crib mattress. They usually have built-in guardrails on all four sides, and some come in creative designs so your child can sleep in a car, castle, boat, or train. The novelty of these can entice an otherwise reluctant child to make the move from a well-loved crib. There are a few disadvantages, though. The guardrails are often fairly short, so if your child moves about in bed, you may have to add additional side rails. Also, your child will outgrow a toddler bed, and a few years from now you'll be looking to buy another bigger bed, though many toddler beds are inexpensive enough to be worth the purchase.

• **Regular bed.** A regular bed with a mattress, box springs, and bed frame is one choice for your child. If you go directly from a crib to a regular bed, though, it's wise to make sure all four sides are protected against falling out. Many companies make bed rails for this purpose, and now you can find them in extra-long lengths or even in soft bolster-type designs. At first, you may want to further protect your child from falls and clumsy climbing by padding the floor around the bed with foam or folded blankets, since one big fall can result in injury or a fear of sleeping in the bed.

While it used to be typical for a child to have a single bed, many families now opt for a double or even bigger size to accommodate the family night-reading ritual, or to provide room for a sibling or eventual overnight guests.

If the bed has a headboard, you may want to securely tie your child's crib bumper to it to maintain a sense of connection to the crib environment that he was used to.

When choosing a bed for your child, be thoughtful about the type of mattress that you acquire. Although children are typically less picky than adults, a comfortable surface is still important (see page 65).

• **Mattress or futon on the floor.** A very common choice for a child who is fresh out of the crib is to place a mattress or futon on the floor. This provides your little one with a big-kid bed, but he can get in and out of it on his own and there isn't a big drop should he fall out of bed. A good size for a floor mattress is a double or larger so that you can join your child for bedtime reading or morning snuggles.

An advantage to placing a mattress on the floor is that it makes a great trampoline. (Oops. Don't tell my mom that I included that benefit!) And keep your trampoline, er, uh, *mattress*, away from any windows or sharp furniture edges.

• **Bunk bed.** Since it's unsafe for children under age six to sleep in an upper bunk, it's wise to avoid even having a bunk bed in the house until your child is close to her sixth birthday. Even if you don't plan to let her sleep there right away, it may be just too enticing for her to wait, and then you'll either find her up there or add a battle to your nighttime routine.

When your child does turn six and you decide to purchase a bunk bed, look for one with high bed rails that surround the top level, or add extra side guardrails yourself. (Look for those designed to accommodate this kind of use, such as fabric bolsters, not bed rails that require box springs for stability.) Look for those with easy-to-use ladders, and if possible, have your child try it out while you watch and gauge her ability to climb the ladder before you purchase the bed.

When shopping for a bunk bed, consider the styles that provide a double size mattress on the bottom and a single on the top. This gives you room to lie beside your child as you tuck her in, read stories, or cuddle for morning wake-ups. It also gives room for a sibling, friend, or cousin to share the space. You can add glow-in-the-dark stars to the underside of the upper bunk to solve any fears of the dark.

Bunk beds invite a whole new set of safety concerns, no matter your child's age, so review the Bunk Bed Safety checklist on page 377.

Safety, Safety, Safety!

No matter when you decide to make the move or what kind of bed you provide for your child, take a look at the safety lists in this book that begin on page 371 to be sure you are providing your child with a completely safe sleep environment. This means his bed is safe, his bedroom is childproofed, and the whole entire house is as safe as possible to welcome any potential nighttime or morning exploring.

How Do We Make the Change?

There are many ways to make the transition from crib to bed. Which one is best for you will depend on your reasons for moving your child out of the crib, your child's personality, and the size and configuration of his bedroom.

No matter which path you choose, be patient and tolerant, and do your best to make it a pleasant experience for your little one. Keep in mind that such big steps toward growth sometimes happen in spurts, and your child may be excited to welcome change one day but wary of it the next. Maintain the important parts of your nightly routine and help your child develop a positive, happy association with his new bed, since he'll be sleeping there for many years to come.

Here are some possible options from which you can create your own plan:

- **Big-kid bed hoopla.** Some children enjoy looking forward to the big event. They love being involved in choosing a new bed and linens and helping set it up. You can even choose an official Big-Kid Bed Day and throw a party. Decorate the room, wrap a few bedtime-related presents, and take pictures. No matter how exciting this all may be, remember that when the actual first night of sleeping there arrives, your child may suddenly be nervous. So provide extra loving attention and reassurance, and help your child enjoy the experience without expecting him to suddenly transform into a big kid overnight.

• **The one-step-at-a-time switcheroo.** A variation of the previous idea (with or without the hoopla) is to take the crib mattress out of the crib and place it in exactly the same place as the crib. This gives your child the security of seeing almost exactly the same view of the room as he's accustomed to. Place temporary guardrails around the sides to create a similar feeling of enclosure as the crib provided. Use all the same bedding and crib toys as your child has been used to. This is a mid-step between the crib and a real bed. After your child is used to this arrangement, you can replace the crib mattress with a bigger mattress. The next step is to add the box springs and, finally, the bed frame. Keep the guardrails up until you're confident that your child is safe from falling out of bed.

• **The gradual introduction.** Plenty of children don't respond well to a major announcement of a change; it creates huge expectations and leaves no room for the back-and-forth process that growing up often involves. They like to gradually work up to the idea and test it out a little bit at a time, like testing the pool water with a toe, then a foot, adding a leg, and finally jumping into the water.

If you think this describes your child's way of thinking, then set up the new bed in the same room along with the crib. Start off by allowing your child to play on the bed. See if she's interested in napping there. Perhaps do your bedtime reading or nightly massage in the new bed. All of this will help your child get used to the new bed over time. Eventually you can suggest that she sleep there all night and see how she responds. If she's excited to try it, then encourage her. If, on the other hand, she expresses horror at the idea, then shelve it for another week or more and then suggest it again.

- **The surprise.** If your child has been coveting an older sibling, cousin, or friend's bed, and you know that he'd be thrilled to have one of his own, you can plan a surprise switch. When your child is off with someone else, perhaps a visit with the grandparents for the day, set up the new bed in place of the crib while he's gone. Include wonderful new bed linens, but keep some old favorites such as a special blanket or the usual bed-pal stuffed animals. For some children, out of sight is out of mind and they'll take right to the new bed without question.

The potential negative to this approach is that your child may panic, and you'll find yourself with a whole new set of bedtime problems or a late-night project of pulling the crib out of the garage and setting it back up again. But if your child usually likes surprises and has been interested in getting a bed, it may be worth the try.

What If He Hates It?

Parenting is filled with decisions, big and little, and parents can't always predict the future. There will be times that what seemed like the right decision turns out to be wrong. Simply reevaluate the situation and revise your decision. Sleep is such a volatile issue, and there are so many sleep- and bedtime-related problems that parents have to deal with in the early years of a child's life. So I vote to avoid an issue if you can. If you've made the change from crib to bed and given it a fair effort, but your child suddenly begins to have many more night wakings, doesn't fall asleep easily, or cries for his crib, then if possible, go ahead and let him go back to his familiar source of comfort. This isn't a failure on anyone's part; it is just a change that your child wasn't quite ready for. If you've planned to use the crib for a new sibling, see if you can come up with an alternative solution, such as putting your newborn into a cradle or portable crib for a while, or even borrowing or buying a second crib.

The Yo-Yo Syndrome

Many children who have been accustomed to the secure environment of a crib and the fact that they have always had to stay in bed all night won't even think to escape from their new bed, even though they could! Simply start out with a consistent bedtime routine, tucking your child in and operating under the assumption that she'll stay there. Make sure that the last fifteen minutes or more of the bedtime routine occur with your child in her bed. This could be reading books, giving back rubs, or storytelling. The key is to leave when your child is very sleepy, half-asleep, or even totally asleep.

If your child does wander out of bed, catch her quickly, explain briefly that she needs to stay in bed, and take her back. If you are very consistent with this return process, your child will quickly learn that she needs to stay in bed once the good nights are completed.

If you find that the process isn't as simple as all this, then read over Bedtime Battles (page 105) or The Night Visitor (page 217) for ideas to curb any night wandering.

Making It Permanent

No matter how well the adjustment goes, new sleep issues are bound to crop up. Some may be in conjunction with the change;

others may appear at this time just as a coincidence. Take each sleep issue individually, and apply solutions to any that arise. It's all part of being a parent.

When you are patient and supportive and allow your child to make a change to a big-kid bed on his own timetable, you'll find this to be a wonderful milestone in your child's exciting and ever-changing growth and development.

Separation Anxiety

My sixteen-month-old daughter has always been a pretty good sleeper, but suddenly our bedtime routine is filled with battles. She gets scared when I leave the room. She clings to me and won't let me leave. During the night she wakes up and cries until I come to her. She's been clingy during the day, as well. Could she have separation anxiety?

It's very likely that separation anxiety is the culprit here, since this normal childhood condition peaks sometime between the first and third birthdays. Nearly all children experience separation anxiety at some point. Some have more intense reactions than others, and the stage lasts longer for some than others. For a number of children, this fear becomes a cause for new bedtime problems. In his book *Sleeping Like a Baby* (Yale University Press, 2001), Dr. Avi Sadeh, director of the Laboratory for Children's Sleep and Arousal Disorders, explains:

> Separation anxiety is one of the main causes of sleep disorders in early childhood. The child often begins to resist sleep immediately at the start of the rituals that lead up to bedtime. Sometimes the source is a problem separating from parents. The refusal to lie down and go to sleep may express anxiety related to the coming separation, the need to continue the pleasurable connection with the parents, or anxieties related to nighttime, darkness, and being alone in the dark.

Why Does a Child Have Separation Anxiety?

The development of separation anxiety demonstrates that your child has formed a healthy, loving attachment to you. It is a beautiful sign that your child associates pleasure, comfort, and security with your presence. It also indicates that your child is developing intellectually (in other words, she's smart!). She has learned that she can have an effect on her world when she makes her needs known, and she doesn't have to passively accept a situation that makes her uncomfortable. She doesn't know enough about the world yet to understand that when you leave her, you'll always come back. She also realizes that she is safest, happiest, and best cared for by you, so her reluctance to part makes perfect sense—especially when viewed from a survival standpoint. Let's put it another way: you are her source of nourishment, both physical and emotional; therefore, her attachment to you is her means of survival, and she realizes this when she reaches a certain level of intellectual maturity.

This stage, like so many others in childhood, will pass. In time, your child will learn that she *can* separate from you for the night, that you will return in the morning, and that everything will be OK between those two points in time. Much of this learning is based on trust, which, as for every human being young or old, takes time to build.

Why Does Separation Anxiety Affect Sleep?

If you stop to think about it, usually the longest separation between you and your child is during her nighttime sleep when the two of you are apart for ten to twelve hours. During this time, your child will have a number of brief awakenings from sleep when she'll open her eyes and realize that she's all alone. This same thing happens every night, so when your child realizes that this long separation is about to occur, it may create struggles at bedtime.

How Do You Know If Your Child Has Separation Anxiety?

Separation anxiety is pretty easy to spot, and you're probably reading this section because you've identified it in your child. The following are typical behaviors of a child with normal separation anxiety:

- Clinginess
- Refusal to go to sleep without a parent nearby
- Crying when a parent is out of sight
- Strong preference for only one parent, shown particularly at bedtime
- Fear of strangers or new situations
- Waking at night crying for a parent
- Being easily comforted in a parent's embrace

How You Can Help Your Child with Separation Anxiety

Children will naturally outgrow separation anxiety, but there are ways for you to support and encourage your child during the process. Many of these ideas will also speed along your child's emotional maturity when it comes to separation.

- Allow your child to be a child. It's perfectly OK—even wonderful—for your child to be so attached to you and for her to desire your constant companionship. Congratulations, Mommy or Daddy: it's evidence that the bond you've worked so hard to create is holding. So politely ignore those who tell you otherwise.

- Don't worry about spoiling him with your love or providing him the attention he needs as he's going to sleep or when he wakes up. The more that you meet his attachment needs at bedtime now, the more quickly he will outgrow his insecurities.

- Minimize separations when possible, especially at bedtime. It's perfectly acceptable for now—better, in fact—to avoid those situations that would have you separate from your child at his bedtime. All too soon, your child will move past this phase and on to the next developmental milestone. Most children outgrow the worst of separation anxiety by their third birthday, and for many it disappears by the time they turn five.

- Practice with quick, safe separations. Throughout the day, create situations of brief separation. When you are in the middle of your child's bedtime routine or just after she gets into bed, take brief trips to another room and whistle, sing, or talk to your child so she knows you're still there even though she can't see you.

- Don't sneak away when you have to leave her, whether it's for a brief jaunt to another room or to go to your own bed. It may seem easier than dealing with a tearful good-bye, but it will just cause her constant worry that you're going to disappear without warning at any given moment.

- Tell your child what to expect. If you are going out for the evening and leaving her at home with Grandma, explain where you are going and tell her when you'll be back. Don't expect her to go to sleep easily while you are away, and prepare Grandma so she'll know what to expect. One night of a late bedtime may be better than having Grandma deal with a crying child.

• Express a positive attitude when leaving him. If you're off to work or an evening out, leave with a smile. Your child will absorb your emotions, so if you're nervous about leaving him, he'll be nervous as well. Your confidence, on the other hand, will help alleviate his fears.

• Leave your child with familiar people. If you must leave your child, especially at bedtime, try to leave her with a familiar care-giver. If you must leave her with someone new, arrange a few vis-its when you'll all be together before you leave the two of them alone for the first time.

• Make sure that any caregiver who will put your child to bed knows her exact bedtime routine. Write it down so that the con-sistency of the nighttime ritual can be kept the same as usual. This will bring comfort and security and ward off anxiety.

• During the day, allow your child the separation that she ini-tiates. If she goes off to play in another room, don't rush after her. Listen and peek, of course, to make sure that she's safe, but let her know it's fine for her to go off exploring on her own. These prac-tice sessions will build her confidence in separations from you.

• Encourage her relationship with a special blanket, stuffed animal, or toy, if she seems to have one. These lovies can be a comfort to her at naptime and bedtime since they create a feeling of security.

• Don't take it personally if only one parent is accepted easily for the bedtime routine. Many children go through a stage of attaching themselves to one parent or the other, and it can be most pronounced when the child is tired. The other parent, as well as grandparents, siblings, and friends, can find this difficult to accept, but try to reassure them that it's just a temporary and nor-mal phase of development, and with a little time and gentle patience it will pass.

• If you have an older toddler or preschooler with a vivid imag-ination, you can take advantage of this by adding a new step to her bedtime routine. Before you leave the room, give your child a "Little Mommy" or a "Little Daddy" to sleep with her. Simply cup your hands as if you are holding something and pretend to give her a tiny version of yourself. Ask her if you can have one of her to take to your own room. This Little Mommy idea can come in handy for daytime separations, too.

Teething

My toddler was sleeping much better than ever, but suddenly he's waking up several times a night and crying out. I suspect that teething pain is the culprit. How can I know if this is really the case, and what can I do to help him feel better and sleep better?

The process of teething is a common reason that toddlers have trouble falling asleep and staying asleep. Think back to the last time you had a toothache, headache, sore back, or stiff neck. Any of these discomforts can disrupt your ability to sleep, just as teething can disturb a child's rest. Toddlers can't always tell us what the problem is. They simply feel uncomfortable but don't understand why; so they cry or fuss. Often this behavior starts long before you see a tooth pop out, so it can be hard to tell whether teething is contributing to your child's sleep issues.

You can't compare one child's teething experience to another's. Some children have no visual indication of a tooth coming until that pearly white pops through. Others have swollen gums that are purple, red, white, or bumpy. They chew incessantly, whine constantly, and wake frequently at night. Some children have more difficulty with eye teeth and molars than they had with earlier teeth because of the location and size of these teeth.

What Are the Symptoms?

A number of typical symptoms accompany the teething process:

- Difficulty falling asleep or staying asleep
- Fussiness
- Drooling
- Runny nose
- Rash on the chin or around the mouth
- Biting, mouthing, and chewing toys or clothes
- Red cheeks
- Rejecting the breast or bottle
- Increased need to suck
- Swollen, discolored gums
- Softer-than-usual bowel movements
- Evidence of pain all the way up the jaw to the ear

Some parents report that slight fever, diarrhea, vomiting, or dia-per rashes accompany teething, but because these symptoms also may signal an infection or virus, they should always be reported to your health care provider.

Mother-Speak

"After tons of extra nursing, lots of fussing, shortened naps, and many awakenings Malcolm's new molar finally popped through, so he slept much better last night. My poor little guy takes teething hard, and it always disrupts his sleep. Why can't babies be born with all their teeth?!"

—Angelique, mother of seventeen-month-old Malcolm

How to Help Your Child Feel Better

If you suspect that your child is teething, here are some things you can do to help relieve her discomfort so that she can relax enough to sleep:

- Give her a clean, cool washcloth to chew on.
- Let her chew on a teething ring that is either room temperature or chilled in the refrigerator—but never frozen, as it may cause cracking.
- If your child uses a pacifier, try chilling it, and see how he likes that.
- Frequently and gently pat her chin dry.
- Offer a cup of cold water.
- Rub her gums with a clean, wet finger.
- Use a specially made, soft baby or toddler toothbrush to clean the gums.
- Make frozen treats from apple juice, orange juice, or yogurt. Just fill a small paper cup, a shape-sorter toy piece, or an ice-cube tray, and use a small plastic spoon for a stick. Or purchase frozen-pop molds from the housewares department of your local store. Sucking on this just before bedtime can help numb the pain.
- Dab petroleum jelly or a gentle salve on her chin in the drool area.
- Breastfeed often, for comfort as well as nutrition.

Avoid teething biscuits, as these are really designed for younger, toothless babies—toddlers with teeth can bite off pieces that become choking hazards. For the same reason, don't offer hard foods like carrot sticks or apples unless under direct and constant supervision.

The pain-relief ointments for teething that are available over the counter can be quite potent (put a dab on your lip and you'll notice a tingly, numbing feeling). The ointments can also numb your child's tongue and lips, and they wash out of the mouth quickly, so they don't bring lasting relief. Therefore, use these sparingly and only with an OK from your health care professional, who can also tell you about homeopathic teething tablets, acetaminophen, ibuprofen, and teething tinctures.

Sleep difficulties are most often a convoluted combination of issues; teething may be just one part of the reason that your toddler isn't sleeping as well as he should be. So in addition to using the ideas in this section directly relating to teething, make certain that you are following all the other parts and pieces of your sleep plan.

Children with Special Needs

Our daughter won't go to bed easily; she has frequent night wakings, suffers from night terrors, and wets the bed. She has special needs, which probably create and complicate all these issues. How can we apply what we're learning in this book to our situation?

While sleep issues are common among all children, those with special needs are even more likely to have sleep difficulties. Furthermore, they often require a more intense and committed plan in order to solve their sleep issues. "Children with special needs tend to have at least one sleep disorder," says Dr. Stephen Sheldon, director of the sleep medicine center at Children's Memorial Hospital in Chicago, Illinois. He explains that children with special needs often have health issues that contribute to sleep disorders such as snoring, sleepwalking, sleep apnea, reflux, teeth grinding, night terrors, bed-wetting, and insomnia. In addition, some children are unable to reposition themselves during the night, and some must deal with cramping and muscle spasms. Medical issues such as tube feedings or the use of ventilators can interfere with sleep, and some children might require all-night monitoring.

There are, of course, a wide range and various degrees of special needs, and therefore, it may be helpful to converse with your health professional and parents of children with similar situations. There's tremendous value in sharing tips and ideas with parents who have children who are similar to your own. No matter your situation, a number of general guidelines will apply to most families when it comes to addressing sleep issues.

Abigail, two years old

Define Your Child's Sleep Issues

Take the time to complete the logs and worksheets provided in Part I on page 19. These will help you not only understand how your child is sleeping now but also clearly identify the sleep issues that need to be changed. They will also be important as they help you identify your feelings about your child's sleep patterns. Not all sleep-related issues need to be labeled as problems; some may just require a change of viewpoint, understanding, or even acceptance.

Many sleep problems are not at all related to your child's special needs, even if you may have thought they were. For example, you may have read earlier in this book that the majority of young children are not self-sufficient when it comes to bedtime. They require a parent to get them settled into bed. In the National Sleep Foundation's 2004 *Sleep in America* poll, less than 1 percent of children in the toddler age group and barely 1 percent of preschoolers managed the amazing feat of getting settled for bed on their own. Only 12 percent of school-aged children put themselves to bed. So if you've been thinking that this situation in your house is in any way unique, it may help to know that it's very typical among all families.

Make a Realistic, Thoughtful Plan

As you put together your sleep plan (page 25), be realistic. It would be wonderful if a few minor adjustments would allow you to say "Night night" to your child at 7:00 P.M. and then not hear a peep until 7:00 A.M. when she calls out a cheerful "Good morning." But this is unrealistic in any situation, and you would just be setting yourself up for frustration and disappointment if you aimed for that goal. Instead, be reasonable as you lay out your sleep plan. Aim for short-term goals, and as you achieve these, set a few more.

One Step at a Time

You may have a number of sleep issues that you'd like to change. Trying to fix everything at once may overwhelm you and your child. It may be more productive and less stressful to work on changing just one or two issues before moving on to the next. For example, if your child won't go to bed easily, has numerous night wakings, and wakes up too early in the morning, you may want to deal only with the bedtime battle to begin with. Once you've established a routine that is pleasant and consistent, then you'll have achieved a success worth celebrating. So remember to enjoy every small victory that makes bedtime issues a little easier to deal with. With a pleasant frame of mind and the knowledge that you can make good improvements, you can then move on to the next issue.

Choosing the Steps to Address

You have several choices as you choose which issues to begin with. You can either pick the problem that bothers you the most or choose the one that may be easiest to correct. For example, if your child is waking you up every few hours all night and draining all the energy you have so that your days are a struggle, then address that issue first and deal with that issue alone. Or you can choose a problem that is relatively easy to fix, such as the early bird syndrome, resistance to napping, or a change in timing or type of a medication that might be causing sleeplessness. Once you've had success with one issue, move on to the next. Keep in mind that gradually applying all that you've learned in this book will bring the best long-term success. There's no reason, however, to add stress to your life by trying to do it all at once.

Focus on Routines and Rituals

Your child may respond best when all her sleep-related activities are choreographed to occur in exactly the same way every night. A bedtime chart as described on page 114 may be helpful by involving your child in the process and giving her a sense of control over her bedtime routines.

Design your child's bedtime routine to meet her needs, strengths, and developmental capabilities. If something seems dif-

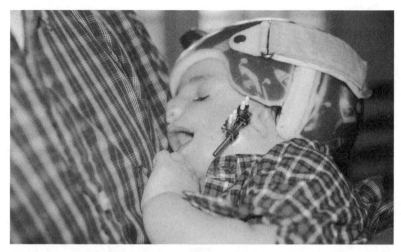

Jim holding Sam, twelve months old

ficult for her or if she's learning a new task, choosing to encourage her independence at the time of day when she and you are most tired and impatient will just complicate your bedtime routine. Save new or challenging tasks for the daytime, and do what you can to make the bedtime routine pleasant and stress-free, even if it means doing things for her that you know she can do herself.

Dig Deep for More Patience

Although you are struggling with the effects of your child's sleep-related problems, your child is likely burdened as well. It's possible that he's just as unhappy with his sleep disruptions as you are, and he's looking to you to solve them. He even may be concerned because of your emotions over his sleep problems. "Children can sense if their parent is upset or angry because they have been woken up, have to change the sheets, or have to lose sleep to tend to the child," says Dr. Sheldon. These complex emotions can even add more depth and confusion to your child's sleep issues. So take a deep breath, and take it one night at a time. While your child's sleep patterns may be frustrating for you today, there are many steps you can take to improve your child's sleep. It just can't be done overnight. If you present a calm, methodical approach, and sprinkle it with plenty of patience and encouragement, it's likely your child will relax about the issues, which will in turn invite more sleep successes.

Ask for Help

There are times when problems are due to sleep disorders that won't improve until they are identified and addressed. If you've made a sleep plan and followed it consistently for several months without any positive results, then read the section on sleep disorders (page 382) to determine if your child might be served by a professional who can provide a more extensive evaluation and specialized remedies. Even if you don't suspect a sleep disorder, you can still gain wonderful insight and ideas from a professional.

Mother-Speak
"If things aren't working in your house, get help and get it now. There are plenty of people who are ready and willing to give you a hand."

—Carol, mother and twenty-five-year veteran special-education teacher

Ear Infections

Our toddler has been particularly fussy and is waking up much more than usual. He wakes up crying as if he's in pain, so we're wondering if he might have an ear infection.

It's quite possible, since ear infections are common in young children. Their ear tubes are short, wide, and horizontal—giving bacteria from the nose and throat an easy path to the ears. Ear infections are often associated with a cold or allergies, which create more mucus in the middle ear.

Two-thirds of children under age three have had an ear infection, and half of them have multiple infections. As children get older and their ear tubes mature, they will no longer be so susceptible to ear infections. In the meantime, an untreated ear infection will prevent your child from sleeping well, since the pain is more intense when lying down versus being upright.

What Causes Ear Infections?

Ear infections happen when bacteria and fluid build up in the inner ear. This situation often occurs following a cold, sinus infection, or other respiratory illness, or in conjunction with allergies. The fluids get trapped in the ear, causing a throbbing pain.

How to Tell If Your Child Has an Ear Infection

Your child may exhibit all, some, or even none of the following symptoms. It's always important to see your health care provider if you even suspect an ear infection. These symptoms *may* indicate an ear infection:

- A sudden change in temperament: more fussiness, crying, or clinginess
- Increased night waking
- Waking up crying as if in pain
- Fever
- Diarrhea
- Reduced appetite or difficulty swallowing
- Runny nose that continues after a cold
- Drainage from the ear
- Fussiness when lying down that goes away when child is upright
- Difficulty with balance, frequent falling, sensations of dizziness (these symptoms should be discussed with your health care professional)
- Signs of difficulty hearing (this should always be checked by a doctor)

These symptoms almost always indicate an ear infection:

- Ear pain or frequent pulling, grabbing, or batting at the ears
- Green, yellow, or white fluid draining from the ear
- A dry crust on the outer portion of the ear after sleeping
- An unpleasant odor emanating from the ear

What to Do About an Ear Infection

If your child is exhibiting any of the preceding symptoms and you suspect an ear infection, make an appointment with your health care provider right away. This is important because an untreated ear infection can lead to speech difficulties, hearing loss, meningitis, or other complications.

Your doctor may suggest some of the following treatments if your child does have an ear infection (*but don't try to solve this problem on your own without an expert's direction*):

- Give your child a pain reliever, such as acetaminophen (Tylenol) or ibuprofen. (Never give your child aspirin unless a doctor tells you to, as it can be hazardous.)
- Keep your child's head elevated for sleep. You can do this by raising one end of her mattress (try taping tuna cans under one end).
- Place a warm compress over the affected ear.
- Keep the ears dry and out of water.
- Offer plenty of liquids.
- Administer prescribed antibiotics or instill prescribed ear drops.
- Provide homeopathic remedies such as echinacea, goldenseal, chamomile, or herbal oil ear drops.

How You Can Reduce the Chance of Ear Infections

Any child can get an ear infection, but a few measures can reduce the likelihood:

- Prevent the colds and flu that introduce the bacteria into your child's system. Wash your hands and your child's hands frequently. When possible, keep your child away from any-one who is obviously sick with a cold or flu.

- Keep your child away from cigarette smoke. Just one after-noon spent with secondhand smoke can increase your child's chances of developing an ear infection.
- Never let your child sleep with a bottle unless it is filled with water. Milk or juice can pool in the mouth and seep into the ear canals. (Plus it might cause tooth decay.)

Sleep Adjustments When Adopting a Toddler or Preschooler

We are in the process of adopting a two-year-old girl from Guatemala. If everything goes smoothly, our little daughter will be joining our family next month. What advice can you give us about helping her make the adjustments needed for good sleep?

Children adopted during the toddler and preschooler years have very different needs than do newborns or school-aged children. "Yet, the available adoption literature talks primarily about infants and older children," explains Mary Hopkins-Best, the author of *Toddler Adoption: The Weaver's Craft* (Perspectives Press, 1998). She goes on to explain some of the unique challenges that these little people present to their parents: "Toddlers are a bundle of contradictions. Many keep their adoptive parents at bay through their anger, grief, and natural urge toward independence. Encouraging a newly adopted toddler's dependence and trust, while supporting his emerging independence is a confounding task for both the child and parent."

Sleep issues are common during the toddler and preschool years, and adoption during this time period adds an additional layer of complexity. Part of the process involves adjusting to the loss of former caregivers or creating the type of family attachment that has yet to be experienced in the child's life. Children who are adopted internationally have even more of an adjustment to make because of jet lag and the effort required to take in all the new sounds, sights, smells, and tastes that fill her new world.

Adopting a toddler or preschooler is as emotionally over-whelming as bringing a baby or child of any age into your family. It will also likely be the most fulfilling and wonderful experience of your life. You can help your child most when you are prepared with information, so it is beneficial to read books, join an online or in-person support group, and visit a family counselor. Many aspects to this new relationship require far more discussion than can be had here, so please keep in mind that I'll cover sleep-related adjustments specifically, and you and your child will best be served by a comprehensive plan for the creation of your new family.

In regard to your child's sleep, you can help her adjust by creating a two-part sleep plan for her. The first segment should be to initiate and bond with your child during the fragile period of adjustment, without pressing the need for changes to her sleep patterns. The second segment is to use the other sections in this book to address any sleep-specific issues, such as going to sleep alone, sleeping through the night, napping, or waking too early in the morning.

Learning Your Child's Sleep History

It's not always possible to learn the details of your child's sleeping situation before he or she joins the family. When you can, however, learning your child's sleep history can give you some helpful background for transitioning your child to a new sleeping situation and may lessen adjustment-related sleep problems. Try to discover the answers to as many of these questions as possible in advance of bringing your child home:

- What time does my child normally go to bed at night?
- What things are normally done before bed: brush teeth, read a book, change into pajamas, sing songs, play music (what songs or music specifically)?
- What does my child usually have in bed with her? A blanket, pillow, stuffed animal, doll, pacifier, bottle?
- When my child falls asleep, is the room usually quiet or noisy? Is the television or a radio on? Are people talking in another room?
- Does my child sleep in the dark or with a night-light?
- How does she fall asleep—is she fed a bottle, rocked, sung to, or placed in her bed awake?
- Does my child now sleep alone? Where does she sleep—in a crib or a regular bed (what size mattress?)? Is the mattress on a bed frame or on the floor?
- Does anyone else sleep in the same room as my child? How close are the beds?
- Does my child sleep with a caregiver? Does my child like to be cuddled as she is falling asleep or to be near someone without touching? Does she have any falling-asleep rituals?
- During the night when my child wakes up, how is she tended to? Is she talked to, fed, rocked, or patted?
- Does my child currently nap? Does she sleep on a regular schedule? What time are her naps? Does she usually have a meal before napping? How long does she usually sleep? Where does she sleep? Is there a prenaptime routine?

Regardless of what you learn about your child's previous sleeping environment or sleep patterns, understand that it's perfectly normal for these to change during the initial adjustment period at home. It's also common for a child to appear perfectly adjusted during the day but for issues to crop up in the quiet, dark night. Love and patience are the things your child needs most to become trusting, settled, and contented.

Creating a Similar Sleep Situation

If you can learn about your child's existing sleeping environment in advance, it can be helpful to duplicate it as much as possible. Toddlers and preschoolers are at an age when familiarity is soothing, especially at a vulnerable time like falling asleep. Over time you will be able to make changes that better suit your family, but at the start it can help your child become more comfortable in his new home if the surroundings are similar to what he has been accustomed to.

Learn About Normal Developmental Milestones

If you study the typical behavior of young children, you would learn that many of the traits that seem connected to the adoption are really just normal childhood behavior. For example, if your child can't seem to fall asleep alone, you may worry that something is wrong. But once you know that almost half of all toddlers and preschoolers require a parent to stay in their room until they are asleep, you relieve yourself and your child of the pressure to conform to some imagined requirement. So pick up a book or two about the typical development of a child at this age, and you'll feel more confident in your parenting skills.

Observe and Listen

Your child may be newly verbal or just learning a new language. You can learn much about your child by observing her reactions, her body language, and her emotional displays. Watch to see which types of things or actions seem to help her relax and which things create tension. For example, she may visibly relax when holding a blanket or soft toy, or become agitated when the lights are turned out. Take these as important cues to creating a comforting sleep environment.

Mother-Speak

"My advice is to open your eyes, your ears, your heart, and your mind and really, truly listen to your child. You may even learn more about her than she knows about herself."

—**Anna, mother of three-year-old Maya Jun**

Re-Create the Attachment Process

Parents of a newborn are advised to respond to their child's needs on demand and provide holding time and attention whenever the baby needs it. This isn't viewed as spoiling, because it involves love and attention, not material possessions. This same concept can be applied when welcoming your newly adopted child to your home and your heart, regardless of how old your child is. Don't be afraid to provide love and attention whenever your child needs it, even if she needs it in the middle of the night. The ten or twelve hours from bedtime to morning are a very long time for a child to be alone in the dark. Remember that all human beings have night wakings, and when your child wakes in the dark, she needs your reassurance and comfort. In addition, these quiet, undistracted times can provide special opportunities for falling in love.

Consider Co-Sleeping or Close Sleeping

Many adoptive parents report that staying close to their children all night facilitates the bonding process. When everyone's beds are

Mother-Speak

"I was told by my agency to do whatever my baby wanted and needed until she felt comfortable. Since she slept with her foster mother, I wanted to maintain that routine and help her feel safe, so I have been sleeping with her. We both sleep very well this way, and I feel that it has really helped us to attach to each other. I have treasured those special moments."

—**Diana, mother of two-year-old Sonja**

in the same room, it's possible that hearing each other's breathing and night sounds creates a subconscious connection. For those children who are very young or who shared a bed with another adult or with other children, maintaining this arrangement is reassuring to the child.

Staying close to your child all night can also make it easier on you as you respond to your child's night-waking needs. It will also shorten the amount of time it takes for you to arrive at your child's side when he wakes up because of pain, grief, fear, or a bad dream.

There are many options for co-sleeping or close sleeping, and you can see the various styles described on page 273.

Close Sleeping Isn't the Only Option

Keep in mind that every child is different. Some children feel very comforted in having their own special crib or bed in their own special room, and as long as they know someone will come if they need help, they do just fine sleeping alone. Also, some children have always slept in a crib or alone in a bed, and they find that environment soothing and familiar. They will adjust well to a new place when provided with a comforting bedtime routine.

Many children sleep well alone but require that someone stay with them until they fall asleep. If this describes your child, you may want to place a chair beside your child's bed and read with a small book light, knit, or listen to an audiobook or music on a headset until your child is asleep. Just being there may be enough to let your child drift off to sleep peacefully. You might want to read over the suggestions in "Mommy, Stay!": Needing a Parent's Help to Fall Asleep, on page 123.

You should make decisions about your child's sleep that feel right to you, too. If you aren't comfortable with co-sleeping or even with having your child sleep in your bedroom, there's no rule that says you must. Many well-loved and secure children have always slept alone in their own bedrooms. This is just one part of your entire family experience, and it's important that everyone is content with how things are set up.

Encourage Your Child's Attachment to a Lovey

A lovey is a soft toy or blanket that acts as a soother to comfort your child in your absence. The value of a lovey is that it can be controlled by the child and held whenever she feels afraid, unsure, or alone. It can be especially valuable to a child when falling asleep or when she awakens in the middle of the night.

A lovey is not intended to—and couldn't possibly—take your place, but it can provide a sense of security and consistency for your child. It can be carried around and used day and night whenever your child is separated from you. A lovey provides your child with a link to the feelings of safety that you give her.

Keep in mind that your child may come to you with an already established lovey. That scrap of blanket or well-worn doll might just be the thing your child needs to calm her anxiety. So if your child clutches his special toy, don't feel you must replace it with something new. You might want to provide several new options and follow your child's lead to see what cuddly toy she chooses to hold at naptime and bedtime.

Young children have strong imaginations: these lovies can seem very real to them. You can encourage this connection by making the toy sing or talk to your child in play. When you do this, it magnifies the power of the lovey so it can ward off any feelings of being alone that your child may have during the night, or when he first wakes up after a nap or in the morning.

You can find information on how to choose and use a lovey in Tip 5 (page 73).

Create and Maintain Naptime and Bedtime Rituals

Bedtime routines are important for all children, but they are especially important for young children who are newly adopted. A formal bedtime routine can enhance feelings of predictability and stability in your child's life. It will give your child a feeling of control over his environment and his life. Knowing the sequence of events leading to bedtime will also minimize sleeptime troubles.

If your child is an older toddler or preschooler, it can be very helpful to create a bedtime chart (see page 114) or a bedtime book (see page 117). This poster and homemade book will provide the added benefit of reinforcing your child's understanding that her place in your family is permanent and help her see her daily life as a predictable series of events.

View Bedtime as Bonding Time

Bedtime is a very special time. Typically, the house is quiet, everyone is less active, and there are fewer outside distractions. You can use this special time at the end of each day to connect with your child and find comfort in simply being together. Bedtime rituals will be important for the first ten or so years of your child's life, so take advantage of this nightly opportunity to simply relax and absorb the growing love between you.

Night Wakings: Your Chance to Be a Hero

It may give you a new perspective if you view night wakings as a perfect opportunity to show your child that you will always be there for him and that you are his champion. Very often, when children wake in the night, they are a little bit disoriented and sometimes scared or lonely. This is your time to respond quickly to your child's need for reassurance. By consistently responding to your child's nighttime needs, you are cementing your place in his life as the source of his peace. Living with a temporary period of your own sleep deprivation is a small price to pay for a lifetime connection between you and your child.

How long your child will continue to have night wakings is a very individual thing. Up to 47 percent of toddlers and 36 percent of preschoolers wake at least once per night and need an adult's help to fall back to sleep. So be patient.

Once your child is comfortable and secure, you can move on to the second phase of your sleep plan: working with your child to go to sleep easily and stay asleep all night without needing your aid. (Begin with the chapter Develop Your Sleep Plan.)

Ask for Help If You Need It

If your child doesn't appear to be sleeping well or if you are struggling with how to solve any bedtime or sleep-related problems, enlist the help of a counseling professional who specializes in adoption issues. A professional will be able to provide you with additional ideas and support.

Twins: Getting Two to Sleep

What is the best way to approach sleep issues when your children are twins?

Since children in general are alike in many ways, every topic in this book that applies to one child applies to your twins. The biggest issue, of course, is that you can't be in two places at once, and this creates a unique challenge. With knowledge and a plan, though, this is a challenge that you can meet and overcome.

Rely on Routines

Having a dependable bedtime routine and consistent sleep times is important for all children, but it can be especially important for parents of twins, who may already feel pulled in too many directions. A written routine, perhaps displayed as a bedtime poster (see page 114) can help guide your children through the nightly process and keep things running smoothly.

Where Should They Sleep?

Together, apart, same room, different rooms, parent's room? As I researched the best place for twins to sleep, I discovered something very interesting. Based on the experience of parents of twins and the expertise of numerous specialists, I could easily formulate a credible argument for just about *any* sleep arrangement. There are those parents who swear that separating twins from the start prevents them from waking each other up, and then those parents who adamantly insist that having twins sleep together allows them to comfort each other so they both sleep better. The bottom line: do what feels right to you and what works best for your children.

It's perfectly fine to experiment a bit. If your current sleeping situation isn't working, try something different for a month or so and see if a new arrangement works better. If it doesn't, try something else. You'll eventually find the right setup for your children. And don't be surprised if this changes over time. Be open to different sleep arrangements for naptime versus bedtime, too. Keep in mind that as your children get older, their preferences and sleep patterns will change, and it's fine to make adjustments as you go.

Mother-Speak

"What we found is that things change from time to time. At one point the girls will sleep together well; then they won't, so we separate them. Then after a time we start finding them in bed with each other again. My suggestion would be to have the most flexible furniture and room setups so you can make the necessary modifications throughout these transitions."

—Shahin, mother of six-year-old twins, Aria and Rose

What Shahin has learned with her children is very important: pay attention to your children's needs and be flexible as you apply what you learn. How well are your children sleeping? Do they have a preference about where they sleep? If you take your children's desires into consideration, and combine this with their sleep patterns and your own needs, then you can come up with the right solutions.

Maezi and Carli, twenty-two-month-old twins

Synchronizing Sleep Schedules

Twin children are two separate human beings, and each has individual sleep needs. To a certain extent you can't force them to adapt to a schedule just because it would work better for you. The good news, however, is that overall most children in the world have similar sleep needs at the same ages, and this can work in your favor.

In order to guide your children toward the same sleep/wake schedule, make your best effort to coordinate all aspects of their

Rebecca and Thomas, twins, twenty-two months old

daily schedules. They're more likely to respond well to the same bedtime if they wake up, eat, and lie down for an afternoon rest (even if it doesn't result in a nap) at the same time every day.

You can also encourage them to have the same sleep schedule by keeping their room dark during sleep times, brightly lit upon awakening, and by using white noise as a sleep cue and a way to mask outside sounds that could wake them.

Pick Your Battles

It may be most helpful if you take the time to review each of your children's sleep patterns individually and learn what the most important issues are. The forms beginning on page 19 will help you do this. While it would be wonderful to solve every sleep-related problem for both children at once, it might make more sense to choose first those that are most frustrating for you or that are most disruptive to your family. Once those things are solved, move on to the next.

You may want to complete separate forms and outline the details for each of your children. Then create two separate sleep plans; for each plan, think only of the one child for whom you are writing it out. Once you have the two plans, look at them together. How can you address both of their needs while taking into account that you don't have superhuman or magical powers?

Once you have an idea of a family plan, write it down. Create several phases so you have a map of direction. This will also help you celebrate small successes along the way and give you a glimpse of the night-light at the end of the tunnel.

Have Realistic Expectations

Everything is twice as challenging when you have twins, and their sleep issues can doubly affect your own precious sleep. If you are trying to run a perfect household and be a perfect parent, you'll surely set yourself up for disappointment. Take a good look at your daily schedule and adopt these guidelines for yourself:

- Relax your housekeeping standards or get help
- Say "No" more often to outside events that create family stress
- Ask for help from those willing to give it; accept help when it's offered
- Take care of yourself: eat right and exercise
- Give yourself credit for all the things you do right

Get Support

Quite a number of good books and magazines have been written about raising twins. There are also numerous support groups, both in person and online. Check into getting yourself some reading material and some personal support from other parents of twins. Keep in mind that while all parents of twins have that one particular thing in common, they have many different philosophies about child-rearing. Try to align yourself with like-minded parents. When you find support, it can mean the difference between struggling with your problems and being confident that everything you're facing is normal and that you can solve today's challenges.

Allergies, Asthma, and Gastroesophageal Reflux Disease (GERD)

Our son has a persistent night cough. He wakes up a few times a night, plus wakes us several more times because of his night noises. What could be the problem? What can be done to stop his coughing?

If a child has a condition that causes him physical discomfort or affects his breathing, it usually affects his sleeping too. Parents sometimes struggle with a child who doesn't sleep well or wakes frequently at night, without being aware that the cause is medical. Three of the most common culprits are allergies, asthma, and reflux (GERD). Unidentified and untreated medical problems can create ongoing disruption to a child's sleep.

What Are These Health Conditions?

Asthma

Asthma is a chronic disorder of the respiratory system. It causes swelling of the airway, making it difficult to breathe. There are various degrees of symptoms, and the frequency of these can range from daily episodes to occasional flare-ups. Asthma is the most common chronic disorder in children.

Allergies

An allergy is a susceptibility to a specific substance such as fur, dust, chemicals, pollen, or certain foods that causes a reaction such as cold-type symptoms or rash. Food allergy insomnia is a sleep disorder caused by a food intolerance that can be solved by identifying trigger foods and avoiding them. Allergies are common; they affect more than 20 percent of the population.

Gastroesophageal Reflux Disease

Gastroesophageal refers to the stomach and esophagus. *Reflux* means to return or flow back. Gastroesophageal reflux disease (GERD) is when the stomach's contents flow back up into the esophagus. A child with reflux suffers from heartburn-like pains, which will tend to be more uncomfortable when she is lying down for sleep. This makes it hard for her to both fall asleep and stay asleep.

What Are the Symptoms?

If you suspect that your child suffers from something more than normal childhood sniffles, it's wise to take note of all of your child's symptoms and talk over the list with a medical professional. In addition, if either parent has any of these conditions, it's possible that your child has them as well, since they are hereditary.

A list of the signs of allergies and asthma follows. Children may have one, two, or many of these symptoms:

- Runny nose or chronic nasal congestion
- Coughing, often at night
- Sniffling
- Sneezing

- Stuffy nose, especially upon waking
- Itchy eyes, ears, or nose
- Red or watery eyes; puffiness or discoloration around the eyes
- Frequent sore throat
- Wheezing, mouth-breathing, noisy breathing, or shortness of breath
- Snoring or snorting during sleep
- Tightness or pain in the chest
- Skin rash or itchiness
- Diarrhea
- Daytime sleepiness
- Insomnia
- Chronic ear infections
- An increase in these symptoms after contact with animals, being outside near plants and flowers, after running or vigorous play, or when exposed to cigarette smoke

Here are some of the common signs of reflux. Children may have one, two or many of these symptoms:

- Coughing or wheezing at night
- Frequent spitting up, drooling, or vomiting
- Frequent night waking
- Waking up crying or in pain
- Making burping and hiccuping sounds
- Bad breath
- Gagging or choking
- Drooling
- Constant runny nose
- Erosion of tooth enamel
- Recurrent ear infections, sinus infections, or sore throats
- Daytime sleepiness
- Insomnia
- Poor weight gain

Only a medical professional can tell if your child has allergies, asthma, or reflux, since many of the symptoms resemble those normally attributed to a cold, respiratory congestion, or other common childhood conditions, like teething. Symptoms can change, increase, or decrease over time. In addition, all three of these conditions have similar symptoms and can sometimes be misdiagnosed. If you suspect that your child may have any of these conditions, it's important to talk to your health care provider about your concerns. Tests can be performed to determine the source of your child's symptoms, and a variety of remedies are available.

It's best to avoid self-diagnosing your child or using over-the-counter medications, since many would not be appropriate for your child or could even cause harm or aggravate symptoms. A professional can direct you regarding making lifestyle changes, learning how to avoid the triggers that cause symptoms, and choosing between medication options.

If your child's sleep problems are related to a medical condition, it's important to have the situation correctly diagnosed and treated, because any sleep success will likely be difficult to achieve, negligible, or temporary. With proper treatment you can improve not only your child's sleep but his overall health as well. If symptoms continue after a diagnosis and treatment, explore the possibility of the child having one of the other conditions or an unidentified sleep disorder (see the section on sleep disorders on page 382).

Snoring: The Noisy Sleeper

My four-year-old occasionally snores at night. What causes this? Is it something I should be concerned about?

Most children snore from time to time, especially if they have a cold or stuffy nose. It's estimated that up to 20 percent of young children snore frequently, and about 10 percent snore every night. Snoring can run the gamut from minor, harmless noisy breathing to a symptom of a heath problem that needs to be addressed. For about 2 to 3 percent of children, snoring is an indication of a sleep disorder or a breathing problem that requires medical attention.

Why Snoring Happens

Snoring occurs when the soft tissues at the back of the throat relax during sleep and vibrate. A number of things can cause this condition:

- The airway being squeezed during a cold
- Excessive thickness of throat tissues
- Enlarged tonsils and adenoids
- Repeated exposure to secondhand cigarette smoke
- Health issues such as allergies, asthma, reflux (GERD), some neurological conditions, or sleep apnea

Sleep Apnea

If your child is a very restless, noisy sleeper, breathes through his mouth, and snores or snorts loudly, he may be suffering from a sleep condition called sleep apnea (obstructive sleep apnea syndrome, OSA, or OSAS). *Apnea* means "absence of breath." The most disturbing symptom of this sleep disorder is that the sleeper actually stops breathing for up to thirty seconds, occasionally longer, then takes a noisy breath. This is very frightening for a parent to witness and should be taken very seriously, but in general, it is not life threatening and can be treated. The main causes of sleep apnea include a narrow throat or airway, enlarged tonsils or lymph nodes, obesity, and facial abnormalities.

Not every child who snores has sleep apnea. Generally, however, if snoring is loud or combined with other symptoms, apnea could be the problem. Conversely, not all children with narrow airways, enlarged tonsils, or excess weight have sleep apnea.

Apnea can cause significant sleep deprivation and compound other sleep difficulties. *Continued untreated* apnea can cause heart problems, high blood pressure, slowed growth, hyperactive behavior, bed-wetting, and learning disabilities.

What Is the Cure?

The most common remedy for childhood sleep apnea is removal or reduction of the tonsils, adenoids, or both. Other typical treatments are enlarging the air passage, holding the passage open during sleep, or (when the condition is caused by obesity) weight loss.

When to Check with a Doctor

If any of the following describe your child, it would be wise to discuss your child's snoring and any other sleep symptoms with a medical professional. You should contact your pediatrician, a sleep clinic, or an ear, nose, and throat specialist if your child demonstrates any of the following:

- Snores almost every night
- Snores loudly
- Is a very restless, noisy sleeper, and breathes through his mouth
- Chokes, gasps, wheezes, or holds her breath in her sleep
- Appears to be tired even after a good night's sleep
- Sweats heavily during sleep
- Frequently wakes up with a headache
- Has a nasal sound to his voice and regularly breathes through his mouth

For more information, refer to the chapter When a Sleep Plan Doesn't Work.

Setbacks

Things had been going very well, and we enjoyed wonderful improvements in our child's sleep. Suddenly, though, we seem to be going backward. What's happening?

Oh the amazing twists, turns, and surprises of parenthood! Children grow and change from day to day; they can be unpredictable, irrational, illogical, and downright baffling at times. On any given day, just when you feel you've figured it all out, your child changes the whole scoop on you, sending you back to square one.

The journey to a good night's sleep is almost never a straight path. It's more like a dance: two steps forward, one step back, and even a few sidesteps in between. It's also as much a process of learning about your child as it is learning about sleep facts—and then applying what you've learned about both to bring about the best results.

You may have started out motivated to follow your plan entirely, and then life's challenges disrupted your efforts. Illness, vacations, visitors, schedule disruptions, the birth of a sibling, and teething are just a few examples. When these things happen and your child responds with difficulty falling asleep or numerous night wakings, you may find yourself giving up in the middle of the night and then berating yourself in the morning for abandoning your plan—an exercise in frustration that just adds tension and stress, which further prevent your success. But keep in mind that setbacks happen, and they happen to everyone.

Figure Out Why

When sleep setbacks occur, it can be helpful to try to identify the reasons, if you can. Check your child's gums for telltale signs of teething, review the changes that have occurred in your household, or do another log to pinpoint more clearly what's happening. If you can identify the issues, take steps to handle those things first and then return to your sleep plan. Sometimes you'll just be left scratching your head, unable to discern exactly what's up. If that's the case, simply start from the beginning and organize a sleep plan incorporating any of the solutions that have brought you success in the past or tying in something new that you may have missed before.

Is It Your Commitment That Has Had a Setback?

Sometimes you just won't have the time, the ability, or the heart to organize and follow your plan. You may realize that the reason that things were going so well before is that you were consistent. But now you've become lax with the bedtime routine, daily naps, or other details, and that's affecting your child's sleep. A recommitment to your plan is what you'll need to get back on the right track.

Is It Really a Setback?

Sometimes setbacks aren't really setbacks at all. Sometimes the only thing that needs adjustment is your expectation. Are you being realistic about what you expect from your child? Have you been comparing your child's sleep patterns to another child who happens to be a fabulous sleeper? Every human being is different, and patience is a parental requirement.

Are You Experiencing a New Problem?

Maybe what you're dealing with is not a setback at all but a brand-new problem. For example, both good sleepers and night wakers can be adversely affected by bouts of illness or teething, vacations, or schedule upsets. Perhaps his biology is dictating a switch from two daily naps to one or he's ready to give up naps entirely. So while it may seem like a step backward, it's just one of those side-steps that happen during your dance.

Do You Need to Refocus?

Have you taken the time to celebrate the sleep successes you've had so far? Sometimes being focused on the things that bother you will prevent you from seeing that overall, things really are changing for the better. Give yourself—and your child—a pat on the back for the good changes that are occurring.

Is Focusing on Sleep Problems Preventing Daily Joy?

At times your child may be having wonderful successes and leaps in development in other parts of his life, but you've become so focused on sleep issues that you're not open to enjoying those daily triumphs and delights that your child is demonstrating. Stop for a minute and smell the roses. If you've been too stressed about the sleep issues in your home, you may even want to back off your plan for a day or two, or even more, and catch your breath.

Should You Use This Time as a Running Start?

Regardless of the details or reasons for sleep setbacks, keep in mind that even if you only follow *part* of your plan, and even if you can't be 100 percent consistent, you will still see sleep *improvement*. Even a few changes in your routines and habits can bring better sleep. Then when things settle down around your house, you'll have a running start to really focus on your sleep plan. So take a deep breath, go back over all the successes that you have experienced, and slide through these inevitable setbacks. Have faith in yourself and confidence in your sleep plan: you will eventually achieve the goals you are reaching for.

Adjusting to Changes

We've finally mastered a bedtime routine. When we're at home, things go smoothly and according to plan. We completely lose our rhythm, though, whenever we have to be away from home or when something new or unusual is happening in the family. How do we help our little one adjust to these changes so that we don't mess up our sleep routines?

No matter how perfect your sleep routines are or how consistent you are in implementing them, you're bound to see an impact whenever something disrupts your usual pattern and flow. If you'll think about it, this is true for you, too. Most people find that their sleep is disrupted whenever they travel or deal with major life changes. The key is to aim for as close to a usual routine as possible, and then to relax and go with the flow. Once life settles back to normal, you can get back on track with sleep, as well. I'll go over some of the typical sleep-disrupters, and I'll give you a few pointers to help you through these bumps in your sleep plan.

Family Changes: Divorce, Marriage, Moving, Day Care, Sickness, and Other Life Events

Any major family change is likely to cause an increase in bedtime battles and disruptions to your child's sleep. The combination of stress, heightened emotions, disrupted schedules, and unfamiliar routines can wreak havoc on even the best sleeper's patterns. A number of things can help your child settle into any new life situation:

- Thoughtfully approach the changes to your child's routine, don't just let things happen and get swept along.
- Maintain as much of your child's original routines as possible. Consistency will help make the changes easier to adapt to.
- Delay any additional changes, such as potty-training, weaning, or moving to a toddler bed, until life has settled into a comfortable new pattern.
- Acknowledge those things that must change. Consider how to best orchestrate them to support your child's need to have consistent nap and nighttime routines.
- Create familiar environments wherever your child sleeps. If the change is due to a move, the organization of two separate households, or the start of day care, try to duplicate your child's sleeping place as closely as possible in the new location.
- Write down your child's naptime and bedtime routine, sleep-related issues, and sleep plan. Request that all caregivers approach sleep in the same way whenever possible. The more consistency there is from place to place, the more quickly your child will adapt to necessary changes.
- Encourage your child's attachment to a special lovey, such as a blanket or stuffed animal. Having one such item will give your child a feeling of security no matter where he is. You can read more about lovies in Tip 5 (page 73).
- Be patient. Your child may have an adjustment period of several weeks, a month, or even more, especially if she is sensitive to new situations. Some extra one-on-one attention and a few more daily cuddles can provide just what she needs to feel comfortable and get settled into new patterns.

- Once things have settled back to normal, review your bed-time routines and rituals and consistently follow them each night.

A New Baby in the House: Making Sleep Adjustments

Having one child is like having one child, but having two is like having five! And if they are both keeping you up at night, it can be more like having a *dozen*! Keeping an open mind, being flexible, and having realistic expectations can help you deal more easily with sleep issues during this transition period.

Consider those things that are disruptive to your sleep. Decide which are the most difficult or troubling issues for you. Determine which of these issues are the easiest to fix. Consider your own needs, those of your partner, and any necessary schedules. Take all of this into consideration as you work toward creating a new schedule. Don't try to fix everything at once, as that can be overwhelming.

Remember that this is a temporary stage—the first few months of having a new baby in the house are the most challenging. What is important for you to focus on is the creation of your new family. Make a mental adjustment to be flexible. Don't sweat the small stuff. Enlist the help of others when possible. Make it easy on yourself whenever you can. Stop adhering to other people's advice unless it meshes with your beliefs, and do what works for you.

Coordinate Sibling Routines

My older three children are close in age, so I remember what it was like to try to coordinate a new baby's nonschedule with two children's bedtime routines. The key to having success with this monumental task is *planning*. If you simply go with the flow, every night will be different, the kids will be going off in all directions, and you'll likely be stressed and unhappy. Once you've passed the initial transition period, take the time to consider each child's needs along with your own, and set a plan.

Like many families, I found that choosing a bedtime that came close to meeting all three children's actual needs and then arranging naptimes and mealtimes to support the chosen bedtime was most effective for me. I prepared snacks for three, put on three pairs of pajamas, brushed three mouthfuls of teeth (actually, two plus gums), and read bedtime stories with a child on each side and one nursing on my lap.

Other parents find that putting one child to bed at a time works best for them. Many report tag-teaming with a partner, each taking on one child's routine. Some talk of using a favorite video to keep an older child happy while putting the baby to sleep first.

No matter which method you choose, do *choose* a method. No rule says you must *forever* follow the path you decide on, though. This may vary once you've figured out what works best or may change over time as your children get older. No matter what, it does help to keep your sense of humor, to keep your eye on the important things in life, and to grab a nap whenever you can.

Weaning Time: Saying Good-Bye to the Nighttime Bottle

Weaning from a bottle isn't only about a method of feeding. It's about saying good-bye to a part of babyhood, a familiar comfort object, and very likely, an important part of your child's sleep-time ritual. Because of this, weaning shouldn't be something that happens suddenly. The cold-turkey approach may only confuse your child and make both of you miserable. A more loving and gradual process is much easier on your child and on you, too.

Many people find that daytime weaning is the easiest step in the process because of the distraction of daytime activities and the available substitution of food and drinking cups. Weaning from the naptime and nighttime bottles is often the more challenging part of weaning. The following tips may help when weaning your child from a sleep-time bottle:

- Add a little water to each nightly bottle over a period of weeks until it becomes 100 percent water. The water is less enticing than milk or juice so your child will likely use it less, and when he does use it, it will be fine: there won't be any concern about tooth decay.
- Substitute a smaller bottle by switching to a four-ounce version or a fancy style that holds less fluid. Once your child is accustomed to the smaller bottle, fill it only three-quarters full, then half. You can also use the previous idea of watering down the milk or juice.
- Replace the bottle with a pacifier or teething toy.
- Try offering your child a cup at the times he normally would have a bottle, or give him both: use the cup for milk and the bottle for water.
- Provide your child with a snack and something to drink right before he gets ready for bed. If his tummy is full, he may be less interested in a bottle of milk or juice. Then at bedtime, offer a bottle or sippy cup of water only.
- Revise your bedtime routine so that you avoid the usual places and situations where your child typically has a bottle. For example, read bedtime stories in a new location, such as sitting on the sofa. Use distraction and a new routine that leaves out the bottle.

- Try the family bestseller idea from page 117.
- Be patient. Some children take longer to wean from the nighttime bottle than others. If the issue becomes a frustration for both of you, take a month or two off from the weaning effort and then try again.

Helping Your Child Give Up the Pacifier

Some professionals recommend weaning a child from the pacifier by age one as a preventive measure, with the argument that the older the child gets, the more attached to the pacifier he will become. Others advise that in the absence of developing dental or speech problems, you can wait until your child is two or three years old, or even older, since you can then use reasoning along with an incentive chart or distraction. Most professionals are less concerned about pacifier use if it is used only at bedtime and not an all-day habit. In the end, the decision is yours. You know your child better than anyone else does. When no medical issues are involved, only you can accurately assess what role the pacifier plays in your child's life and in her sleep, and how you can best wean her from it. Here are a few ideas for getting the process going when you're ready to start weaning:

- Unless there is a specific reason why you must take away your child's pacifier, it's best to do it slowly but surely. Try to choose a time when no other major changes are happening in your child's life, such as the birth of a sibling, potty-training, starting day care, or moving.
- It can help to begin by making the pacifier scarce except during critical times, such as when your child is hurt or falling asleep.

- Use distraction as your chief weapon during the day. When your toddler asks for her pacifier, first try to distract her: sing a song, give her a toy, or go for a walk to get her focused on something other than her sucking urge.
- Gradually reduce your child's use by keeping the pacifiers in her bed or only in certain areas of the house. Some families have a "no pacifiers downstairs" or "only in your car seat" rule.
- Give your child an alternative to help soothe her when she feels upset or tired. A cuddle, blanket, stuffed animal, or favorite toy may comfort her instead of the pacifier.
- Establish new bedtime routines that are different from usual so that the cues for pacifier use aren't as evident. For example, if your child typically is rocked with a pacifier, move your prebedtime routine to the sofa or bed instead. If she usually sucks during the bedtime story, offer a sippy cup of water or teething toy instead.
- If your child falls asleep with a pacifier in his mouth and then wakes crying for it during the night, you can wean him of this need by using Pantley's Gentle Removal Plan described on page 171.
- Some children embrace the idea of a Pacifier Fairy. She, of course, collects pacifiers left under the pillow by children who no longer need them and leaves wonderful toys behind in their place.

Trips, Vacations, and Sleepovers

There can be tremendous fun and memory making when you travel with your children, but keep in mind that even the best-laid plans can be disrupted. It's best to get organized as much as possible in advance, but then try to stay relaxed, accept changes, and go with the flow during travel and your vacation.

In the hustle that precedes a trip, it can be easy to *let* things happen, instead of *make* things happen. Be proactive in making your trip decisions in regard to all the details, including sleep-related issues. Contemplating the following questions and coming up with the right answers can help make your trip more successful:

- Does your child sleep well in the car? If yes, plan your travel time to coincide with a nap or bedtime so your child can sleep through part of the journey. If not, plan to leave immediately after a nap or upon waking in the morning. Don't fool yourself into thinking your child will behave differently than usual just because it's a special occasion. If your child sleeps well in his car seat, dress him comfortably, take off his shoes, and give him a blanket. He'll likely fall asleep to the hum and vibration of the ride. If you have a finicky sleeper, plan your trip during the daytime hours and bring along plenty of toys and activities to keep your child happy.
- Is it necessary to make the trip all at once, or can you break it up with stops along the way? The longer your child is strapped in her seat, the more likely she'll become fussy and the less likely she'll sleep when you need her to. Planning a few breaks can give her the activity and exercise necessary to bring on tiredness. If you're on a long airplane or train voyage, use the hallways for walks when your child gets antsy.
- Do you have everything you need to make sleep during the trip possible? Include items like:
  - Window shades to help create a darker, nap-inducing atmosphere
  - A cooler for cold drinks; a bottle warmer if needed
  - Your child's favorite blanket, pillow, stuffed animals, and pajamas

- Music, lullabies, or white noise on tape or CD
- A rearview car mirror to keep on eye on your child (unless a second person will be sitting with your little one)
- Books to read to your child
- Adult audiobooks or quiet music to use during the times when your child is sleeping
- A battery-operated night-light or flashlight if you'll be traveling in the dark

Sleeping in an Unfamiliar Place

Preparation is the key to the tricky issue of getting your child to sleep in an unfamiliar place. Obviously, you can't use the exact same routines that work for you at home, but you can follow much of your usual routine and you may be able to create a *similar* sleep setting for your child. If your little one sleeps in a crib, for example, you may want to bring along a portable folding crib and ask if you can set it up in a bedroom. (Let your child sleep in it a few times at home so that it's familiar.) Bring along your child's typical crib-mates, such as his blanket, crib sheets, pillow, stuffed animals, lullaby tape, or white-noise clock. Pack a night-light to make middle-of-the-night potty runs and diaper changes easier, and so that you can avoid turning on bright lights at night and disrupting sleep cycles. Your night-light can also be used during the tucking-in process.

For co-sleepers, your first order of business is to create a safe sleeping place for your child. Check out the room where you will be sleeping, and look at the furniture placement. If you know that pushing the bed against the wall, moving a dresser, or replacing a fluffy comforter with a blanket would make the situation safer, then politely explain to your host. Let her know that you'll move things back before you leave (and then remember to do so). If you're staying in a hotel, the housekeeping staff will often help with this if you ask politely.

Remember that many daily cues help keep sleep consistent. Serving meals of familiar foods at regular times, exposing your child to daylight in the morning and keeping things dimly lit at night, and avoiding prebedtime wrestling matches can all help keep bedtime and sleep time more natural.

Traveling the Zones: What to Do About Jet Lag

Traveling with a young child can be a challenge because of the disruption to the daily routine, the excitement of activity, plus anxiety over meeting new people and adjusting to new surroundings. When you add a leap across time zones, you complicate matters even more, since your child's biological clock (which tells him when to feel awake and when to feel tired) is forced out of sync with the clock on the wall and the day's activities. If you're already struggling with sleep issues, you'll likely find that travel of any kind intensifies your dilemma. Because of this, the very first and most important rule is *be flexible and be patient*. A few other tips may help your child overcome jet lag more quickly:

- Keep your child well-hydrated with plenty of water, milk, juice, or breastfeeding sessions. Have plenty of healthy, nonsugary snacks in your carry-on bag. Don't use any over-the-counter products such as those designed for jet lag, sleep aids, or antihistamines without your doctor's specific approval and instructions. Many of these can be harmful to young children.
- Switch to the new time once you've arrived in your destination or even on the trip over. Powerful biological cues, such as the timing of meals and naps, plus exposure to day-

light and darkness will help all of you adjust to the change in time more quickly.

- Avoid letting your child take excessively long naps at the wrong times. This will just prolong the adjustment. Keep naps to their regular length and wake your child gently. Typically, the excitement of the new environment will ease him out of sleep.
- Watch the time. It's easy to miss mealtimes, naptimes, and bedtime when you're on vacation yourself. If you stick to your child's usual pattern, however, you'll be able to avoid any major meltdowns from a hungry, overtired child.
- Keep in mind that no matter what you do, it will take a few days to find a new rhythm. Don't over-schedule your first few days, if possible. To avoid the temper tantrums and fussiness of an out-of-sync child, give him a day or two to adjust to the new time zone before embarking on a full schedule of activities.

Part IV

Family Sleep: Safe and Sound

Adult Sleep:
Now It's Your Turn

While many sleep issues disappear with childhood, a whole new crop of problems can arise in adulthood. In addition, having a child who doesn't sleep well and who disrupts your sleep regularly can exacerbate your own sleep problems or create new sleep troubles for you. Once you feel you have a handle on your child's sleep issues and you've seen some success with your solutions, you may want to take some time to improve your own sleep.

What's Happening?

You may have even gotten into the habit of waking up during the night, so now, even when your child sleeps, you're up. It has probably been a long time since you've had a full night's sleep. Almost certainly even longer than you realize! Many parents actually forget what their sleep patterns were like before children entered their lives. Many assume that they used to get eight straight hours consistently and without interruption. In reality, though, at least half of all adults have trouble sleeping—falling asleep and staying asleep. In other words, if you weren't sleeping like a log before children entered your home, you won't be sleeping like a log now, even if your children are.

There's another aspect to your current sleep situation to consider. As people age, the amount of sleep they need and the amount of sleep they get tend to decline, and sleep problems increase. Studies by the National Sleep Foundation have acknowledged how the ebb and flow of hormones have an impact on sleep. In their studies, 43 percent of women reported disturbed sleep during the week *before* their period; 71 percent reported sleep problems *during* their period. In addition, 79 percent of women reported sleep problems during pregnancy.

According to sleep experts, it's not only age or hormones but also the stresses of adult life that contribute to sleep problems. Add all of these situations together and there seem to be few nights when adult sleep is not disrupted for some reason.

So now you know *the rest of the story*. You can't blame *all* your nighttime problems on parenthood!

How to Get a Good Night's Sleep

Just as it does for your child, the quality and quantity of your sleep can affect your entire life. Getting adequate, restful sleep is essential to your health and well-being, and adds to your ability to be a good parent. Everyone has different sleep requirements. Let your own body tell you what it needs, and listen to it.

Following are a few helpful tips for improving adult sleep. Sift through the list, and use as many as you wish. Applying even one or two of these suggestions should prove helpful. Review the ideas, check off the ones that appeal to you, and create your *own* plan for healthy sleep.

Stop Worrying About Sleep

In cruel irony, lying in bed worrying because you can't fall or stay asleep will just keep you awake. So relax. Turn your clock away from your bed, and don't agonize over whether you are sleeping or not. You can't force yourself to sleep by fretting about it. The best you can do is to establish good sleeping habits and follow them nightly.

As a busy parent, you may be compounding your problem by worrying that your sleep time is taking up productive time that you should be spending doing other things. You either get yourself to bed much too late or lie in bed and feel guilty about it, thinking about all those other things you "should" be doing. Give yourself permission to sleep. It's necessary for your body, important for your health, and good for your soul. Remember that your child will benefit if you are well rested, too, because you'll be a happier parent. And if you're breastfeeding or pregnant, your improved sleep will be beneficial to both you and your children.

Set Your Body Clock

Just as it does for your child, the consistency of your sleep schedule sets your biological clock and makes it work for you. If your bedtime and awake time are different every day, the effectiveness of this amazing gift of nature is undermined—your clock is out of sync. You'll find yourself tired or alert at inappropriate times, sometimes feeling as if you could fall asleep standing up during the day, but then lying wide awake in bed at night.

This explains why many people have trouble waking up on Monday morning. If you have specific wake and sleep times during the week, you probably find that by Friday morning you are waking up just before your alarm goes off and on Friday night it's an effort to stay awake during the late-night movie. Then come Monday morning, you're groggy and exhausted when your morning alarm goes off. What has happened is that by the end of the week, your biological clock has taken control because of your consistent wake/sleep schedule during the week. But come the weekend, you push your bedtime later, and if you're lucky enough to

Steve and Nikole, three years old

manage it, you sleep late in the morning as well. This effectively cancels the setting on your biological clock, and by Monday you have to start all over again.

This imbalance is an easy one to fix. Choose a specific bedtime and time to wake up for yourself, and stick to it as closely as possible, seven days a week. Obviously, your busy life will alter this routine sometimes. You can deviate from your plan once in a while without doing too much to upset things. But on the whole, if you adhere to your schedule as consistently as possible, your sleep will be more refreshing and you'll be more energetic and alert. Your body clock will function as it should, allowing you to tick through your day productively and wind down at night calmly.

Naturally, a few lucky people can function perfectly with a varying sleep schedule, but they're the exception. Most people are helped immensely by this simple, effective suggestion.

Get Organized

When your days are hectic and disorganized, your stress level increases; the natural physiological and emotional responses to this stress hamper your ability to sleep. So you can attack this kind of sleeplessness by getting at the root of it: become more organized and purposeful during the day.

A formal daily to-do list or calendar can help you feel more in control of your days. With the myriad critical details of each day written down, you'll be able to relax somewhat. Think of it as moving all the dates, times, and tasks out of your head and onto paper, freeing up a little breathing room upstairs. Keep a pad and a pen near your bed in case an important idea or task *does* pop into your mind as you're trying to drift off. Write it down—then *let it go until morning.*

Avoid Caffeine Late in the Day

Here's an interesting tidbit: caffeine stays in your bloodstream between six and fourteen hours! The caffeine in that after-dinner cup of coffee is still hanging around in your system at midnight and beyond. Caffeine contains a chemical that causes hyperactivity and wakefulness, which is why many people find their morning coffee so stimulating. Tolerance levels for caffeine vary; so you'll need to experiment and find out how much you can drink and how late you can drink it without disrupting your sleep.

If you are a nursing mother, watch your child carefully to see if she, too, is being affected by caffeine. While no study has proved the connection between caffeine and a nursling's sleeplessness, it is known that diet affects the quality, quantity, and palatability of breast milk—so such a connection is very possible.

Keep in mind that caffeine is an ingredient in more than just coffee but that each substance has different levels of caffeine. Coffee and cola have the most caffeine. Black tea has about half that of coffee, and green tea has even less. Some other soft drinks (even root beer and orange pop—check the labels), chocolate, and some over-the-counter painkillers contain it, albeit in smaller amounts.

Quit Smoking

If you are a smoker and you don't sleep well, there may be a connection between the two. Studies show that on the average, smokers take longer to fall asleep, wake up more often during the night, and have more bouts of insomnia. Smokers are also more likely to have breathing problems that disrupt their sleep.

If you want to improve your health day and night, and make yourself a good role model for your child, consider taking the steps to quit.

Watch Out for the Effects of Drugs and Alcohol

If you are taking any medication, ask your doctor or pharmacist if it has any side effects. People often are aware of what medications make them drowsy, but they don't realize that some have the opposite effect and act as a stimulant.

Likewise, an evening glass or two of wine or beer usually won't affect sleep and might bring it on. But more than that can have a rebound effect, causing an episode of insomnia a few hours later, in the middle of the night. Alcohol also can disturb the *quality* of your sleep, making it shallow and disrupting normal dream cycles.

Make Exercise a Part of Your Day

Fitting regular exercise into your day has many benefits, and improved sleep is at the top of the list. Many studies have shown that moderate, regular exercise reduces insomnia and improves the quality of sleep.

The key to using exercise to improve sleep is to maintain a regular pattern: thirty to forty-five minutes of moderate aerobic exercise three to five times a week. For best results, make sure you complete your exercise at least three hours before bedtime; exercise leaves most people too energized for sleep right after. (Once again, there are exceptions. Some people find that strenuous exercise helps them fall asleep quickly soon afterward. Experiment to learn if this applies to you.)

Make Your Environment Favorable to Sleep

Take a good look at your bedroom and make sure that it is conducive to relaxation and healthy sleep. Every person is different, but here's a checklist for you to review:

- **Comfort.** Is your mattress comfortable to you? Does it provide the amount of support that you need? Do you like your blanket or comforter, or is it a source of aggravation in the night? Is your pillow the right softness and thickness? Do you find its material cozy and soothing? Do what you can to improve these details.
- **Temperature.** If you are too cold or too hot during sleep, you will wake frequently. Experiment until you find the best temperature. If your partner or co-sleeping children have different preferences, find a way to please everyone by changing the type of pajamas you wear, using a fan, or piling on extra blankets.
- **Noise.** Some people sleep better in perfect silence, while some prefer background music or white noise. Again, if one sleeper likes noise, but others sleep better with silence, experiment: try earplugs or a personal headset for music or sound.
- **Light.** If you sleep better in complete darkness, cover your windows. If you like light, open the blinds or use a night-light. (Be

cautious about using lights during the night if you wake up to use the bathroom or tend your children. Bright light will fool your biological clock into thinking it is morning.) Here again, if your partner likes the blinds open and you or your children sleep better with them shut, find a compromise. You might buy yourself a soft eye mask made just for that purpose or leave the blinds open on one side of the room, closed on the other—facing the closed window will give you more of a sense of darkness.

• **Activity.** Many people use their beds for varied activities, from watching television to catching up on work on their laptop computer. If you can designate your bed for reading, sex, and sleeping only, you will create a better association between your bed and sleep.

Have Your Own Bedtime Routine

Ideally, you have implemented a successful bedtime routine to help your child sleep better. This same idea can work for you, too. Often, we parents have a very pleasant routine for putting our children to bed. After that relaxing hour, when we have just about fallen to sleep reading the bedtime story, we jam into high gear and rush about the house tending to all those duties that await our attention until we look up and—oh *no!* It's midnight!

Your own prebedtime routine can greatly improve your ability to fall asleep and stay asleep. It can include anything that relaxes you, such as reading, listening to music, or sitting down to enjoy a cup of tea. Avoid stimulating your mind or body in the hour before bed. Tasks like answering your e-mail, doing heavy housecleaning, or watching television can keep you awake long after you've finished them.

If possible, try to keep the lights dim in the hour before bed, as bright light strongly signals your body to leap into daytime action.

Lower lights and quieter sounds will help prepare you for a good night's sleep.

Eat Right and Eat Light Before Sleep

You will sleep best with your stomach neither too full nor too empty. A large meal can make you feel tired but will keep your body working to digest it, thus disturbing sleep. An empty stomach can keep you up with hunger pains. A happy medium is usually best. Have a light snack about an hour or two before bedtime. Lists of the best nighttime food choices are listed on page 81.

Encourage Relaxation and the Onset of Sleep

Often, when we lie in bed waiting for sleep, our mind and body are primed for action. The wheels are turning and our thoughts keep us awake. A helpful method for bringing on sleep is to focus your mind on peaceful, relaxing thoughts. Here are a few ways to accomplish this:

- Repeat a familiar meditation or prayer to release the mind from daily action and prime it for sleep. Yoga stretches can help relax your muscles.
- Focus on your breathing while repeating the word *relax* in a slow pattern tied to your exhales. Or imagine your breathing is moving in and out along with a wave at the beach.
- Use progressive relaxation to coax all the parts of your body to relax. Begin at your feet. Feel the weight of your feet, have them go limp and relaxed, and then imagine that they have warmth moving over them. Then progress to your right leg, repeat the process. Move on to your left leg, and continue on up to your head. (Most people are asleep or nearly asleep by the time they get that far!)

Nap Appropriately

If you're a person who likes to nap and who *can* nap during the day, go right ahead. Choose the time when you have your normal dip in energy, usually mid-afternoon. Keep your naps brief—ten to thirty minutes to achieve the best benefits. Naps that are too long or too late in the day will create insomnia at bedtime.

Pay Attention to Your Own Health

If you have chronic insomnia or other sleep problems, or other health problems, be smart: see a health care professional.

Sleeping-Safety Checklists

The following safety information comes from a wide variety of reputable sources and authorities, including the Consumer Product Safety Commission (CPSC), the National SAFE Kids Campaign, and the American Academy of Pediatrics (AAP). Please read over this section, and give it serious consideration. Keep in mind that these lists cover safety issues relating to the *bedroom* and *sleep at home*. You should, of course, be aware of many other safety issues—at home and away. Also, because safety precautions are updated constantly, and because all children and their families are different, no checklist is fully complete and appropriate for every household. Do your homework, and please, *put safety first*.

General Sleeping-Safety Precautions for All Families

- Do not use large, heavy blankets or comforters under or over your child, as these can entangle him or become a suffocation hazard. Instead, dress your child in warm sleeper pajamas layered with an undershirt when the temperature warrants them, and use small child-sized blankets. Have your child use a firm child-sized pillow (for children over eighteen months old).
- Keep the bedroom at a comfortable sleeping temperature, usually between 65°F and 72°F (18°C to 22°C). Be careful not to let your child get overheated or chilled.
- Do not allow anyone to smoke around your child. This holds true whether your child is asleep or awake. Children exposed

to secondhand smoke face an increased risk of health complications, such as sleep apnea, allergies, and asthma.

- Dress your child in flame-resistant or snug-fitting sleepwear, not oversize, loose-fitting cotton clothing. Billowy or cotton fabrics pose a burn hazard in case of fire.
- Do not allow your child to sleep on a very soft sleeping surface such as a pillow, water bed, beanbag chair, foam pad, feather bed, or any other flexible surface. Young children should sleep only on a firm, flat mattress, with a smooth, wrinkle-free sheet that stays securely fastened around the mattress.
- Keep night-lights, lamps, and all electrical items away from where your child sleeps.
- Make sure you have a working smoke detector in your child's sleeping room, and check it as often as the manufacturer suggests. Have a carbon monoxide alarm in the home if necessary. Replace batteries as recommended.
- Do not put a child to sleep near a window, window blinds, cords, or draperies.
- Keep your child's regular appointments for checkups. If your child is sick or feverish, call your doctor or hospital promptly.
- Never shake or hit your child. (Child abuse often occurs when a parent is sleep-deprived and at the end of the rope. If you feel like you may lose your temper with your child, put your child in a safe place or with another caregiver, and go take a breather.)
- Never tie a pacifier to your child with a string, ribbon, or cord, as any of these can become wound around your child's finger, hand, or neck.
- Follow all safety precautions when your child is sleeping away from home, whether in a car seat, stroller, or unfamiliar place.
- Never leave a child unattended while in a stroller, child seat, swing, or car seat.

- Never leave a pet with access to a sleeping toddler. Use caution when inviting a pet into bed with a preschooler.
- Learn how to perform cardiopulmonary resuscitation (CPR). Be sure that all other caregivers for your child are also trained in CPR.
- If your child spends time with a child-care provider, babysitter, grandparent, or anyone else, insist that safety guidelines are followed in that environment also.
- Keep your child's environment clean. Wash bedding often. Wash your hands after diapering your child and before preparing food. Wash your child's hands and face frequently.
- Pay attention to your own health and well-being.

General Safety Precautions for Cradles and Cribs

- Make certain your child's crib meets all federal safety regulations, industry standards, and guidelines of the CPSC's most recent recommendations (cpsc.gov). Look for a safety certification seal. Avoid using an old or used crib.
- Make sure the mattress fits tightly to the crib, without gaps on any side. (If you can fit more than two fingers between the mattress and side of the crib, the mattress does not fit properly.)
- Make certain that your crib sheets fit securely and cannot be pulled loose by your child, which may create a dangerous tangle of fabric. Do not use plastic mattress covers or any plastic bags near the crib.
- Remove any decorative ribbons, bows, or strings. If you use bumper pads, make certain they surround the entire crib and that they are secured in many places—at a minimum, at

each corner and in the middle of each side. Tie securely and cut off dangling string ties.

- Remove bumper pads before your child is old enough to get up on his hands and knees, so that these pads are not used for climbing out of the crib. If your child can pull himself to stand, make sure the mattress is on the lowest possible setting. Also, inspect the area around the crib to make sure no dangers await him if he does climb out of the crib. When your child is capable of climbing out, it's time to change to a floor mattress or bed.
- Be certain that all screws, bolts, springs, and other hardware and attachments are tightly secured, and check them from time to time. Replace any broken or missing pieces immediately. (Contact the manufacturer for replacement parts.) Make sure your crib has a sturdy bottom and wide, stable base so it does not wobble or tilt when your child moves around. Check to see that all slats are in place, firm, and stable—and that they are spaced no more than 2⅜ inches (60 millimeters) apart.
- Make sure that corner posts do not extend more than ¹⁄₁₆ inch (1½ millimeters) above the top of the end panel. Don't use a crib that has decorative knobs on the corner posts, or headboard and footboard designs that present a hazard, such as sharp edges, points, or pieces that can be loosened or removed. Always raise the side rail and lock it into position. Make sure your child cannot operate the drop-side latches.
- Don't hang objects over a sleeping or unattended child— that includes mobiles and other crib toys. There is a risk of the toy falling on your child or of your child reaching up and pulling the toy down into the crib.
- If you are using a portable crib, make sure the locking devices are properly and securely locked.

- Make sure your child is within hearing distance of your bed or that you have a reliable baby monitor turned on.
- Check the manufacturer's instructions on suggested size and weight limits for any crib. If there is no tag on the crib, call or write the manufacturer for this information.
- Make sure that any crib your child sleeps in when away from home meets all of the preceding safety requirements.

General Safety Precautions for Co-Sleeping

If your child sleeps with you, or any adult or other child, either for naps or at nighttime, you should adhere to the following safety guidelines:

- Your bed must be absolutely safe for your child. The best choice for toddlers is to place the mattress on the floor, making sure there are no crevices that your child can become wedged in. Make certain your mattress is flat, firm, and smooth. Do not allow your child to sleep on a soft surface such as a water bed, beanbag chair, or any other flexible surface.
- Make certain that your fitted sheets stay secure and cannot be pulled loose.
- If your bed is raised off the floor, use guardrails to prevent your child from rolling off the bed, and be especially careful that there is no space between the mattress and headboard or footboard.
- If your bed is placed against a wall or against other furniture, check every night to be sure there is no space between the mattress and wall or furniture where your child could become stuck.
- Use a large mattress to provide ample room for everyone's movement.

- Consider a sidecar arrangement in which the child's crib, bed, or mattress sits beside or close to your bed.
- Make certain that the room your child sleeps in, and any room she might have access to, is child-safe. (Imagine your child crawling out of bed as you sleep to explore the house. Even if she has not done this—yet—you can be certain she eventually will!)
- Do not ever sleep with your child if you have been drinking alcohol, if you have used any drugs or medications, if you are an especially sound sleeper, or if you are suffering from sleep deprivation and find it difficult to awaken.
- Do not sleep with your toddler if you are a large person, as a parent's excess weight has been determined to pose a risk to a child in a co-sleeping situation. Examine how you and your child settle in next to each other. If your child rolls toward you, if there is a large dip in the mattress, or if you suspect any other dangerous situations, play it safe and move your child to a bedside crib or his own bed.
- Use caution regarding pillows and blankets. Blankets shouldn't be too large or heavy. Pillows shouldn't be too large, deep, or soft. Keep in mind that body heat will add warmth during the night. Make sure your child doesn't become overheated.
- Do not wear any night clothes with strings or long ribbons. Don't wear jewelry to bed, and if your hair is long, put it up.
- Do not allow pets to sleep in bed with your toddler, and use caution when inviting a pet into bed with your preschooler.
- Never leave your child alone in an adult bed unless that bed is perfectly safe for your child, such as a mattress on the floor in a childproof room, and you are nearby or listening in on your child with a reliable child monitor.

Bunk Bed Safety

- Never allow a child under six years of age to sleep in an upper bunk.
- Make sure the mattress is the proper size for the bed and that there is no space between the mattress and headboard or footboard.
- Use a bunk bed with high guardrails that surround the top level (all four sides) and that are screwed, bolted, or otherwise firmly attached to the bed. If all sides are not protected, add extra guards yourself. (Use those designed to accommodate this kind of use, such as fabric bolsters or additional boards. Don't use bed rails that require a box spring for stability.) Make sure your child cannot slip through the space between the guardrails.
- Do not place a bunk bed without side rails next to a wall as a child can become trapped between the two.
- Make sure the cross ties under the mattress are secure and can't fall out.
- Purchase a bed with an easy-to-use ladder, and if possible, have your child try it out while you watch and gauge her ability to climb the ladder.
- Teach children to use only the ladder to go up and down from the top bunk and to never jump from the upper bunk.

Childproofing Checklist for the Bedroom

Imagine your child exploring the bedroom alone. Even if your child is sleeping in your bedroom, she could be up and about while you sleep. Is everything perfectly safe? Use this checklist to be sure.

- Install childproof covers over electrical outlets.
- Secure any furniture to prevent it from tipping. This includes all dressers and bookcases. (See meghanshope.org/cms for more information.)
- Use corner bumpers on sharp furniture edges.
- Keep curtain and blind cords out of reach.
- Use a childproof night-light that is cool to the touch.
- Install childproof latches on drawers that contain toiletries, solutions, or potential choking hazards, or keep these things secured in another room.
- Use wire guards or safety covers for electrical cords.
- Keep houseplants out of reach.
- Keep cribs and furniture away from windows.
- Use open toy boxes or those with child-safe lids.
- Keep large, heavy objects and enticing toys off high shelves.
- Do not use an electric blanket or electric heating pad with a young child.
- Install window guards. (Screens do not prevent accidents.)
- Do away with any removable plastic or rubber ends from doorstops.
- Use a monitor, intercom, or a bell on the door so that you know if your child leaves the bedroom.
- Keep all small toys and potential choking hazards out of the bedroom.
- Use a Tot Finder window sticker on the outside of the window to alert firefighters that it is a child's bedroom. (These are available through fire departments or safety catalogs.)
- Don't use bunk beds for children under six years old.
- Have a fire-escape ladder for rooms above the first story.
- Block stairways with childproof gates.
- Consider hiring a specialized company to help you childproof your home.

When a Sleep Plan Doesn't Work: Analyzing Problems and Identifying Sleep Disorders

We've followed some of the ideas from this book for two months, but our child's sleep problems have hardly improved at all. Are we doing something wrong, or could our child have a real sleep disorder?

It is possible that making changes in your approach will bring sleep success, but it is also possible that your child has a sleep disorder that must be addressed before you can have that success. The best place to start is to think about what has happened since you began working on your child's sleep issues. Since you and I can't sit down over a cup of coffee or tea and talk about your child (wouldn't that be nice!), I've created this chapter to help you figure out what parts of your plan are working, which parts need to be changed, and ways to find out if there really is a sleep disorder standing in your way. Start by using the information from your logs (pages 19–21) to complete the comparison chart on the next page. Fill in the information from both logs and the amount of change that has taken place since you've begun.

Then take a few minutes to answer the following questions. Doing so will help you analyze what's happening. If you can, it may be helpful to talk over the information with your spouse, parenting partner, or someone else you trust. You may even want to search out a group of parents and create a support group—either in person, by e-mail, or through a message board. The support of other parents who are going through the same things that you are right now can be very helpful and enlightening. (Check my website for a list of support groups or to list your new group.)

Comparison Chart

	First log	Current	Amount of change
Number of naps			
Length of naps			
Bedtime: Asleep time			
Morning: Awake time			
Number of awakenings			
Longest sleep span			
Total hours of sleep			

Questions to Help You Analyze Your Child's Sleep Situation

Since you've started, how closely have you followed your plan?

- ☐ I followed all parts of my plan exactly.
- ☐ I followed some parts of my plan but not everything.
- ☐ I started out great but reverted back to my old habits.
- ☐ Plan? What plan? (Oops, better start over and make a plan!)

Have you seen positive changes in at least one area (for example: a thirty-minute increase in naptime or sleep span, an earlier bedtime, a reduction in the number of night wakings)? _____

What area(s) shows the most change? _____

_____

Why do you think that's true? (What have you done to influence this? What solutions have brought about the change?) ____

_____

_____

What area(s) shows the least change? _____

_____

Why do you think that's true? (Have you done anything to influence this? What solutions have you applied to this situation?)

_____

_____

What have you learned about your child's sleep habits? _____

_____

_____

What parts of your plan seem to be having the best influence on your child's sleep? _____

_____

_____

Are there areas that you've not addressed with specific solutions? What sections from the book do you think you should incorporate into your plan? _____

_____

_____

How are you going to make these changes? What solutions are you going to add to your plan? How can you approach this to consistently adhere to your plan? _____

_____

_____

Could It Be a Sleep Disorder?

Do you feel that your sleep plan has been clear, specific, and accurately targeted? Do you feel that you've been committed and consistent in following the plan you've created? Despite all this, does your child continue to have sleep-related problems? If this is the case, it is possible that there is an underlying sleep disorder or medical reason that your child isn't sleeping well. About 10 percent of children have a true sleep disorder, and their sleep problems cannot be solved without it being identified and treated.

A sleep disorder is a physiological condition that disturbs sleep, and some studies show that almost 90 percent of sleep disorders go undiagnosed and untreated. When a sleep disorder is correctly identified and treated, however, then a child—and the parents—can all get a good night's sleep.

Signs That Your Child May Have a Sleep Disorder

The following is a list of symptoms associated with the more common children's sleep disorders. These may also indicate a health problem, such as asthma, allergies, or reflux (page 335); plus, these conditions can create or exacerbate sleep problems. A review of these indicators can help you decide if you should seek medical advice about your child's health and sleep. Determine if any of these apply to your child:

- Snores almost every night
- Snores loudly
- Is a very restless, noisy sleeper
- Often breathes through the mouth during sleep
- Chokes, snorts, gasps, wheezes, or holds his breath in his sleep
- Has a persistent night cough
- Frequently has trouble falling asleep even when tired
- Wakes up every hour or two during the night and a sleep plan has not made an improvement
- Appears to be tired or lethargic even after a good night's sleep
- Sweats heavily during sleep
- Has frequent and intense night terrors or nightmares
- Sleeps in strange or contorted positions
- Frequently wakes up with a headache, heartburn, or sore throat
- Has a nasal sound to her voice and regularly breathes through her mouth
- Uses the toilet confidently during the day but is over six years old and is a chronic bed-wetter (Night wetting under age six is usually due to normal immature bladder control.)
- Is difficult to awaken even after a full night's sleep, or remains groggy for a long time after waking up

- Sometimes experiences muscle weakness when highly emotional (during laughter or crying)
- Is often inattentive, irritable, depressed, or hyperactive during the day
- Frequently falls asleep in front of the television or while in the car
- Has sleep problems that are almost unbearable for you to handle, even though you have tried many solutions

Solutions for Children with Sleep Disorders

If you suspect that your child may have a sleep disorder, it is best not to attempt to diagnose the problem yourself. In addition, it's never wise to give a child any kind of sleep aid, medication, or herbal remedy without a medical professional's advice, as some remedies could pose a danger to your child.

There are a number of places where you can find help determining if your child has a sleep disorder. These professionals can also assist you in mapping out a treatment plan. Depending on your child's issues, your family's approach to health care, and the results you have along the way, it may take visits to more than one of these professionals to settle on the best answer. But don't give up. This is an important issue to solve for the sake of your child's health and well-being.

Your General Health Provider

The pediatrician or health care provider who handles your child's regular checkups may be able to help you determine if a sleep disorder exists, what treatment to use, and if your child should see a specialist. Not all general-medical professionals are versed in sleep medicine, though, so if you aren't confident in the information you receive, then seek out a second opinion.

A Sleep Disorders Center

Specialized sleep centers are staffed with medical professionals who have specific training in sleep medicine. They are set up with the equipment necessary to perform diagnostic tests and sleep studies. Look for a center that specializes in pediatric sleep disorders if possible. You can acquire information about sleep centers from your local hospital, your health care provider, or one of these organizations:

National Sleep Foundation
1522 K Street NW
Washington, DC 20005
sleepfoundation.org

American Academy of Sleep Medicine
One Westbrook Corporate Center, Ste. 920
Westchester, IL 60154
aasmnet.org

Alternative Medicine

Alternative medicine is made up of a variety of practices that are outside the realm of conventional medicine. If they suit your family's approach to health care, many are able to effectively treat sleep problems. Some of the choices are as follows:

• **Holistic medicine and homeopathy** is completely natural medicine that treats the whole person. A homeopathic practitioner will take into account your child's temperament, eating habits, prior illnesses, vaccination history, and family health history to determine which remedy and lifestyle changes would most improve your child's sleep situation. Homeopathic remedies are numerous and made from minerals, plants, and animals.

• **Naturopathy** is an integration of natural medicine with medical diagnostic science. Naturopathic health care is the practice performed by naturopaths for the diagnosis, prevention, and treatment of the disorders of the body, including sleep-related problems. Treatment includes the use of such physical forces as air, light, water, vibration, heat, or electricity; hydrotherapy, psychotherapy, dietetics, or massage; the administration of botanical and biological drugs, natural food, and herbs; and lifestyle changes.

• **Chiropractic care** focuses on treating disease and other health problems by making adjustments to the bony framework of the skeleton, particularly the spine. Chiropractic doctors can be effective in diagnosing sleep disorders and delivering treatments for a better night's sleep.

• **Acupuncture** is a natural therapy used to heal illness and improve well-being. Tiny, hair-thin needles are inserted into specific points in the body where they are stimulated to trigger the body's natural healing response. Acupuncture can be useful for the treatment of some sleep disorders.

• **Craniosacral therapy (CST), craniopathy, or cranial osteopathy** are holistic therapies that focus on the skull, membranes, and fluids that surround the brain and spinal cord. They involve massaging a child's head and spine. This is practiced by a physical therapist, massage therapist, or chiropractor and is believed to reduce stress, enhance the body's functioning, and improve the quality of sleep. You may want to talk with your health care provider about looking into this option and locate a doctor who specializes in using this method for children.

• **Pediatric psychologists and family therapists** can often help to diagnose sleep problems and recommend treatment.

Choosing the Right Answer

Every family approaches health care in its own unique way. What-ever way you choose to handle your child's sleep problems, make sure that you take the time to investigate your choice thoroughly. When you select a method of care, give it enough time to work before evaluating your results. Sleep disorders are rarely corrected in one day or even one month. These take time, care, and patience to remedy, but you may be providing your child a lifelong benefit by taking the necessary time to solve his sleep problems.

For More Information

You can read interviews with many of the original test mommies at the author's website: www.pantley.com.

To obtain a free catalog of parenting books, videos, audiotapes, and newsletters; or information about lecture services available by Elizabeth Pantley; or to contact the author:

Write to the author at:
5720 127th Avenue NE
Kirkland, WA 98033-8741

E-mail the author at:
elizabeth@pantley.com

Call the toll-free order line:
800-422-5820

Fax your request:
425-828-4833

Visit the website:
pantley.com

Search the Internet for articles by "Elizabeth Pantley"

Index